Children and Languages:

Research, Practice, and Rationale
for the Early Grades

compiled by

Rosemarie Benya

and edited by

Kurt E. Müller

National Council on Foreign Language and International Studies

The American Forum
45 John Street, Suite 1200, New York, New York 10038

The National Council on Foreign Language and International Studies is grateful to the following foundations, whose financial support has made this publication possible:

Charles E. Culpeper Foundation

Exxon Education Foundation

Ford Foundation

William and Flora Hewlitt Foundation

Henry Luce Foundation

Andrew W. Mellon Foundation

Rockefeller Foundation

The editor owes a debt of gratitude to Rosemarie Benya for all the effort that went into the conference that produced this collection of papers. He appreciates the assistance of Annette Dieli and Sarah Egan during the production of this book. A final word of thanks is due for the extensive editorial assistance provided by Elizabeth A. Coriell.

This is the third volume in the National Concil's International Education Series, originally titled Occasional Papers Series.

ISBN 0-944675-37-9 clothbound

ISBN 0-944675-07-7 paperback

Contents

Compiler's Preface
Rosemarie Benya v

Language Education for Children
Kurt E. Müller 1

Why FLES Fails: Lack of Funds or Provincialism?
Maureen Regan 8

Foreign Language in the Elementary School: A Comparison of Achievement
Nancy C. Rhodes and Marguerite Ann Snow 17

A Comparison of Three Second Language Programs
Magdelhayne F. Buteau and Helen Gougeon 24

Fairview German Bilingual School: A Model for Elementary-School Language Learning
Frederick P. Veidt 43

A Model Foreign Language Experience Program for the Elementary School
Patricia Davis Wiley 51

The Public Loves Foreign Languages for Children
Gladys C. Lipton 59

Languages for Children at Tarrant County Junior College
Jane Harper 65

Launching Foreign Language Programs in Elementary Schools: Highpoints and Headaches
Ulrike Criminale 69

Assimilative Motivation and the Development of Second Languages in Children
C. Ray Graham 72

Should We Teach Children Grammar?
Mervin R. Barnes 78

The Pappenheimers: A Multimedia German Program for Children
Christian P. Stehr and Tamara D. Stehr 90

Speak It, Read It: Simultaneous Acquisition of Language and Reading Skills
Lucille R. Guckes and Barbara Kandaras 95

To Read You Must Write: Language Acquisition among Limited-English- Proficient Children
Curtis W. Hayes, Robert Bahruth, and Carolyn Kessler 105

Testing in Beginning FLES: Listening
Loren Alexander 117

Individual Differences in Second Language Learning among Korean Immigrant Children
Heesoon Jun-Aust 124

A Discourse Analysis of Interactions of Spanish-English Bilingual Children
Carol A. Klee 142

Age of Second Language Acquisition and Hemispheric Asymmetry
Stuart J. Anderson, Rory P. Plunkett, and E. John Hammond 155

Classroom Management: Maintaining A Viable Learning Environment
Donald R. Jacoby 177

Laying the Foundation: German in the First Grade
Marianne Ryan 185

Fairy Tales in the ESL Classroom
April Haulman 194

Short Stories in the Elementary Classroom: "El camello que se perdió"
Cida S. Chase 199

Teaching Methodology: A Child-Centered Approach
Marcia H. Rosenbusch 204

Bilingual Language Arts through Music
Sheryl L. Santos 218

Grammar and the Reluctant Learner: A Games Approach
Robert Williston 231

A Practical Project in Studying Foreign Languages in the Elementary School: Students Teaching Parents
Ivy A. Mitchell 240

Compiler's Preface

The conference on second or foreign language acquisition by children, held in Oklahoma City in March, 1985, responded to a nationwide rebirth of interest in this topic as well as a manifestation of our "coming of age."

Organizations such as the American Council on the Teaching of Foreign Languages (ACTFL), regional conferences such as Central States and Northeast, and others have begun to pay greater attention to second/foreign language acquisition by children by including more relevant sessions in their respective programs. Because of this growth of interest, the time appeared ripe for having a conference devoted exclusively to this topic. The idea for holding such a conference seemed so right, so current. From the moment this idea was proposed, it was received enthusiastically by the key representatives of the co-sponsoring organizations: John Folks, Mary Reid, and Al Gage of the Oklahoma State Department of Education; Ralph Downs of the Oklahoma Curriculum Improvement Commission; the members of the Executive Board of the Oklahoma Foreign Language Teachers Association; Stanley Wagner, Gene Stephenson, Doug Nelson, and Lucile Morse of East Central University. Their outstanding support and that of their organizations continued throughout the entire planning phase and into the ultimate realization of the conference itself.

Nearly 200 conferees representing 29 states and two foreign countries attended the sessions in Oklahoma City. A cross-section of those attending includes teachers from preschool to university, as well as interested parents, students, and administrators. The presentations covered a wide variety of topics both theoretical and practical: administration of and advocacy for second/foreign language programs for children, medical and educational research in relevant areas, as well as classroom methods and materials.

Because of the superb caliber of papers presented, many found that they had to make some difficult choices of sessions to attend. Both Nancy Rhodes and James Asher, the keynote speakers, shared valuable information from and insights into their respective areas of expertise.

v

During the conference, it was gratifying to see the many professionals who are dedicating themselves to this vital area of second/foreign language acquisition. A spirit of camaraderie and cordiality permeated the conference. The conference was as successful as it was primarily because of the outstanding attendees, presenters as well as participants.

Overall reaction to this International Conference on Second/Foreign Language Acquisition by Children was very favorable. A number of conferees expressed a desire to make the conference an annual event. This interest led to a November 1986 meeting in Dallas, held in conjunction with the annual meeting of ACTFL.

The story about the 1985 conference, however, does not end here. Part of the plans for the 1985 conference included the publication of the papers given by the presenters. Because the conference did not generate enough income for this purpose, the realization of this dream had to be postponed.

After some time had passed and plans for the 1986 conference were progressing well, Kurt Müller of the National Council on Foreign Language and International Studies (NCFLIS) phoned to say that one of the National Council's chief emphases for 1986-87 was to be early language acquisition. As a result of this focus, NCFLIS was very interested in publishing the papers from the 1985 conference. The rest, then, is history, reflected in this publication. Indeed a sincere debt of gratitude is owed to Kurt Müller and the National Council on Foreign Language and International Studies for their interest in and commitment to this project. The willingness of the National Council to finance this publication is a truly significant step in serving and addressing the area of second/foreign language acquisition by children.

Before finishing this message, I want to mention my own personal indebtedness to two of my former teachers: Lucille Colianni, formerly of Notre Dame College in Cleveland, Ohio, and Melba Woodruff, professor emerita of foreign language education at Ohio State University. Both these women were responsible for instilling in me an interest in second/foreign language acquisition by children. Through my own career I hope to nurture this interest among others.

I would be remiss if I did not include the names of others who contributed, in their special ways, to the success of the 1985 conference and to this publication: Rose Hayden of NCFLIS, Ralph Pohlmeier of Educational Media, Inc., Nita West, Wanda Burke, Gail Cox, and Christy Gregory, Ed Scebold, Mark Goodin, Herman Scharf, David Barrow, Karen Benya Smith, Joyce Blankenship, May Lou Aylor, Lucille Freeman, Curtiss Baker, Kenneth Clinton, Evelyn Collins, and Marty Fulk.

Rosemarie Benya
East Central University
Ada, Oklahoma

Language Education for Children

Kurt E. Müller

Language education is a sorely underdeveloped, inadequately defined subject in the United States. Most of us have little sense of language as the carrier of national culture. Not only do we demonstrate little appreciation for other languages, but we often show little sense of a distinctly American idiom. Although our dictionaries clearly demonstrate the demarcation between British and American usage of English, many writers are ill at ease with the distinctions. It usually strikes me as an unnecessary affectation that many theaters spell their names as "X Theatre," as if the British/French spelling were somehow better than our own. It is often left to editors to impose a house style on the writing of educated Americans, bringing consistency to an otherwise incomplete sense of language identity. The utilitarianism in our national character seems to have prevented us from taking notice of matters of verbal style. More accurately, we do not acknowledge our prejudices in evaluating the speech of others. Some school districts have wrestled with the treatment of black English, questioning whether speakers of this nonstandard dialect should enter ESL programs. Linguists based in the social sciences have long affirmed the equality of nonstandard dialects with the dominant language or prestigious dialect of a given country. But affirming the value or pointing out the artistic achievements of an undervalued dialect is not the same as facilitating a child's upward mobility by giving that child the verbal key to the power structure. If we accepted the linguists' value-neutral assessment of a nonstandard dialect, we might be led to according it equal validity in our education system. Such a policy would be as unwise as accepting Spanish as a substitute for English skills among Hispanics in American society. For while we were according these ethnic groups their political due, we would be limiting their opportunities for advancement. The practice in several countries of speaking a dialect at home and using a standard pronunciation and lexicon in the office—or of using one language socially and another for business—facilitates mobility only so long as the individual is sufficiently skilled in the appropriate language for each set of circumstances.

Lest someone misread my intentions, I hasten to add that if we were concerned with developing the abilities of all students to their

1

Kurt E. Müller is Executive Vice President of the National Council on Foreign Language and International Studies.

fullest potential—a goal that is only consonant with the values underlying a meritocracy—we would also facilitate the development of a child's native language if it is not English. Unfortunately, bilingual education has a long but tortured history in America. Our experience with immigration was such that often the schools were used to teach newcomers English so that they could quickly join in the task of nation building. Mistakenly, education officials and second-generation Americans often construed as a corollary of this goal the eradication of native languages. Consequently, it is hardly surprising that "language development" as a topic in education is too often restricted to the teaching of English.

Since *Lau v. Nichols,* the general public has become accustomed to calling schoolchildren with limited proficiency in English "bilinguals," often conflating the term with the more accurate label "limited-English-proficient" (LEP). Yet, the Bilingual Education Act was passed not to ensure that native speakers of other languages would grow up bilingual but to facilitate the replacement of their native tongue with English. As Ernest Boyer, president of the Carnegie Foundation for the Advancement of Teaching and former U.S. Commissioner of Education, has eloquently pointed out in board meetings of the National Council on Foreign Language and International Studies, anyone who would deny linguistic-minority children the opportunity to become fully proficient in English is restricting seriously the future prospects of these children. Concerned with different languages at different times in our history, the general public has repeatedly questioned whether children in bilingual schools achieve sufficient mastery of English. This debate continues, most recently with staff of the U.S. Department of Education taking the "con" position and the General Accounting Office taking the "pro." We have accepted the misnomer "bilingual education" so completely that language professionals now distinguish between "additive" and "subtractive bilingualism." The latter oxymoron betrays an underlying public attitude that maintaining the home language is not in the public interest.

In contrast to efforts to maintain or develop minority languages, foreign language education arouses few contentious opponents. "Additive bilingualism" is clearly perceived as a noble venture; it contributes to the international competitiveness of all our children. There should be no question that adding the ability to use another language is in the national interest diplomatically, economically, militarily, and culturally.

All American children must grow up fully proficient in English, and all should have the opportunity to learn an additional language as well. If they are to understand the nature of language, they must be exposed to a comparative dimension, i.e., to understand their own, they must see how another language functions. If the subject of "language arts" is supposed to familiarize students with the structure of language, but the phenomenon of communication is examined from within the boundaries of only one language, the investigator can take no critical distance from the subject.

Since the 1979 report of the President's Commission on Foreign Language and International Studies (Perkins Commission), numerous commissions, boards, and individual investigators have called for sequenced programs of foreign language study to begin in the elementary schools. In a study for the President's Commission, the University of Michigan Survey Research Center found overwhelming support for language insturction: 93% of the American public thought languages should be offered in high schools; 76% (82% of the college-educated) thought languages should be offered in the elementary schools (Eddy, "Attitudes toward Foreign Language Study" 8). Subsequent reports have continued to promote the desirability of begining language instruction early, but these reports have not catalyzed the education community to respond to their urgings. In its 1983 report, *A Nation at Risk*, the National Commission on Excellence in Education wrote:

> Achieving proficiency in a *foreign language* ordinarily requires from 4 to 6 years of study and should, therefore, be started in the elementary grades. We believe it is desirable that students achieve such proficiency because study of a foreign language introduces students to non-English-speaking cultures, heightens awareness and comprehension of one's native tongue, and serves the Nation's needs in commerce, diplomacy, defense, and education. (26)

In late 1983, the National Advisory Board on International Education Programs, chaired by James Holderman, president of the University of South Carolina, issued its report, *Critical Needs in International Education: Recommendations for Action*. In this report, the board observed:

> The groundwork must be laid in the elementary schools. Unfortunately the majority of our elementary schools do not offer any foreign language instruction, nor do a fifth of our secondary schools [the latter situation has improved since the Holderman Board's report—Ed.] Even where foreign language instruction is offered, courses have been reduced. We believe that foreign language instruction should be offered to all students. (6)

The Holderman Board's mandate was to look at international education needs in higher education. In support of its work, it is notable that the board's first recommendation concerns the elementary schools:

> Local school districts should provide every student with the opportunity to begin the study of a foreign language in the earliest years of formal education and to continue study of the same language until a functionally useful level of measured proficiency has been achieved. (9)

In his report on secondary education in America, Ernest L. Boyer recommends, "language study should begin early—by the fourth grade and preferably before—and it should be sustained" (Boyer

3

100). Some states have begun to respond to such calls for early exposure to foreign languages by mandating the expansion into the lower grades of language programs. Under New York's Regents' Action Plan, all students must now have two years of a foreign language prior to grade 9. In Louisiana, foreign language study now is mandated from grade 4, and in Hawaii, from grade 3. North Carolina is working on a plan for a sequence of language study that will run from kindergarten through high school. Under this initiative, all students in grades K-4 must take a foreign language, and all schools must offer a foreign language in grades 5-12.

Despite national calls for starting earlier, obsolete attitudes toward language instruction persist. Rather than serving all students, some districts continue to reserve foreign language offerings for the college bound. Some systems avoid offering languages to students with low scores in English. The attitude of "they have enough trouble with English, how can we expect poor students to handle a foreign language?" is reminiscent of attempts to communicate with foreigners by continuing to speak English but to do so more slowly and more loudly. Rather than offer an added perspective on language structure by exposing students to a comparative dimension, such restrictions simply offer added opportunities for failure. When investigations into the effect of prolonged language study on verbal achievement in English clearly demonstrate gains on the verbal tests of the American College Testing (ACT) Program and the Scholastic Aptitude Test (SAT), the reluctance of some school systems to provide sequential programs of language study is difficult to fathom. An investigation into SAT performance by the Center for Applied Linguistics in 1979-80 concluded

> that the length of time of foreign language study is a significant predictor of performance on the SAT-Verbal and various sub-tests. We may infer that a person who studies a foreign language for a long period of time will do better on the SAT than a person having studied for a shorter period of time, other things being equal. (Eddy, *Effect of Foreign Language Study* 88)

In an investigation into performance by students at Southern Illinois University on the ACT, Eugene Timpe found that the greatest improvement on verbal test scores as a correlate of exposure to foreign language study was evidenced by those students who were least likely candidates for success in college, i.e., those who were not in college preparatory programs, who did not maintain a high school grade-point average of B or better, and who were not in the top of their high school class.

Passive support for curriculum, such as is evident in the survey questionnaire administered by the University of Michigan, differs from active advocacy for expansion of curricular offerings in a given school district. If elementary-school language programs entail hiring additional staff, districts may be reluctant to seek funding to be able to add specialty teachers. Across the nation, parents have been overcoming the lethargy of school administrations that fail to offer language programs during the school day. By paying separate tuition for before- or after-school programs, often run by parent-teacher associations or by associations for the gifted and talented, parent groups are ensuring the opportunities that administrations may be reluctant to provide: Ulrike Criminale's paper describes a language school that was funded by parents who were convinced that their children should have earlier exposure to languages; even enrollment declines in her school are attributed to increased interest as parents began urging local PTAs to coordinate new language programs for neighborhood children, creating competition for Criminale's language school.

The papers in this volume are such that some are likely to appeal to parents and school board members while others are likely to be read only by researchers. They range from research in neurophysiology and in language choice to video support for school foreign language programs. The inclusion of papers concerning ESL instruction as well as those concerned with teaching anglophones an additional language offers the opportunity to appreciate the similarities as well as major differences in these two distinct sets of language-education circumstances. Although foreign language education, "bilingual" education, and ESL instruction all intend to enable students to use a language they could not use before, their approaches and clienteles are quite different, and their methods may not be transferable. Teachers in these programs often do not perceive themselves as belonging to the same discipline and typically do not read each other's professional literature. Consequently, to the ESL teacher, the foreign language professional's work seems uninformed by the rich experience of the last two decades while to the foreign language teacher, the literature on ESL methods seems parochial.

For the language teacher, the joint appearance of these papers should occasion some reflection on the acceptability of current practices in their field(s). In their paper, for example, Hayes, Bahruth, and Kessler relate their experience with a class of children of migrant farmworkers in which they deliberately avoided correcting spelling and grammar mistakes in children's dialogue journals but included corrections in their responding comments. This approach to error correction is generally accepted in the ESL community but has been questioned in the foreign language teaching profession. Students learning the dominant language of a society may well hear enough of the language outside the classroom to correct their own speech patterns, whereas a teacher's failure to correct an error in a foreign language class may result in "error fossilization" that will inhibit the student's progress toward functional proficiency in the language.

Several of the papers should offer opportunities for professional debate on issues such as staffing, curriculum, age for starting a program, and teaching methods. Gladys Lipton describes efforts to introduce language sequences without adding staffing costs to a district's budget. An approach to language instruction using solely non-professional volunteers seems fraught with problems, not the least of which is the lack of commitment from the district administration that one anticipates in such a program. Nevertheless, using volunteers, her district was able to introduce language study where it otherwise would not have been, and we hope the inclusion of her report prompts a dialogue on the promises and pitfalls of volunteer labor in support of curricula. Nancy Rhodes and Ann Snow compare the achievements of students in immersion, partial immersion, and traditional FLES programs; Magdelhayne Buteau and Helen Gougeon look at early and late immersion in Canada and compare these programs with traditional Canadian programs in French as a Second Language. Papers by Patricia Wiley, Gladys Lipton, Jane Harper, Ulrike Criminale, and Frederick Veidt present information on curricular and other considerations in a specific program type, from limited exposure to a foreign language to the most exciting development in early language education: immersion. Mervin Barnes and Robert Williston both concern themselves with the role of grammar in language instruction. Grammar has long been a scapegoat in education. Overemphasis on grammatical accuracy has impeded the development of fluency in a foreign language, but underemphasis on English grammar has been blamed for the current inability of high school and college graduates to write coherently. Current research in the teaching of (English) writing is cited by English teachers as showing no correlation between the ability to recognize grammar rules and the ability to write well. Being one of those foreign language teachers who is relatively uninformed on ESL matters, I am in no position to refute this research to the satisfaction of the English profession, but I am skeptical enough to hypothesize that inattention to the structure of English has led to a degeneration of graduates' expressive capacity. Certainly, unfamiliarity with grammatical terms encumbers the learning of a second or third language in an academic context. To keep us from losing sight of the major purpose of language, Ray Graham emphasizes the communicative motivation of children. I hope the inclusion of these papers sparks further interest in the topic.

Academic practice is often inimical to the collection of information from diverse research specialties. Language education is no exception to this tendency. Foreign language teachers are usually trained in foreign language departments, often in departments of "national literatures," e.g., French or German; ESL teachers may be trained in English, ESL, or applied linguistics programs. The preparation of foreign language teachers is overwhelmingly oriented toward secondary and postsecondary instruction, reflecting the disciplinary boundaries of the institutions that train these teachers; seldom do the teacher-training programs reflect the integrative approach that typifies elementary education. We hope this collection of papers is used to cross some of these boundaries.

References

Baker, Keith A., and Adriana A. deKanter. *Effectiveness of Bilingual Education: A Review of the Literature.* Washington, D.C.: U.S. Department of Education, 1981.

Boyer, Ernest L. *High School: Secondary Education in America.* New York: Harper and Row, 1983.

Eddy, Peter A. "Attitudes toward Foreign Language Study and Requirements in American Schools and Colleges: Results of a National Survey." *ADFL Bulletin 11.2 (1979): 4-9.*

————. *The Effect of Foreign Language Study in High School on Verbal Ability as Measured by the Scholastic Aptitude Test-Verbal.* Final Report to U.S. Department of Education under Grant No. G0077901701. Washington, DC: Center for Applied Linguistics, 1980.

General Accounting Office. *Bilingual Education: A New Look at the Research Evidence.* Briefing Report to the Chairman, Committee on Education and Labor, House of Representatives. Washington, D.C.: GAO, 1987.

National Advisory Board on International Education Programs. *Critical Needs in International Education: Recommendations for Action.* [Washington, DC: GPO], 1983.

National Commission on Excellence in Education. *A Nation at Risk: The Imperative for Educational Reform.* Washington, DC: GPO, 1983.

President's Commission on Foreign Language and International Studies. *Strength through Wisdom: A Critique of U.S. Capability.* Washington, DC: GPO, 1979.

Timpe, Eugene F. "The Effect of Foreign Language Study on ACT Scores." *ADFL Bulletin* 11.2 (1979): 10-11.

7

Why FLES Fails: Lack of Funds or American Provincialism?

Maureen Regan

Teaching Foreign Languages in the Elementary School has come of age . . . again. From Maine to California the word is out, FLES is in. No matter that second language instruction for the youngest American is neither new nor innovative—the first program began in the 1800's in the Ohio Public Schools—the notion remains determinedly novel, frighteningly trendy, and regrettably cyclic. If college language courses remain, FLES programs come and go, dependent on financial and professional whim or on the curricular bandwagon the school district happens to be riding. Beginners in language, it would seem, are destined to be old; the "age" of the learner apparently determines the "quality" of the academic experience. Yet when the nation's educators are periodically cajoled or frightened into reevaluating the means by which they reach those hearts and minds to which tomorrow's hopes are inalterably tied, the case for FLES is tried and wins.

America's schools are once again ready for early language instruction. Better informed and genuinely concerned, they are anxious not to repeat past mistakes. If they are indeed back to basics, they are also running scared. There is, quite simply, too much at stake to fail again. Embassies, once inviolate, have become the terrorist's playground. Developing nations have the cheek to want their own customs respected and their own language used. No longer unchallenged in the world market, monolingual American business is losing out to its multilingual competition; "American technology," announces the New York Times, "is losing technological ground." In this age of instant information, we have come to realize that instant annihilation is only as far away as the nearest panic button. The experts' warnings plus concern for American peace, power, and prosperity have finally given the public pause. No longer to be considered luxuries for an elitist few, understanding, communicating with, and relating to our world neighbors have become mandates not to be ignored if we intend to survive yet another generation.

The experts have spoken. The youngest student is an ideal language candidate. Proficiency is not an overnight process; the road to fluency is long and hard. The child is in fact our most avid word

Maureen Regan is an Associate Professor at the Potsdam College of Arts and Science of the State University of New York, where she teaches French in the Campus School.

8

collector. How many adults integrate 400 new items into their vocabularies in a six-month period? We know the arguments; we may not know the answers. The issues are clear; the solutions are less so. Why are so many FLES programs initiated in the heyday of language renewal now defunct? Why are these programs, which research supports and the public wants, not healthy enough to endure trends and cycles and budgetary crises? According to Senator Paul Simon, 84% of those with children sixteen and under would encourage their children to take a foreign language; 74% believe knowing a foreign language would help Americans have a better awareness and understanding of people from other nations.[1]

The cause for secondary language learning has indeed been thoroughly documented. The cause of early foreign language learning, however, even among language professionals, remains an enigmatic, gray area haunted by past failures. The last curricular area to be funded and the first to have financial support withdrawn, it is perceived as educationally sound, yet not academically rigorous. At best a perquisite for the affluent school district, FLES often eludes the efforts of language-sensitive legislators and serious language scholars, whose attention seems ever riveted on high schools and universities. We are dedicated to the belief that the only real language learner is the older language learner. And when, in response to public pressure or academic conscience, language programs for children are initiated, we fail our most natural learners by denying them academically challenging, culturally rich curricula supported by pedagogically sound, appropriately designed materials. Then programs fail and we name lack of funds and American provincialism the culprits. However, funds are far from the main issue, and American provincialism is a curable, if life-threatening, disease.

Good programs weather hard times. Master teachers are helped but not made by media packages or visual aids. And funds can be found where commitment endures. Potsdam College of Arts and Science, the oldest unit of the university system of the State of New York, has supported a children's language program on its campus for nearly forty years. Set in rural, relatively isolated, sometimes welfare-ridden northern New York, the campus has known its share of budget crises. Located in small-town America, in an area as prone to small ideas as any other its size, Potsdam College has maintained an active, viable FLES program since the mid-1940s. When the Children's Learning Center nearly closed in 1975, threatening to take the language program with it, the program director sought help from the National Endowment for the Humanities to extend the Potsdam FLES experience through television. The Endowment did help; Potsdam language classes continued, and others began in fourteen states across the nation. Money, then, can be found, and creative use of existing materials and personnel resources soothes the sting of a meager purse. If budget is our handiest excuse, it is not our most formidable enemy.

Provincialism is the far more dangerous adversary. Its protagonists are the products of an education system that says language courses need not be part and parcel of the American school curriculum at every level. If colleges in the '70s dropped language requirements for the most part, they did not drop language courses. High schools of any academic reputation similarly may have de-emphasized second languages, but they did not remove them from the curriculum. Why then is language instruction basic to the curriculum only of the student who research says is past his or her linguistic prime? More than giving American students the opportunity for eventual fluency, more than influencing them to continue language study, more than laying a solid foundation on which later language learning can be built, FLES can effect a change in the prevailing antilanguage attitude before it emerges. It is this attitude that keeps the school administrator and our neighbors, the business person in the world market and the diplomat at the conference table, monolingual.

If the speech patterns of the very young are malleable, so are their priorities, their tastes, their perceptions of the world about them. There exists in the early language classroom an unparalleled opportunity to raise the international conscience of a new generation of Americans. The young student represents the nearly blank page on which we can still write our history as we wish to read it. Language instruction can be the window through which the child sees the rest of the world. But as long as the learning of a new language remains an adjunct, after school, sporadic or infrequent activity, the change in attitude which could reform America's language posture will be forever out of reach. When FLES is as routine a part of the elementary school day as reading and writing, we reach all children. In high school and college language courses, we reach only a chosen few whose life course is nearly charted.

Knowing all this to be true is one thing. Making it all come true is another. I suggest three target areas which merit our undivided professional attention: administrative support, teacher training, and material and curriculum development.

Administrative Support

In the final analysis, it is an administrative decision that establishes or terminates an elementary language program. Even master teachers conducting model programs are at the mercy of administrative support. Too many American public school administrators operate from an English-only base. Monolingually trained and functional, they cannot be expected to share the polyglot's conviction that a multicultural perspective is required to achieve international literacy. But administrators care about children and sincerely believe children's total development to be their responsibility. It is on this level, as conscientious caretakers of tomorrow's citizens, that we must appeal to them.

There are two kinds of administrative support. In one, the administrator believes totally in the teacher who will plan, organize, and implement the language program. Yet, lacking background in language acquisition or language learning and insecure about their own ability to speak a second language—a feeling unfortunately encouraged by those elitists who do—these principals absent themselves from the FLES process. Then when trends change and budgets shift, it is easy to disband programs about which they know relatively little and in which they have made marginal, if any, personal investment. The second type of administrative support comprises those who openly and independently affirm the value of early language learning and seek staff and curricula that confirm what they know to be true.

In either case, rule number one is to deliberately and personally involve those who choose to make FLES a genuine and lasting component of the curriculum. Remember that administrators, as Americans first and public school officials second, are prey to the same myths and misconceptions as any other citizen. They believe that as a nation we are not only language deficient but linguistically unable. Not true. We are not less able; we are less willing. American children are not stupid, yet their peers in practically every other country in the world are given the opportunity to learn other languages easily and expertly. Every child is language gifted. Such misconceptions can and must be corrected.

The administrator should be approached as American to American and educator to educator, not as bilingual to monolingual. The American may care that we spend billions of dollars on weaponry to kill the Russians and less than it takes to repair three-quarters of a mile of interstate highway to get to know them (Simon 45). The American will care about the balance-of-payments deficit in the amount of $25 billion - $30 billion going to those whose languages are different from our own. The American will care if most area specialists in the executive branch of the federal government, including the intelligence services, do not or cannot read the materials of greatest concern to them in the original. The American will be interested in a 1975 survey revealing that 1,261 U.S.-based companies needed or preferred to have language skills for 60,678 positions. The American will care that one out of every eight manufacturing jobs is dependent on exports, that one out of every three American acres grows produce for export (Simon 23).

The educator will care that transfer from second language study contributes to improved performance in English vocabulary, that students of second language in the elementary schools out-perform other students on measures of English vocabulary knowledge, reading, and comprehension. The educator will be interested in the association between foreign language proficiency and the level at which studies started, that those who start in elementary school do the best, that students who have had a foreign language exposure in grade school are more likely to take a language in high school, that the child who studies a language early may also listen more carefully, read more widely, judge more fairly, select different items from a menu, different books from a library, or elect a trip to a museum over one to the television set.

If foreign languages in the elementary school are your cause, know the facts. However well-intentioned, uninformed emotional support is useless. Read the experts. Know your opponents. Send frequent factual information regarding the national language profile to those in your district who keep FLES alive. Build a "visual" professional library and use it. Locate model programs through ACTFL, ERIC, MLA, NCFLIS, or your state language association and visit them with your supervisors or administrators. Teach with your door open literally and figuratively. Know as much about why you are teaching young students as what you are teaching.

The FLES Teacher

Like the subject they teach, teachers of FLES have a serious image problem—regrettably, sometimes deserved. No matter that wide-eyed, six-year-old language learners in no way resemble their sleepy-eyed, glazed-over college counterparts. No matter that the course content closely resembles that of a beginning college course; when the student is eighteen, it's language 101, when the student is eight, it's fun and games. The secondary or college language teacher hopefully has a wealth of background in the content area. The FLES teacher may make an impressive presentation based on an impoverished second language background that may not withstand a long language-learning sequence. It is a common belief that anyone can teach a child and, sadly, sometimes does. A bona fide language teacher must have bona fide credentials. A FLES teacher apparently can be anyone from your next-door neighbor who "once studied" to the non-teacher native speaker. Neither is an ideal candidate. The best FLES teachers are specialists who know children and are trained to teach them. Professionals who consider any language learning a serious academic endeavor, they should be orally superior and pedagogically skilled (methods do matter), with diversified cultural backgrounds. I do believe parents and paraprofessionals can help, guided by a professional, but staffing programs without professional input gives FLES/FLEX a bad name.

Where are these unusual professionals, and lacking them in sufficient number, how do we recycle our available personnel resources? First, consult our teacher-training institutions. Encourage language majors to combine language and elementary education. After establishing a history of providing special training for FLES teachers, Potsdam College now offers just such a dual major. Teachers with such training will be increasingly in demand in the decade ahead. The state of Louisiana with a mandated elementary language program expected a shortage of over 100 FLES teachers in the 1985-86 academic year. As of 1989, New York State will require two units of language of every student before entering high school. Require in-service methods courses and adequate elementary classroom observation of those natives, secondary language teachers, or non-professionals who hope to teach second languages to children. "Walk-ins" or "stand-ins" should no more be allowed to tamper with elementary school language programs than with programs in high school or college. The potential for permanent harm is far greater with the child learner.

Children's initial language experience will have significant impact on the way they view the world, those who inhabit it, and their role in it, not to mention their motivation for further language study. Children at the Potsdam College Campus Learning Center, who are students of French, wear name tags during Foreign Language Week that identify them as "Bilingual Americans and World Citizens." They are taught from the earliest age to think of themselves as Americans who must contribute to, and be part of, a much larger and more significant picture than the northern New York countryside that surrounds them.

Make use of the media. When televised, model teachers and model programs can reach many at little expense. Ask master teachers to videotape their work. In an attempt to share expertise gleaned from its forty-year-old language program for children, Potsdam College has developed a televised teacher-training package. Entitled "Mon Atelier," this series of video cassettes features eighty children, age six through thirteen, in a classroom setting. It was filmed without a script and is supported by a running commentary. Investigate federal funds for teacher training. During July 1986, forty teachers from Illinois, New York, and Ohio participated in an NEH-supported inter-disciplinary summer institute held at SUNY, Potsdam, designed to train and retrain elementary and secondary teachers to teach French to young learners. Funded proposals are most often those that identify strong district needs; funds are available both for teacher training and improved language instruction.

Last, look to our Canadian neighbors whose numerous successful core and immersion experiences have led to important research, an abundance of excellent materials, and exacting teacher-certification requirements.

Until such time as FLES teachers understand, speak, write, and read a second language expertly; know and understand the cultures of that language well and have the on-paper, in-the-field credentials to prove it, they forever will be song and dance men.

Curriculum and Materials

American children have been routinely cheated—not only of the opportunity to learn a second language during what research says is their finest academic hour—but also by the quality of the curriculum and materials purported to enhance that learning. By tradition we remove or exclude from the children's language study a whole host of items that could make the learning of another language the child's richest academic experience. Very little is too complex for young language learners if presented in a manner and with vocabulary appropriate to their age and interest levels. Children, particularly today's children, are far more sophisticated than they are commonly believed to be. Commercial and instructional media are aware of this—educational specialists should be as well. When the children learn by rote, must all they learn be in the *présent* or even in the *passé composé*? Is there an unwritten law that says a child cannot parrot a *plusque-parfait* or a *subjonctif*? Must games be limited to the learning of vocabulary or

13

could they set grammatical habits as well? A child can be aware of gender, understand the phenomenon of agreement, know that verbs change form and perceive why and when elision takes place. Must the color red be taught only with apples, or would Matisse's "Red Studio" do the job as well?

Caught by children's marvelous facility for mimicry, we often lock them in an oral vacuum, denying them access to the reading and writing that will continue to whet their language appetite. We limit their cultural background to the habits of everyday living when in fact we should be attaching hooks on which a multitude of ideas, concepts, and even philosophies can later be hung. However important the communicative skills, the students must come away with much, much more. In a small town with no major museum, they can still look at fine art; lacking access to food specialty shops, they can still sample gourmet delights. They can be aware of famous people and important events long before they sit in a history class. They can learn to look at that which is different with a open mind. Young language students at Potsdam look at a Renoir and know it's not a van Gogh. They know the smell of French perfume, the taste and texture of a croissant. They know the name of the French president though the five-year-olds agree unanimously that our own president is named George Washington. And if what is taught to the younger language learner is lacking in quality, it is equally lacking in quantity. Syllabi, when they exist, stop far short of a FLES student's capabilities. Children not only can count to ten; they can spell and compute the numbers to one hundred while using them to give cultural information. Not only can children learn over thirty parts of their own body, but they can apply them to expressions and situations that have nothing to do with physical description. When children learn the verb "to think," they can learn about great thinkers as well.

We need realistic expectations. The first question posed any teacher of FLES is, "Do the students in your program speak the language in question?" An honest answer is, "No." Can they at any given moment truly and accurately express their thoughts and ideas? No. Do they form original statements? Yes. Can they ask and answer questions? Yes. Can they supply information, given adequate stimuli? Yes. Can they recite, translate, and express a limited range of emotions? Yes. Do they understand oral and some written communication? Yes. Do they know much about the land and people whose language they are studying? Yes. Do they have a better chance of becoming fluent, having started young? Yes!

I suggest that FLES programs do not fail because funds are not available to keep them afloat. If a project lacks money to hire resident language professionals, expertise can be borrowed. Potsdam College, with the help of the National Endowment for the Humanities, has created a media series, *Madame, Merci et Mou* for just such a purpose. Programs fail because of the prevailing notion that Americans cannot learn languages well and that if young Americans attempt to, they are not involved in a serious task.

As language professionals, we must climb down from our ivory towers. Americans first and language teachers second, we must take a hard look at the language-learning site that represents the greatest potential for the citizenry of the next generation: the elementary school classroom. While continuing to support language learning at every level, we must beware putting the roof on a house not yet built. I suggest we teach what we believe a child can learn rather than what others have told us a child can learn. The curriculum must grow with the child. Learning another's language is serious business, an academic, interdisciplinary, rigorous concern, be the learner two or twenty-two. The best teacher, whose superior command of language and facts is supported by an equally superior methodology, belongs in the classroom of the youngest language learners. We cannot, must not fail again.

Notes

[1]Paul Simon, *The Tongue-Tied American: Confronting the Foreign Language Crisis* (New York: Continuum, 1980) 73.

[2] Maureen Regan, *Mon Atelier: Language Learning, a Creative Experience,* State University of New York, College at Potsdam, New York Network.

[3]Maureen Regan, *A Multi-media Foreign Language Project for Children with a Humanistic Approach.* Created with the support of the National Endowment for the Humanities, Division of Educational Programs, State University of New York, New York Network, Albany.

15

Suggested Readings

Asher, James, and R. Garcia. "The Optimal Age to Learn a Foreign Language." *Modern Language Journal* 53(1969):334-41.

Boyd, Rachel. "Influences of Foreign Language Study on English." *Babel* 13 (April, 1977):19-22.

Carroll, John. "Implications of Aptitude Research and Psycholinguistic Theory for Foreign Language Teaching." *Linguistics* 112 (1973):5-13.

Gessell, Arnold, and Francis Ilg. *The Child from 5-10.* New York: Harper, 1946.

Guiora, Alexander Z., et al. "Empathy and Second Language Learning." *Language Learning* 22(1972):111-30.

Krashen, Stephen, et al., *Language Two.* New York: Oxford Univ. Press, 1982.

Lenneberg, E. "Understanding Language without Ability to Speak: A Case Report." *Journal of Abnormal and Social Psychology* 65(1962):419-25.

Masciantonio, Rudolph. "Tangible Benefits of the Study of Latin: A Review of Research." Washington, D.C.: Eric Document Reproduction Service, 1978. ED 143200.

National Commission on Excellence in Education. *A Nation at Risk: The Imperative for Educational Reform.* Washington, D.C.:GPO, 1983.

Oyama, S. *Sensitive Period for the Acquisition of a Second Language.* Diss. Harvard Univ. 1973.

Penfield, Wilder G., and L. Roberts. *Speech and Brain-Mechanisms.* London: Princeton Univ. Press, 1959.

President's Commission on Foreign Language and International Studies. *Strength through Wisdom: A Critique of U.S. Capability.* Washington, D.C.:GPO, 1979.

Scovel, Thomas. "Foreign Accents, Language Acquisition, and Cerebral Dominance." *Language Learning* 19(1969):245-54.

Sullivan, Edmund. *Piaget and the School Curriculum: A Critical Appraisal.* Toronto: Ontario Institute for Studies in Education, 1967.

Foreign Language in the Elementary School: A Comparison of Achievement

Nancy C. Rhodes and Marguerite Ann Snow

"Elementary school students can pick up languages much quicker than high school students." "They're not as inhibited and their pronunciation and proficiency are better." "Young students have a greater aptitude for learning foreign language." These comments are often heard about the language capabilities of young children. But not until now has there been a nationwide study comparing language learning of elementary school children and high school students. Nor has there been any comparison of proficiency levels attained by elementary school students enrolled in different types of programs.

There has been much speculation on the most successful way to teach foreign language to children. Some suggest a totally oral approach, others a combination of the four skills—listening, speaking, reading, and writing. Some advocate teaching the language three days a week for twenty minutes; others every day for fifty minutes. Some even claim that the best way to teach the language is not to teach it at all but, rather to teach regular subjects (e.g., geography, math, science) in the foreign language.

Not all approaches aim at achieving fluency and, as a result, all must be examined in view of their stated goals. But the question remains, do different methods result in different levels of fluency in elementary school students? And if so, what conditions and/or teaching methods contribute to the highest level of fluency?

With these questions in mind, researchers at the Center for Applied Linguistics, in conjunction with UCLA scholars, set out to gather information and to test students who were participating in various elementary school foreign language programs. This seminal research was funded by the U.S. Department of Education and the Hazen Foundation. The researchers wanted to compare the foreign language achievement of elementary school students in different types of programs. They also wanted to compare this achievement with that of students who had been studying a foreign language in high school. Students in three types of elementary school programs were tested: immersion, FLES (revitalized Foreign Language in the Elementary School), and partial immersion. The most important differences among these programs are (1) the time spent per day in the

17

Nancy C. Rhodes is Language Researcher at the Center for Applied Linguistics. Marguerite Ann Snow is Visiting Assistant Professor in the Department of TESL and Applied Linguistics at the University of California at Los Angeles.

study of foreign language; (2) the language used by the teacher (English or the foreign language); and (3) whether or not the students are taught basic subjects (math, science, social studies) in the foreign language.

The three programs had the following characteristics:

Immersion. Starting in kindergarten, children are taught most of their subjects in the foreign language. The foreign language is not taught as a subject per se but is used as the medium for teaching the other subjects. English language arts is introduced in second or third grade, and the number of subjects taught in English is gradually increased until the sixth grade. Of all the programs, immersion sets the highest proficiency goal. The goal is that students master the material in the regular curriculum as well as become functionally fluent in the foreign language. This means that sixth graders should be able to communicate in the foreign language on topics appropriate to their age almost as well as children their age in French- or Spanish-speaking countries.

FLES. While the proficiency goals are not as ambitious as those of immersion, FLES programs emphasize oral communication and set more precise goals than their forerunners in the 1960s. The primary goal is that students acquire a certain level of listening and speaking skills (depending on the program) and an awareness of the foreign culture. Reading and writing skills may also be emphasized in some programs. In general, the degree of proficiency anticipated in a particular FLES program depends on the time available for language instruction. Typically, the instructor teaches in English. FLES programs observed for this study taught language for 20-45 minutes daily.

Partial Immersion. This program type possesses characteristics of both immersion and FLES, and the proficiency goals fall somewhere between the two. Like immersion, a portion of the school curriculum is taught in the foreign language. Like FLES, a portion of the school day is also devoted to formal language instruction. In partial immersion, it is typical to have up to 50% of the school subjects taught in the foreign language. For the purpose of this study, however, the definition of partial immersion was broadened to include schools that teach foreign language per se for at least seventy minutes a day, during which time only the foreign language is spoken. Thus, a range of partial immersion programs is represented in this study.

Methodology

The study focused on 382 elementary school students (and some junior high students) who had studied French or Spanish for 4-7 years. The students were selected from 15 schools that teach foreign language in immersion, FLES, or partial immersion programs. The schools represented a diverse sampling: 8 schools were in the Midwest, 6 on the West Coast, 1 on the East Coast; 12 were public, 3 private; and the socioeconomic status of the students ranged from lower to upper class. A total of 179 immersion students, 105 FLES students, and 98 partial immersion students were tested.

One obstacle to the research was that there is no foreign language test for elementary school students that assesses the four skills. As a result, it was decided to use the Modern Language Association (MLA) Cooperative Foreign Language Exam (1963) designed for high school students. Because it was meant for older students, it was first tested with young students to make sure that it was appropriate. The pilot test showed that students of that age did not have problems with the mechanics of the test.

The MLA test consists of four subtests. The listening subtest measures comprehension skills via multiple-choice questions on cassette tape. The reading subtest contains multiple-choice questions based on short passages as well as fill-in-the-blank sentences. The writing subtest includes structured items that require the student to fill in verb tenses and make grammatical corrections and less controlled writing of a short dialogue. The speaking subtest, administered to 13% of the students, includes word repetitions, oral reading, and story telling. In addition to taking the test, the students were asked to rate themselves on how well they thought they perform, in general, on the four skills. They could rate their skills as "none," "a little bit," "fairly well," "very well," and "fluently."

Results

The test results for French and Spanish students will be discussed separately for each of the research questions addressed in the study. Although both the French and Spanish tests have the same format, they were not developed for comparative purposes so cannot validly be compared. Also, only two types of French programs were involved in the testing (FLES and immersion), while three types of Spanish programs were involved (FLES, immersion, and partial immersion). The test results are reported in terms of mean percentile scores which are based on the original high school students' performance upon which the test was normed.

19

Performance on the MLA Test

French students. Figure 1 displays the mean percentile scores on the four subtests for French FLES and immersion students. Students in the French immersion programs significantly outperformed their FLES peers on all four language tests by more than two to one in terms of scores attained on each of the subtests. For example, in the reading subtest, immersion students scored at the 77th percentile and FLES students at the 22nd percentile. Clearly, the findings indicate that the amount of exposure to a foreign language has a positive effect on student performance. In fact, an additional analysis revealed that students who had studied French in immersion programs for 4-6 years out-performed their FLES counterparts who had studied French for 7-9 years. Thus, the intensity of immersion programs (an average of 75% of their total instruction per week in French compared to approximately 10% for FLES) and use of the

Figure 1

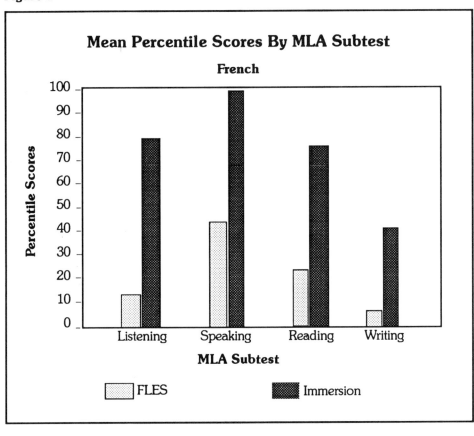

Mean Percentile Scores By MLA Subtest

French

foreign language to study basic subjects have resulted in substantial differences in performance in all four skill areas of the MLA test.

The percentile scores were also used to compare performance of the elementary school students with high school students who took the test in 1963. French immersion students scored at the 80th percentile in listening, i.e., 80% of the high school students in the norming group earned scores lower than that score. In the FLES group, 14% percent of the high school students scored lower in listening. Immersion students also ranked very high in comparison to high school students in speaking (99th percentile) and reading (77th percentile).

Spanish students. Figure 2 displays the mean percentile scores on the four subtests for Spanish FLES, partial immersion, and immersion students. As with the French programs, students in the Spanish immersion programs outperformed their peers on all four language subtests. Immersion students were followed by partial immersion students and then by the students in FLES.

Several results are of particular interest. First, Spanish immersion students outperformed the FLES students by more than two to one on the listening, reading, and writing subtests. The differences were most pronounced on the reading subtest, with a range from the 14th

Figure 2

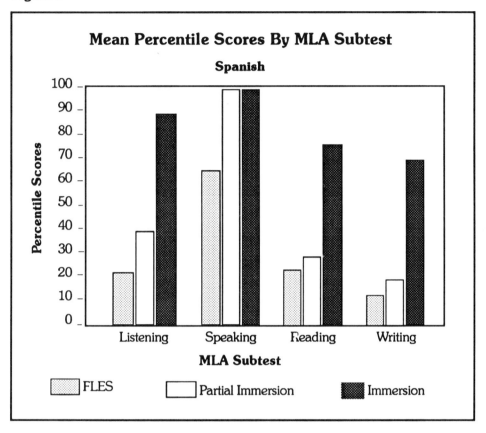

Mean Percentile Scores By MLA Subtest

Spanish

percentile for FLES students to the 75th percentile for immersion students. Students in the partial immersion program performed better on the test overall than FLES students. These differences, however, were significant only on the listening and speaking sections. Finally, a comparison of Spanish immersion and partial immersion reveals significant differences in student performance on the listening, reading, and writing subtests.

Again, a discussion of these findings must take into account the amount of exposure to the foreign language that students have experienced. While immersion and FLES represent opposite ends of the continuum, partial immersion falls somewhere in the middle. Given the variation among the partial immersion programs, it is difficult to quantify the exposure received by these students. The range, however, extends from 1.5 to 3 hours (23% to 60%) of instruction per day. Therefore, findings from all three Spanish programs are consistent with the claim that the amount of exposure to a foreign language has a measurable effect on student performance.

In comparison with high school students, Spanish immersion students performed very well, scoring higher than the 70th percentile in all skills. Partial immersion and FLES students also did well in comparison on the speaking test.

Difference in Student Performance among Schools having the Same Type of Program

French students. There are, indeed, significant differences among students from schools with the same type of program. In other words, differences in student performance may be due to individual school factors as well as to the type of foreign language program. We can speculate from visits to the schools that factors such as program longevity, articulation among grades, and teacher turnover might account for program variation. It is interesting to note that there is more variation in test results between the two French immersion programs than among the three French FLES schools. Perhaps this is because of the greater similarity in FLES program design in which listening and speaking skills are emphasized.

Spanish students. Again, there are significant differences in student scores among the individual schools. Of the three programs, the scores from the FLES schools are the most homogeneous. Factors such as low socioeconomic status and no courses in which Spanish was the language of instruction might explain the variation found among the partial immersion schools. Students in the Spanish immersion junior high significantly outperformed their elementary school counterparts on listening, reading, and writing. While students in all three immersion schools had studied Spanish the same number of years, the age factor may explain the superior performance of the junior high students.

Correlation between Students' Self-assessment of Language Skills and Actual Performance on the MLA Test.

French students. The degree of exposure to the language did improve the self-assessment abilities of French students. There was a strong positive correlation between student performance and self-assessment ratings for the French immersion students on three of the four subtests—listening, reading, and writing. On the other hand, a significant positive correlation was found only on the listening score for FLES students. Thus, the immersion students were more adept at evaluating their language skills than the FLES students who had had less exposure to French.

Spanish students. Spanish immersion and partial immersion students were better able to predict their performance on the MLA test than FLES students were. There were significant correlations for the listening and writing tests. In contrast, the scores from the Spanish FLES students showed no significant correlations on any of the four subtests.

In short, the reliability of self-assessment reports for language is related to the degree of exposure and proficiency in the foreign language. It is also evident that some of the students, particularly those in FLES programs, had inflated perceptions of their language skills.

Conclusion

This study set out to compare three approaches to the foreign language education of elementary school children in communities across the country. The research is timely, given the increasing awareness of the critical importance of foreign language resources as they relate to our academic, commercial, and sociopolitical interests both at home and abroad. A second purpose was to provide information that decisionmakers such as school adminstrators and parents could use to make informed choices about foreign language programs in their communities. The results of this study provide clear indications of the student gains that can be reasonably expected from the three approaches. Furthermore, a favorable comparison with high school students' proficiency is apparent for at least the immersion programs.

There is little doubt as to the relative efficacy of the three methods when students' overall language proficiency is the objective. Immersion, setting the most ambitious language fluency goals, provides the highest level of proficiency. Partial immersion ranks second in promoting proficiency attainment, and FLES, whose goals are the least ambitious, ranks third.

References

Campbell, R. N. "The Immersion Approach to Foreign Language Teaching." *Studies on Immersion Education: A Collection for United States Educators.* Sacramento: California Department of Education, Office of Bilingual Bicultural Education, 1984.

Gray, Tracy, and R. N. Campbell. *Results of Preliminary Evaluation of Modern Language Association Cooperative Test of Spanish Proficiency.* Final Report to the Hazen Foundation, 1982.

Met, Myriam, et al. "Elementary School Foreign Language: Key Link in the Chain of Learning." *Foreign Languages: Key Links in the Chain of Learning.* Middlebury, Vt: Northeast Conference on the Teaching of Foreign Languages, 1983.

Rhodes, Nancy C., and Audrey R. Schreibstein. *Foreign Language in the Elementary School: A Practical Guide.* Washington, D.C.: Center for Applied Linguistics, 1983. ED 225 403.

Rhodes, Nancy C., G. Richard Tucker, and John L. D. Clark. *Elementary School Foreign Language Instruction in the United States: Innovative Approaches for the 1980s. Final Report.* Washington, D.C.: Center for Applied Linguistics, 1981. ED 209 940.

A Comparison of Three Second Language Programs

Magdelhayne F. Buteau and Helen Gougeon

During the past ten years traditional school subjects taught in French have been the vehicle through which a large segment of Canada's English-speaking student population has learned a second language. This has been achieved by (1) enrolling in French language schools with the resultant "submersion" in French language and culture, (2) by participating in the linguistically less effective but culturally more acceptable French Immersion programs offered within the context of the English-language education system, or (3) by selecting one of a variety of limited bilingual or enriched French-language programs that are currently accessible to most anglophone students.

Professional opinion is divided as to when intensive instruction in a second language should begin and the extent to which knowledge of content suffers as a consequence of being transmitted in a student's weaker language. Decisions to implement a particular program must take into consideration the best advice of researchers, the goals of parents, and the practical problems of enrollment, teacher availability, and program development.

Each of the three programs described in this paper has been initiated as a result of dissatisfaction with the limitations of traditional French as a second language (FSL) programs and in response to parental demands to increase the quantity and quality of French available to their child. The age of onset, intensity, and duration of each program have been a function of a number of considerations both theoretical and practical. Elsewhere we have provided the details of the methodology employed and the presentation and discussion of results.[1] Our intention here is simply to describe the programs, the theoretical and practical considerations which prompted their implementation, to summarize the trends in the results, and to discuss implications for second language learning and teaching.

Rationale for Program Development

A province in which over eighty percent of the citizens speak French as a first language, Quebec has been promoting the use of French in commerce and industry during the past ten years. As a

Magdelhayne F. Buteau is Professor Emerita of Education in Second Languages and Helen Gougeon is Dean of Admissions and Associate Professor of Educational Psychology at McGill University.

24

result, most English-speaking parents want their children to become functionally fluent in French. In their judgment and in that of educators, the regular French as a second language (FSL) program within the English school system does not provide the opportunity to attain such proficiency. Attending a French school in which an anglophone student could expect to attain a high level of fluency in French is considered by some parents as impractical or undesirable. Consequently the need has arisen for alternative French language programs within the English sector that conforms to current thought on bilingual education with respect to the impact on second language learning of age, ability, time, motivation, and other circumstances. The implementation of such programs must also take into account the more practical administrative restrictions and the unique community setting in which the program is being offered.

In the case of the first experimental program, in Kindergarten, parents and administrators have opted to explore and experiment with a French-language program which interferes as little as possible with the regular English instruction while offering an intensive second language experience at an age where the child is, according to research, favourably disposed to second language acquisition.

The selection of grade four as the starting point for the second experimental program was based on the assumption that first language skills were well entrenched by this time and yet the learner was young enough to benefit from an intensive second language experience. Somewhat similar reasoning has been applied to the development of the third innovative program, the secondary immersion program. Youngsters who have opted for this program are young enough to benefit from the advantages of youth in the area of language learning and old enough to be self-motivated and to be capable of making the most of an enriched second language program.

Program Onset, Duration, and Intensity

Figure 1 provides information on the grade of onset, duration, and intensity of the French language instruction within the three experimental programs.

In the Bilingual Kindergarten, the regular morning half-day English-language kindergarten was extended to a full day in order to accommodate the complementary second language program. This program focuses on a number of interesting activities in the natural and social sciences. In the follow-up program in grades one and two, pupils take approximately fifty minutes of instruction per day of an integrated French language and social studies program. In grades three, four, and five, an enriched French as a second language program as well as a social studies program taught in French is part of the curriculum. At grade six, pupils are given the option to take either a total French immersion program (i.e., all subjects in the curriculum are taught in French) or a regular English program where French is taught as a second language. Although it is likely to include some subjects taught

---

Figure 1
Onset, Duration, and Intensity of Experimental Programs

Bilingual Kindergarten and Follow-up Programs

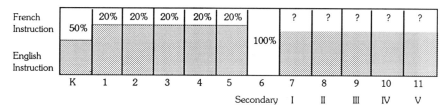

Elementary French Immersion Program

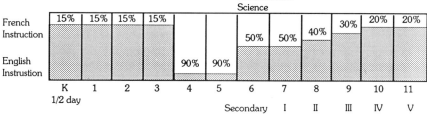

Secondary French Immersion Program

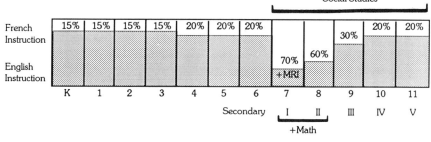

---

through French, the program at the secondary level has not yet been developed.

The second innovative French program depicted in the diagram is the Elementary French Immersion Program. After following a regular FSL program from kindergarten through grade three, pupils are "immersed" in grades four and five in a program in which over ninety percent of the curriculum is taught through French and, in grade six, in a program in which fifty percent of the curriculum is in French with the focus on mathematics, history, geography, and moral and religious instruction. Subsequently there is a reduction in the number of subjects taught in French with approximately twenty percent of the curriculum in French in the graduating year (secondary five, or grade eleven).

The Secondary French Immersion Program is implemented in

secondary one (grade seven) after seven years (K-6) of the regular FSL program. At secondary one, mathematics, history, geography, and moral and religious instruction are among the subjects taught in French. By the graduating year, twenty percent of the curriculum is taught through French.

Description of Programs

Following from the overview of the program provided in the section above, a more detailed description of the major characteristics and objectives of the three innovative programs is provided. Included is a brief description of the traditional FSL program, followed by students in the regular English stream.

French as a Second Language

According to provincial regulations, the teaching of FSL in the English schools is compulsory from grade one to seven (secondary five). Daily periods vary from twenty to thirty minutes in the six levels of elementary school and from forty to fifty minutes in secondary schools. Oral skills are emphasized at both the elementary and secondary levels. At the secondary level, these skills are supplemented by instruction in reading and writing, and the French program comprises a variety of options to suit the needs of different types of learners. In addition to the regular French language program, pupils in secondary three, four, and five may opt to take one or two subjects in French.

Generally, French is taught by French specialists. At the elementary school, however, there are a number of classroom teachers who have this subject included in their teaching load. Although they enjoy considerable freedom in the selection and use of material, teachers usually follow the progression and use the material and techniques provided in the French series by Helen Kerr et al. entitled *Ici on parle français*.

27

Bilingual Kindergarten and Follow-Up Programs

The French component of the kindergarten program does not repeat or review what has been taught in the English kindergarten. Time is spent in pleasant educational activities conducted in French with a view to developing auditory comprehension of directives and explanations associated with the physical and social aspects of school life and with short story comprehension. The pupils are gradually and naturally initiated in French oral production through songs, nursery rhymes, games, and so forth.

Special attention is paid to the development of positive attitudes towards learning French. The teacher is advised to center on the children's interests and characteristics and to provide means for acquiring French naturally in integrated and functional situations. Individual and group projects, out-of-school visits, adequate use of materials and audio-visual media are expected to provide the variety of experience that is necessary to ensure attentive cooperation from the children during the French session.

The general and intermediate objectives of the French component of the Bilingual Kindergarten program as well as the content of the syllabus and guidelines for implementation are provided in separate documents.[2] The content of the program is based on ten themes (e.g., animals, health and food, buildings, and community life) which are fully developed in ten modules available to the teacher and corresponding to each month of the school year.

The Follow-up Program (or Curriculum) consists of the integrated teaching of social studies and FSL in grades one and two.

The aim of this experimental program is to maintain and reenforce the skills and favourable attitudes that the children have developed through their 300-hour contact with a French-speaking kindergarten teacher.

As the pupils have been initiated in the use of French through an experimental approach based on natural activities and concrete materials, it was assumed that the follow-up program would adopt a similar approach. The integration of social studies and FSL daily periods seems to provide a suitable framework to this end. It provides the child with the possibility of learning French more intensively in a communicative context, without being deprived of any components of the regular curriculum. Moreoever, as the regular social studies curriculum is designed to arouse children's curiosity for, and awareness of, persons, things, and experiences close to them, it is anticipated that the integration of these two subjects will serve as motivational factors toward enjoying the learning of French through authentic discovery of facts and phenonema. This integrative approach falls in line with a school-board policy of teaching social studies in French at grades four and five in preparation for the grade six total French immersion option. The general pedagogical objectives, the terminal and intermediate objectives, as well as comments on the syllabus and some guidelines and reference materials are available.[3]

Elementary French Immersion Program

At grades four and five, the French immersion program is so designed that over ninety percent of the learning activities can be conducted in French. Although some modifications have been recently introduced, in the original proposal class time was allocated as follows:

1. Twenty percent to a highly structured second language core program;
2. Twenty percent to four interest centers oriented towards mathematics, science, social studies, and art;
3. Ten percent to free activities such as singing, watching TV, etc.;

4. Forty percent to activities focusing on a thematic or integrated approach to curriculum.

The bulk of instruction time is devoted to the integrated approach in order to facilitate oral interaction in the target language—a major goal of the first two years of the program—and to provide for a new and stimulating method of instruction. Prepared by the curriculum development division of the school board, extensive materials using an integrated approach of teaching around a theme, are used for approximately forty percent of the school work. To give a simplistic example, the theme "bicycle" would be used as a means of teaching science, mathematics, and social studies, and as a medium for learning vocabulary and grammar. Teachers are very enthusiastic about this approach and are inclined to adopt it in developing their own materials.

The expectation is that the first few months of the elementary immersion program will constitute quite a challenge for both teacher and students. Instructional objectives specify that, by the end of the year, the content of the grade four program should be assimilated by the majority of students and that, by the end of grade five, almost all students should achieve such facility in French that their academic growth is not impaired by the exclusive use of French as a teaching and learning medium. On the other hand, they are expected to develop such quality of bilingualism that their achievement in French skills gradually approximates those of native speakers.

In grade six, those continuing in the program take approximately fifty percent of their instruction in French. In addition to language arts, courses in social studies and natural science are taught in French. Art, music, and physical education would be taught in either language, depending on the availability of teaching personnel. In secondary one, the program and instruction time vary depending on the school. For most schools approximately forty percent of time is allotted to instruction via the second language. Social studies, science, and, in some schools, moral instruction are taught in French. There is also a period devoted to instruction in French language arts. At secondary two a similar program is implemented.

Secondary French Immersion Program

The introduction of immersion classes at the elementary level has given rise to a number of administrative problems, such as bussing of pupils, assignment of teaching loads, purchase and design of new teaching materials, and space and budget allocations. Encouraged by the success of other immersion programs initiated at the secondary level and in search of alternative solutions to bilingual education for their pupils, school officials have introduced a second experimental program, this one at the onset of secondary school. This immersion program is implemented at secondary one. Instruction time in French varies among schools from approximately sixty to eighty percent. Mathematics, social studies, moral instruction, and language arts are taught in French. Pupils in their fourth year of immersion are instructed separately from those in their first year of immersion. Secondary two students in their second year of immersion are enrolled in a substantially similar program. In secondary three, students within the two immersion programs, the elementary and the secondary, are brought together for instruction in all subjects including the one or two they continue to take in French. Pupils returning to the regular English program are given the traditional fifty-minute FSL period, but an accelerated course has been designed for these returning students. (Additional information is available in a series of unpublished documents).[4]

Other Programs

Students in each of the three experimental programs who took part in the testing were compared with students following other programs within the same school system or in neighboring school systems. The most important programs from which students were selected for comparison purposes are described below.

Regular English Program. This program is found within the English school system where students receive approximately thirty to forty minutes per day of FSL from kindergarten through grade six and approximately fifty minutes thereafter.

Regular French Program. This program exists within the French school system. The teaching of English as a second language parallels the teaching of French within the regular program in the English system. The majority of students within this program are francophones. The anglophone students enrolled in this French system are described as being "submersed" with respect to French language instruction.

Reception Kindergarten Program. A special kindergarten program within the French system, this option prepares non-francophone students for integration with French-speaking students. For the purpose of this investigation only those students whose mother tongue was English were selected for comparison.

Design of Evaluation

Evaluations of student performance are to accomplish three major goals. The first is to assess the development of proficiency in French of pupils participating in one of the three innovative programs and, at some point, to make comparisons among programs with regard to achievement in the target language. A second goal is to assess English and subject-area skills (e.g., mathematics, social studies) of pupils in the experimental programs in order to determine whether the programs have had a detrimental effect on English-language skills or on performance in a basic subject. A third goal is to assess the pupils' attitude towards program, their perception of their second language proficiency vis-à-vis pupils in other programs, and their attitudes towards the learning and value of the second language.

30

In order to guard against drawing conclusions based on spurious results, it was decided to follow three cohorts of pupils within each of the three evaluation studies. Within each investigation, comparisons are made for each cohort and at each grade level among pupils attending the experimental program and those attending the comparison programs either within the same or at neighboring schools.

For each cohort of the elementary and secondary immersion programs, a random sample from each school was selected at the beginning of the programs (grade four and grade seven) from each of the comparison groups. For each cohort, populations had to be resampled at the beginning of secondary one because approximately forty percent of the pupils who had been in the regular English program chose to enter the secondary French immersion program. Approximately 300 pupils were tested at grade four in the experimental group. By grade eight, with the introduction of the second French immersion program, the sample was reduced to about 150. At any one grade level, from fifteen to twenty-five percent of the population was included in the sample.

In the case of the bilingual kindergarten and follow-up programs, a total population of one class was tested and compared to comparison groups (classes) from a similar socioeconomic status.

The voluntary nature of the program at each level did not permit random arrangement of pupils to treatments (programs). Consequently, because of the probability of the initial differences between experimental and comparison groups and the shifting samples as pupils left the program for various reasons, most tests were administered at the beginning and the end of each year and, where possible, an analysis of covariance designs was used in the statistical treatment of data. In most cases, either the Raven's Progressive Matrices or the Canadian Lorge Thorndike Test was used to adjust achievement test means for any differences in general ability between samples.

Six categories of tests were used, including tests of general mental ability, tests of subject content (e.g., mathematics, social studies), tests of English language proficiency, tests of French language proficiency, classroom observation techniques, and attitude questionnaires (pupils, parents, teachers). These tests covered a range and combination of types including standardized and nonstandardized, individual and group, oral and written.

Tests were administered and scored by trained graduate students whom we supervised on all aspects of these operations. Open-ended tests were scored blindly and independently by two raters, and measures of inter-judge reliability were calculated. All interpretations of results and subsequent writing of articles and reports other than theses were undertaken by the major investigators.

A list of tests administered to students in the experimental and comparison groups is provided in Table 1. We developed, pretested, and validated the nonstandardized instruments. A description of the tests and, where appropriate, the scoring and validation procedure are available in the annual reports.

31

Table 1.
Types of Tests *

Bilingual K & Follow-Up (K, Grades 1, 2, 3, 4)	Elementary Immersion (Grades 4, 5, 6)	Secondary Immersion (Grades 7, 8, 9, 10, 11)
Standardized	*Standardized*	*Standardized*
Raven	Raven	Raven
Peabody Picture Vocabulary	Lorge-Thorndike	Lorge-Thorndike
Bilingual Syntax Measure	Canadian Tests of Basic Skills	Metropolitan Achievement Tests
Metropolitan Achievement Tests	Vocabulary	World Knowledge
Reading	Reading	Reading
Language	Spelling	Language
French Comprehension (OISE)	Capitalization	Spelling
French Reading Comprehension (OISE)	Punctuation	Math 1 (Computation)
	Language Usage	Math 2 (Concepts)
	Mathematics	Math 3 (Problems)
	Je Sais (Auditory Comprehension Test)	
	Test de Rendement en français	Je Sais
	Tests de Français (CECM)	Tests de Rendement en Français
	Epreuve de Lecture Silencieuse	Tests de Français (CECM)
	Tests de Lecture "California"	Epreuve de Lecture Silencieuse
	Tests de Compréhension (I.O.P.F.)	Epreuve de Lecture Rapide (SLP)
		Tests de Lecture "California"
Nonstandardized		
Peabody Picture Vocabulary (French)	*Nonstandardized*	*Nonstandardized*
Echelle de Syntaxe Bilingue (ESB)	French Oral Comprhension and Expression (Buteau-Gougeon)	French Oral Language Measure
Oral Language Measure (Eng. & Fr)		English Cloze
Buteau-Gougeon French Reading Comp. Test		French Cloze
Content Exam (in French)		English Written Expression
Verbal Interaction Analysis		French Written Expression
Pupil Attitude Questionnaire		French Oral Language Interview (analysed for content & language)
Teacher Questionnaire		Student Attitude Questionnaire
Parent Questionnaire		

*Tests listed not used at all grade levels

Overview of Test Results

For a precise presentation of the results within each cohort, the reader is referred to the annual reports. Here, we shall provide only a summary of the findings in the evaluation of the bilingual kindergarten program and of the two French immersion programs.

Bilingual Kindergarten and Follow-up Programs

At the kindergarten level there are no statistically significant differences between the groups on any of the English language tests. Differences in the expected direction are apparent on the French language measures. Generally, the pupils in the regular French (RF) kindergarten achieve significantly better results than do those in the reception (R) kindergarten who in turn perform better—but not significantly so—than those in the experimental (Exp.) bilingual kindergarten.

A pattern similar to that in kindergarten is observed in grade one. Again, on English language tests there are no significant between-group differences, while on French language tests the differences between the groups (reception, experimental, regular English) are in the expected direction. Although differences in French comprehension indicate that the post-reception group have an advantage over the experimental group, there are no significant differences on measures of French oral language.

In grades two and three the reception kindergarten group moves firmly ahead of the experimental and the regular English group on French language tests. The French immersion group maintains its lead over the regular English group on the French tests. In addition, in the area of social studies, the immersion group has not suffered any detriment to their content knowledge as compared to the other groups.

The results of an attitude questionnaire administered at grade four reveal a willingness to use French outside school in situations which warrant its use (e.g., in shops). The positive identification with the French language and culture is not as apparent as one would have anticipated.

From the perspective of the parents, the program was evaluated as advantageous, and nearly all parents would recommend the program to others. The teachers who participated in the implementation of the programs identified specific deficiencies, particularly in the area of the clarification of certain linguistic objectives, but are of the opinion that the programs are viable and should be maintained.

Elementary and Secondary French Immersion Programs

Based on the results of ability tests and pretests in English language and mathematics, it appears that the immersion program is attracting

33

more of the academically more able students and fewer of the academically less able students. Pretest scores (baseline data for each of the cohorts) consistently favor the immersion groups. Students leaving the immersion program during the first year are frequently those who are experiencing difficulty, thus further reducing the heterogeneity of the sample.

At the elementary level, participation in immersion results in some temporary effects on performance in English language tests. At the beginning of grade four, prior to participating in the immersion program, the immersion sample for each cohort was achieving subtest means which were significantly greater than those obtained by the regular English sample. By the end of grade four and the beginning of grade five the two samples were equivalent in performance. On certain specific English-language skills (e.g., spelling, capitalization, punctuation) significant differences between means favoured the regular English sample. Participation by immersion students in the fifty-fifty program at level six resulted in their regaining the more dominant position held by this group at the beginning of grade four. At the secondary level, the differences on English-language skills between the students in the secondary immersion program and those in the regular English program are less marked. The fact that, in the secondary immersion program, students follow approximately thirty-five percent of the curriculum in English may be responsible for maintaining language skills to the level of counterparts within the regular program.

On standardized tests of French language skills, the results of the statistical analysis of mean scores reveal that at the end of secondary three, the students who opted for the secondary French immersion program had reached about the same level of proficiency as students who entered French immersion in grade four, even though most differential trends favoured the latter. On nonstandardized tests of French oral and written expression, there is a consistent trend which reveals that the elementary immersion group is ahead of the secondary group.

On the attitude questionnaire, secondary five students who had begun immersion in grade four rated themselves more highly on French language achievement than did students who began in secondary one (grade seven). With regard to the selection of preferred programs, a greater percentage of the former seemed more satisfied with their own program than did those in the latter group or in the regular program. Respondents did not believe that instruction in a weaker language had negative effects on academic success. They did consider some subjects (e.g., history, geography) as more suitable than others (e.g., science, math) for inclusion in immersion programs.

Implications for Teaching and Learning

Since the major goal of the bilingual kindergarten and follow-up programs was simply to provide an enriched early experience in French in order to develop more positive attitudes towards using the language and a greater facility in comprehension and expression than that permitted in the regular FSL program, this program could be considered a success. Because the program, after kindergarten and until immersion in grade six, contributes to only a small portion of the pupil's day, it is imperative that an enriched FSL program is implemented and monitored from grades three to five so that the positive outcomes of the early intensive experience in French can continue to develop.

The option to attend either of the French immersion programs is made available to all students within a large school district. The subtle form of streaming which results when more of the academically more able students select an experimental program can lead to classes following the regular program that are composed of an unusually high number of academically weaker students. If regular programs are to remain a viable option within the system, special attention needs to be paid to pupils in these programs.

Based on the evidence provided by the results on the French reading tests, the tests of free written expression, and the oral language measures, the investigators have identified a type of interlanguage in some students. In order that native-like competence may be facilitated, broader exposure to the second language as well as systematic training in certain aspects of written French should be encouraged. This could be achieved through a special bilingual language arts course which would incorporate a contrastive study of the features of English and French as well as vocabulary development strategies and general communication techniques that could lead to excellence in the use of both languages.

A maintenance program must include a number of experiences with the language in the French-speaking community so that students have the opportunity to enhance their oral skills and to be exposed to a variety of second language models.

In view of the favorable reports on immersion across Canada and our own findings in this area and in the early bilingual program, one can only give support to the implementation of programs which provide a more successful pedagogical practice of teaching French than does the traditional curriculum. This finding is all the more impressive when accompanied by results that indicate no long-term negative effects on first language skills and little or no apparent detrimental effects on the learning of the traditional subjects through which French is taught. Although the findings in our investigation corroborate those in other studies, there are questions which can be raised about the academic and cognitive development of students who take subjects such as science and history through a weaker language and about the linguistic skills of students subjected to a curriculum emphasizing content over language. An attempt to respond to these critical questions goes beyond the scope of this paper.

Notes

[1]Magdelhayne F. Buteau and Helen Gougeon, "Tip of the Iceberg on French Immersion," paper presented at Canadian Learned Societies Conference (CLSC), Toronto, June 1974; "A Balance Sheet: Report on a Longitudinal Evaluation of Two Partial French Immersion Programs," paper, CLSC, London, June 1978; "Two French Immersion Programs: A Longitudianl Evaluation of Student Achievement on English and French Language Tests," paper, Eastern Educational Research Association, Norfolk, Virginia, March 1980; "An Analysis of the Opinions of Three Groups of Secondary Five Students on Their Study of French," paper, CLSC, Vancouver, June 1984; "The Use of the Cloze Procedure in Evaluating Global Language Proficiency in Bilingual Contexts," paper, Third Annual Conference on the Teaching of Reading in Bilingual Education, Texas Women's Univ., Denton, Tex., June 1984; "The Assessment of Some Aspects of Verbal Behaviour in a Bilingual Kindergarten Program," in M. Lutjeharms and T. Culhane, eds., *Practice and Problems in Language Testing* (Brussels: Vrije Universiteit Brussel, 1982):193-203; *L'Evaluation de la compréhension du français oral chez les élèves d'origine portuguaise inscrits dans les classes d'accueil et de francisation*, (Quebec: Direction générale des réseaux, Ministère de L'Education, 1982); "Le Test de closure en langue première et en langue seconde; son utilisation dans l'évaluation de différents programmes d'immersion," *Mesure et Evaluation en Education* 5(1982):4-15 (unpublished English version available on request); "Maternelle Bilingue: Evaluation Longitudinale des progrès en français langue seconde," *Les Annales de l'ACFAS* 50.3(1983):81 (English version available); "Enseignement du français par immersion partielle: Analyse d'observations," *Les Annales de l'ACFAS* 51.1(1985):85 (English version available). See also annual progress reports for the St. Croix School Commission, 1979-84, and for the Lakeshore School Commission, 1972-83.

[2]_____, "Programme expérimental d'enseignement bilingue à la maternelle," soumis au directeur générale, Direction générale du développment pédagogique, le 26 février 1979; "Programme expérimental d'enseignement bilingue à la maternelle," soumis le [1]er février 1980.

[3]_____, "Programme expérimental d'enseignement intégré des sciences humaines et du français langue seconde en première année," préparé pour la Commission scolaire Sainte-Croix, 1980; "Programme expérimental d'enseignement intégré des sciences humaines et du français langue seconde en deuxième année," 1981.

[4]A series of unpublished documents and papers referring to the goals and objectives of the Elementary and Secondary French Immersion programs is available from the Curriculum Development Services Division of the Lakeshore School Board, 257 Beaconfield, Quebec H9W 4A5.

Appendix A.

Description of Nonstandardized Instruments Used in the Evaluation of the Three Innovative French Language Programs

Peabody Picture Vocabulary Test (French Version). The English version of this test provides an estimate of the child's verbal intelligence through the measurement of his hearing vocabulary. Norms are based on results of testing children between two-and-one-half and eighteen years. The test consists of a series of 150 plates each containing four drawings. For each set of four drawings, the subject must indicate the picture which best corresponds to the word presented by the examiner.

The French version of this test consists of a translation adapted for use with francophone children. The raw score is based on the number of correct responses prior to making six errors on eight consecutive items.

L'Echelle de syntaxe bilingue (E.S.B.). This French version of the Bilingual Syntax Measure, developed by Paul Pimsleur and used by his collaborator at the University of Paris III, Elisabeth Bautier-Castaing, uses the same cartoons as the B.S.M. It consists of thirty-four questions and deals with fifty-six syntactic structures. Unlike the original version, the E.S.B. does not, as yet, permit the calculation of a precise level of competence.

Oral Language Measure (OLM). This oral language test consists of an interview of about ten minutes dealing with the events represented in a series of drawings. Partly structured and partly free, the exercise involves the description of drawings, the formulation of possible conversations among characters depicted in these drawings, relating the total story, and the explanation of a specific event depicted in one of the scenes.

Buteau-Gougeon French Reading Comprehension Test. This test was designed to assess French reading comprehension in anglophone students 8 to 10 years of age who have acquired a fairly good level of French oral comprehension through lessons in social studies taught in French. It consists of a text followed by a series of questions. The final form was accepted only after a few trials with francophone and anglophone students.

The text is made up of four paragraphs and includes about 350 words. It is an adapted version of a passage on winter drawn from a French reader. The questions consist of multiple choice items (9) and comprehension items (5). In content, the questions aim at testing lexical (4), inferential (8), and evaluative (2) comprehension.

Content Examination. This oral test was prepared with a view to assessing the acquisition of the ideas provided in the modules (at the kindergarten level) and in the social studies curriculum (at grades one and two). At the kindergarten level, for example, the test consisted of twenty-two questions based on the modules. Approximately fifty percent of the questions referred the children to two series of randomly-arranged drawings representing animals, foods, and a variety of objects. The examiners were instructed to elicit as much information as possible from the children. If necessary, examiners would repeat questions in English. Appropriate responses in English were accepted. The maximum number of correct responses was sixty-nine. Each pupil's score was converted to a percentage.

Verbal Interaction Analysis. This technique is an observational tool that focuses the observer's attention on the frequency and direction of verbal exchanges between pupil and teacher and pupil and pupil. Verbal events (pupil statements, questions, commands, exclamations) through which the child attempts to communicate his thoughts are recorded on a grid. Since only one pupil is observed at a time, verbal behavior and any paralinguistic behavior can be reported in detail. An observer, familiar with the classroom routine and trained in the use of the grid, stays close to the pupil for ten minutes, recording

37

utterances in as much detail as possible, and then moves on to a second pupil.

Pupil Attitude Questionnaire. This is a two-part questionnaire administered for the purpose of determining in a global way the pupil's interest in, enjoyment of, and desire to use French within and outside the school setting. In Part 1, the pupils must respond "yes" or "no" to statements about the relative difficulty of the second language and interest in pursuing the study of the language. Part 2 provides a statement with a multiple-choice response in which the pupils can indicate the extent of their commitment to the use of the language and their interest in using the language in situations outside the school setting.

Tests de Compréhension (I.O.P.F.). These tests are drawn from a set provided in the *Teacher's Textbook* of the *Ici on parle français* series, Level Two. They are group tests consisting of short anecdotes recorded in French on a test tape. The anecdote is played through once while the students listen. The examiner then stops the tape recorder and distributes mimeographed copies of a series of ten multiple-choice questions worded in English. The students may now refer to these questions as the French anecdote is played through a second time. They are then allowed time to underline the completion which makes each English sentence acceptable according to the recorded anecdote. The maximal score is 10, and individual scores are obtained from the number of correct answers.

French Oral Comprehension and Expression (Buteau-Gougeon). This is a tape recorded interview that tests: comprehension (part A tests commands and directions), by asking the examinee to react to questions with gestures and actions judged as appropriate or inappropriate by the examiner; (part B consists in true and false statements); phonemic accuracy, in repeating a few statements; prosodic accuracy, in repeating a few intonation patterns; free expression, elicited by a picture; fluency; and attitude towards learning and using French. Scores are based on predetermined criteria and on descriptive scales.

Cloze Tests (English and French). The cloze test, in which the test-taker is asked to complete a mutilated text, is generally accepted as an excellent measure of global language proficiency. One English and two French tests, approximately 400 words in length, were rigorously selected for linguistic and content appropriateness. This length was determined with a view to providing a few intact sentences before and after the series of 50 blanks obtained by the systematic deletion of every seventh word. The position of the first blank was set after a few trials with a small sample of students.

French Oral Language Interview. This procedure was designed to serve a double purpose. First, the content was expected to draw complementary data from secondary five graduating students on their perception and attitude concerning their schooling particularly insofar as it was related to the French program they had been taught. Second, the linguistic form was to supply a corpus of authentic communication performance that could be analyzed and assessed.

The interview consisted of a twenty-minute semi-structured tape-recorded conversation conducted in French. Using English when the need was felt, the student was to answer six open questions.

Student Attitude Questionnaire. This instrument was devised to elicit from secondary five graduating students their perceptions in retrospective on various aspects of their schooling, particularly those relating to the type of program they chose or were assigned to. It takes the form of a questionnaire made up of twenty-one closed questions and an open one. With the exception of six which deal with factual information such as language(s) spoken at home, sex, proportion of time spent in French activities, and so forth, the others call for responses expressed by checking a Likert-type scale.

Appendix B.
Bilingual Kindergarten Program

General Pedagogical Objectives

1. *Cognitive and Educational*
   - guide and assist children in acquiring elementary notions about
       space (distance, direction, position, etc.)
       time (duration, succession, etc.)
       nature (plants, animals, etc.)
       society (personal identity, family, neighborhood, etc.)
   - help children derive, from their observation of facts, rules of personal and social behaviour.

2. *Linguistic*
   - provide children with a French language experience which helps them understand and eventually use the basic French vocabulary and structures related to attainment of the cognitive and educational objectives.

3 *Socio-Cultural and Affective*
   - help children build an awareness of cultural similarities and differences and develop open-mindedness towards social diversity.

Terminal Learning and
Behavioral Objectives

1. *Notional and Educational (examples)*
(a) - identify, following sensory observation, some space relations
    - distinguish between various locations of persons and things
    - show awareness of directions to be followed in moving from one place to another
    - identify type and use of a few categories of vehicles
(b) - identify time divisions and show awareness of duration
    - show some familiarization with weather facts relative to time and with consequent impact on clothing, nutrition, and general activities
    - relate special events to time continuum: Halloween, birthdays, holidays

39

2. *Linguistic*
(a) Comprehension

- react adequately to about 100 different types of formulation of language functions related to normal classroom interaction in a kindergarten, e.g., sit down, louder, etc.

- react verbally or by gesture to about 50 types of questions related to the identification, description, comparison of space and time phenomena forming part of the program content e.g., what colour is...? What is the use of...?

- manifest comprehension of essential vocabulary and structure used in the presentation of the program content

- express, verbally or otherwise, comprehension of the main trends of stories related by the teacher

(b) Expression

- use appropriately and spontaneously about 200 words (lexical and function) in various contexts of identification

- join relevantly and naturally in verbal exchanges with teacher and other students according to normal kindergarten classroom practice: asking permission or exclamation; expressing needs; emotions; informing, etc.

- describe briefly elementary aspects of persons, things, and phenomena

3. *Cultural*

- sing a few French songs
- recite French short poems, stories, or jokes
- give a few typical French names for boys, girls, street names, etc.

40

Guidelines and Materials

To assist the teacher in the implementation and evaluation of the program, 1 modules developed according to the following format:
- Central Theme and Subthemes.
- Topics corresponding to each subtheme.
- Specific sets of language forms needed to teach the topic.
- Different phases in teacher's activities.
- Corresponding pupils' activities and learning strategies.
- Teaching aids: songs, materials, directions for projects, references, cat. logues, etc.

Appendix C.
Follow-Up Program (or Curriculum)
Integrated Social Studies and
FSL Grades One and Two

General Pedagogical Objectives

1. *Cognitive and Educational*
    - guide and assist the child in further developing notions of time, space and society.
    - initiate the child in the elementary scientific strategies: observation, comparison, ordering, inference.

2. *Linguistic*
    - train the child to develop in understanding and use of French language forms related to efficient classroom interaction
    - provide the child with the opportunity to learn and use the French vocabulary and structures related to the program content in social studies.

3. *Socio-Cultural and Affective*
    - help the child to further develop positive attitudes towards the learning and use of French and openness towards linguistic and cultural pluralism.

41

Terminal Learning Objectives

1. *Cognitive and Educational* (examples)
    - Concept of space
        (a) To identify natural and man-built features of one's immediate local surroundings.
        (b) To situate oneself in one's immediate environment, through the use of cardinal points and landmarks.
        (c) To describe how to move from one place to another, with the use of plan or map, indicating cues and landmarks.
        (d) To situate a place in relation to surrounding natural and man-made features.

    - Concept of time
        (a) To situate in the context of daily, weekly, and yearly cycles, one's own activities and those of the people around.
        (b) To situate along a time continuum familiar events relating to oneself or other people.
        (c) To situate some events in time relative to other events in one's own life or in the life of others.
        (d) To describe from personal observation changes which have taken place with time in one's social or physical environment.

- Concept of life in society
  (a) To identify various ways through which family life provides for the child's material needs.
  (b) To identify various means through which community provides for some of the child's other needs.
  (c) To identify a few cultural and linguistic characteristics of one's surroundings.

2. *Linguistic*

   - To show comprehension, by a verbal or physical response of requests for identification or description of oneself, another person, a group of people, an object, an event, a place;
   of narration or description accompanied by visual support;
   of directives relating to classroom management and interaction;
   of offers concerning assistance; of granting or refusal of permission;
   of words of appreciation, agreement, reprimand.
   - To respond spontaneously to requests.
   - To relate a short story or describe an event or a phenomenon.
   - To express a desire, an emotion, a physical condition, an attitude, an invitation, an appreciation, agreement.
   - To inquire about people, events, facts, justification.
   - To express refusal, blame, reprimand.
   - To reproduce a few rhymes, jokes.
   - To sing a few French songs.

3. *Socio-Cultural and Affective Objectives*

   - To engage in effective conversation with at least one native francophone person.
   - To engage verbally in a group activity requiring French verbal interaction.

42

Fairview German Bilingual School: A Model for Elementary-School Language Learning

Frederick P. Veidt

In 1974, prompted by concern over an increasing degree and number of racially isolated schools and by lack of curricular options, the Board of Education of the Cincinnati Public Schools established the first of a series of alternative or magnet schools with the intention of promoting voluntary integration. Among these early options in education was the first of the district's now highly successful foreign language programs for elementary school pupils—the German-English Bilingual Alternative School. Given the ethnic heritage of the city of Cincinnati, the historical affinity of its public schools for the teaching of German,[1] and the existence of a German FLES program, then in its eighth year of operation, as a source of experience and a base for expansion, the choice of German as the target language for an initial, intensive, elementary-school, second-language program is not surprising. Unlike conventional bilingual programs, the teaching focus of this altenative school is on the monolingual English-speaking child, with bilingualism in German the aim of the overall sequence of instruction. This paper will concentrate on Fairview German Bilingual School, the elementary-school (K-5) segment of the total German Bilingual Alternative Program, with only peripheral mention given to the later stages of the instructional sequence.

43

Goals

Although a significant proportion of curricular time is devoted to second language instruction, academic achievement in the basic skills is also of primary importance. This dual emphasis is expressed in a set of program goals for each element. The German language component endeavors to provide pupils with:
• an opportunity to learn to understand, to speak, to read, and to write German;
• an understanding of and appreciation for the German speaking peoples and their way of life;
• an awareness of the contributions of the German language, German customs, and the German-speaking peoples to American life and society;

Frederick P. Veidt is Principal of the Fairview German Bilingual School in Cincinnati, Ohio.

• a command of a second language as a tool leading toward more career options, both in professional and vocational fields;
• positive multi-ethnic and multi-cultural attitudes.
In the standard English portion of the curriculum, the pupil will:
• gain knowledge of phonics-based English language reading, pronunciation, and spelling;
• demonstrate improved learning habits and study skills as manifested by a lengthening attention span and an increased ability to work independently;
• behave in a manner reflecting increased self-discipline and respect for others;
• attain mean grade level proficiencies in reading and mathematics that are at least equal to the current national average as measured by selected standardized achievement tests.

Enrollment and Student-Body Characteristics

During the 1984-1985 school year a total of 510 pupils were enrolled in grades K-5 at Fairview German Bilingual School. Approximately fifty-four percent of these youngsters were white, forty-four percent were black, and two percent were of Oriental or Spanish descent. More than eighty-five percent of the pupils live in excess of one mile from the school and are eligible for district and state-subsidized transportation service. The school draws its student body from fifty different neighborhoods and, thus, reflects the racial, social, and economic composition of the total Cincinnati school population.

Matriculation is generally at the kindergarten or first grade level. Occasionally, children with no prior German language experience are accepted directly into the second grade on a space-available basis if such youngsters are deemed able to deal with the entire standard curriculum at or above grade level and to catch up on one year of second-language instruction. Children with previous background in German may be admitted beyond the second grade. Kindergarten and first grade admittance is on a first-come, first-served basis. Achieving and maintaining racial balance is also of prime consideration in the acceptance procedures.

Parents who desire a bilingual program for their children are interviewed and are advised that a major strength of the German Bilingual Program is the existence of an active, concerned, and involved parents' group.[2] Parents of potential applicants and their children are encouraged to visit the school, to observe classes in session, to inspect the facilities, and to discuss the German Bilingual Alternative with program administrators, teachers, and other staff members.

Staffing

Instructional personnel fall into two categories: basic classroom teachers and German-language instructors. Basic classroom teachers, of whom there were eighteen on full-time contract during the 1984-1985 school year, are responsible for the standard grade level curriculum. At the primary level a self-contained classroom procedure is utilized. The basic classroom teachers operate in a semidepartmentalized structure at the intermediate level. With a few exceptions, basic classroom teachers have only minimal competence in German. Beyond the kindergarten level, German instruction is given by itinerant language specialists, each of whom is responsible for three or four classes usually at a specific grade level. The German instructors work with small (twelve to fifteen pupils), homogeneous, ability-level groups as well as with entire classes, in specially designated German classrooms. Approximately one hour of the daily schedule is devoted to second language instruction. Four full-time staff members were serving in this category during 1984-1985.

Basic classroom teachers are selected on the basis of their certification, ability, background, experience, interest, and commitment to the alternative-school concept, in general, and to Fairview German Bilingual School, in particular. German language instructors must possess near-native fluency in German, must have had extensive and intensive exposure to the people, culture, and institutions of a German-speaking country, and must hold the appropriate teaching certificate. Furthermore, they must exhibit the willingness, enthusiasm, and ability necessary to instruct elementary school children.

The rationale for the two-pronged approach to staffing is based on several factors. It is extremely difficult to find teachers who meet the German language portions of the above requirements and who also have certification as elementary teachers, especially in the numbers that would be needed to staff the entire school. Therefore, the German language instructors have been selected from the ranks of those who hold certification as secondary German teachers. In Ohio a teacher holding secondary foreign language certification is eligible for special K-12 certification in the same language. Furthermore, the utilization of itinerant second language teachers who visit each of several classrooms on an established schedule helps ensure that second language instruction will occur routinely on a daily basis and that such instruction will not be skipped, slighted or relegated to a position of lesser importance due to the curricular or time demands besetting one teacher who has dual responsibility for both curricula. Finally, the use of two types of teaching personnel aids in fulfilling a school-district policy that about thirty percent of the instructional staff of each school be black. Given the dearth of black German teachers, it would be next to impossible to meet this requirement without the dual approach to staffing.

Philosophically, Fairview German Bilingual School seeks to staff its program with teachers who believe that children in the early grades perform at their best academically in an orderly environment where basic skills and self-discipline are taught as a foundation for the development of creative, self-directed enterprise. In an atmosphere of this nature, the children learn that teachers and peers expect max-

45

imum effort scholastically and behaviorally. Thus, the pupils are imbued with a sense of security and continuity in the realization that, from teacher to teacher and from year to year, the same standards and expectations apply. Indication of staff agreement with this philosophy and of staff satisfaction with an assignment to Fairview German Bilingual School can be seen in the school's low teacher-turnover rate[3] and in the positive replies to school-assignment commitment on districtwide teacher surveys.[4]

Curriculum and Instruction

German instruction at the kindergarten level is given for 20 minutes three times a week and focuses on greetings, common expressions, and basic vocabulary building. The children learn songs, dances and rhymes, play games, and listen to stories. Beginning in the first grade and thereafter, the pupils learn German within the framework of a sequenced and highly structured oral language curriculum. Close cooperation and planning between the classroom and German teachers ensure that instruction in English and German are complementary and that the two curricula are integrated. The first grade instruction emphasizes the development of aural/oral proficiencies. During German class, English is not used by either the pupils or the teacher. In this regard the aim is to take advantage of young children's proclivity to talk, their relative lack of inhibition, their view of a second language as a secret means of communication, the absence of strong peer-group pressures and of related adolescent and pubescent interferences.

Action verbs such as come, go, show, draw, fetch, take, give, sit down, stand up, run, ride, drive, throw, eat, laugh, and cry are stressed. Realia, especially those from the children's home and school environment, are seen, felt, and manipulated by the children. Handpuppets put in constant classroom appearances, and a seemingly endless variety of games are played. The affective domain is included by teaching the children the vocabulary and gestures associated with sharing, taking turns, and other basic courtesies. To aid in the development of the pupils' listening and speaking skills, Hermann Schuh's *Komm bitte*! materials (Munich: Hueber, 1974), which were designed for use with *Gastarbeiter* children, have proven to be an invaluable source of suggestions and practical ideas. Indeed, this series represents the core of our instructional activities at the primary level.

To supplement the core materials, concepts of the first grade social studies curriculum are coordinated with the culture of the German-speaking peoples. Mathematics operations are drilled and practiced and grade-level-appropriate art, music, and physical education activities also occur during German time. No formal reading or writing activities in German take place during the first grade. The rationale for this is based on the intent to estabish a solid aural/oral foundation and to avoid possible interference with the developmental stages of the youngsters' reading and writing skills in English.

In second grade the major emphasis is still on the development of aural/oral skills. In addition, the pupils are introduced to German reading-readiness skills using the same phonics-based approach employed in the English curriculum (see, for example, Charles C. Walcutt and Glen McCracken, *Lippincott Basic Reading* [New York: Harper, 1981]). In an effort to keep the pupils from developing the perception that Germans are just like Americans except that the former talk funny, basic cultural awareness begins to receive increased instructional attention through the use of a variety of devices including slides, filmstrips, and the first few films of the *Guten Tag*[5] series. Included is the concept of country and the comparative sizes and locations of the United States and Germany.

In grade three pupils continue to build their aural/oral proficiencies, to expand their reading skills through the use of German-language readers,[6] and to acquire a core of geography and social studies concepts and terms. At this level work is begun with a supplemental German workbook such as Ilse Herrndobler and Horst Scholz, *Lachen und Lernen mit Uli* (Munich: List, n.d.). Designed as a remedial instrument for use in the Federal Republic of Germany with *Legasteniker*, i.e., children who experience difficulty in learning to read, the workbook provides a variety of German language-arts activities in a colorful, interest-holding, culturally authentic, and difficulty-level-appropriate format.

The fourth and fifth grade German curricula include reading and language arts and a reinforcement of content-area instruction. Mathematics word problems are introduced. Units of the English social studies and science-health curricula are also taught in German, increasing the students' familiarity with terminology and related concepts in the target language. Typical instructional units include map skills, graphs, the city and suburbs, Ohio and Cincinnati history, and animal classifications. Units devoted to the study of mammals and of birds and their habitats culminate in bilingual field trips held in cooperation with the Cincinnati Zoo, which provides facilities, materials, and supplemental instructional personnel. With growing second-language competence, the amount of content-area teaching in German is gradually increased from grade to grade. Some content-area material is taught only in German while other units are treated in both languages with varying degrees of overlap and reinforcement.

To supplement normal classroom pursuits, pupils participate in several traditional American and German holiday festivities. Plays, performances, and spelling bees are presented in both languages. Numerous excursions of cultural and/or educational nature are scheduled throughout the year as an integral part of the curriculum. The school offers a math-science enrichment program to qualified pupils as well as a number of after-school activities, which currently include a computer club, a German chorus, extended-day physical education, a German folk-dance group, and scouting troops.

47

Academic Achievement

The goals of the German Bilingual Program can be summarized as the acquisition of German language skills in a framework of basic academic achievement. In a situation where approximately twenty-five percent of the available instructional time is devoted to an alternative subject, it is essential that basic skills be learned and maintained.

Each spring the Cincinnati Public Schools administers to its pupils the California Achievement Tests (Monterey Cal.: CTB-McGraw-Hill, 1977). Results of these tests are summarized in three stanine groupings, i.e., below average (1-3), average (4-6), and above average (7-9). Annually since 1976, a total of ninety percent to ninety-eight percent of the German Bilingual pupils have scored in the average or above-average categories in both reading and mathematics. This rate is substantially higher than the expected nationwide result of seventy-seven percent in the same categories and supports the contention that German Bilingual pupils are being given the opportunity to learn a second language beginning in elementary school without sacrificing vital, fundamental, basic skills proficiencies.

Assessing the pupils' German language achievement is much more difficult. Applicable standardized test instruments that adequately measure the abilities of the target population are simply nonexistent. Those standardized German-language tests currently available are designed for secondary school and university-level students and measure second language skills in a manner and degree which do not coincide with the instructional philosophy, goals, and emphases of the Cincinnati Public Schools' curriculum. However, in an effort to provide some basic comparative data, pupils completing the eighth grade are administered Form LA of the Modern Language Association-Cooperative Foreign Language Tests for German.[7] An arbitrary application of the second year high school audio-lingual German norms reveals average midpercentile ranks of ninety-five for speaking, eighty for listening, seventy-two for reading, and sixty-three for writing. Since test content validity is low, few interpretations can be made from these data other than to say that the pupils are learning German in accordance with program goals and that the rate of that learning is superior to that of the average American second language learner.

Articulation

Upon completion of Fairview German Bilingual School, pupils in grades six through eight attend Cincinnati Bilingual Academy, the district's bilingual middle school, which serves those who have completed a five-year sequence in German, French or Spanish. The curriculum at the middle school is intended to bridge the gap between the conversational focus of the elementary grades and the expectations of the more traditional secondary and university language programs. Eventually students will attend universities that will expect them to have mastered certain skills and concepts. The curriculum at the middle school begins to prepare pupils for those expectations.

Between the seventh and eighth grades, German Bilingual pupils are given the opportunity to apply for an exchange program with the Donaueschingen (Germany) Middle School. Begun in 1980 through the auspices of the American Association of Teachers of German and the Pädagogischer Austauschdienst as a one-way experience for Cincinnati German Bilingual youngsters, the endeavor has expanded to a full exchange which is now associated with the Goethe Institute-sponsored German-American Partnership Program (GAPP). By the end of the 1984-85 school year, a total of 147 Donaueschingen and Cincinnati pupils will have spent a month in each other's country, lived with each other's family, studied at each other's school, and been exposed to each other's way of life.

In grades nine through twelve, bilingual pupils have three options for continuing their second language studies. The Cincinnati Public Schools' International Studies Academy offers both a globally oriented curriculum as well as the academically rigorous International Baccalaureate program. By attaining a qualifying entrance examination score, pupils can also attend the district's college preparatory secondary school. Lastly, pupils may attend their neighborhood or a private or parochial high school. Approximately forty-five percent of the German Bilingual pupils choose the first option, forty-five percent the second and ten percent the third.

In summary, what began as an alternative school experiment to reduce racial isolation has developed into a unique German language learning opportunity of proven academic success. The student body represents a social, racial, and economic cross section of the district's population. Despite the lack of selection criteria, achievement test results have substantially exceeded the performance of both nationally and locally normed groups on measures of reading and mathematics. Competition for available openings is indicative of strong community interest. An active and committed group of parents, eighty-five percent of whom have chosen to bus their children to an alternative school for, in some cases, as long as an hour one way rather than take a short walk to a neighborhood facility, recognizes and supports the value of learning a second language. For their children who are learning to communicate with our neighbors abroad, positive human relationships and attitudes are being facilitated and a valuable tool leading toward increased career options is being developed.

49

Notes

[1]Cincinnati has been credited by Theodore Andersson, *Foreign Languages in the Elementary School* (Austin: University of Texas Press, 1969), pp. 59-60, as the first city in the United States to introduce optional German language instruction into the curriculum of its public schools. In the late 1880's more than fifty percent of all Cincinnati Public Schools' pupils were receiving German instruction, and by 1900 the system employed almost 180

German teachers to instruct 18,000 pupils. For further details see Edwin H. Zeydel, "The Teaching of German in Cincinnati," *Cincinnati Historical Society Bulletin,* 20 (1962): 29-37.

[2]The parents' organization has formed a non-profit, tax-exempt foundation to provide support for the school. In addition to furnishing financial and fund-raising expertise to supplement public school revenues and to help carry out special activities such as the exchange program, members of the parents' organization and its advisory board also act as school and classroom volunteers, provide needed improvements to the physical facilities, sponsor and assist at extracurricular events, disseminate public-relations information, and serve as liaison between the school and the Board of Education.

[3]Since its inception in 1974, approximately one teacher has left the program every two years.

[4]On a scale of 1.00 to 7.00, Fairview German Bilingual teachers recently accorded their commitment to remain at their present assignment if offered another teaching location a rating of 6.12. Cincinnati Public School System, Evaluation Branch, Teacher Survey, December, 1984.

[5]This set of 26 black and white, 16mm sound films was written by Rudolf Schneider and produced by the *Studienprogramm des Bayerischen Rundfunks* and the Goethe Institute in Munich in 1968. Distribution rights in the United States are held by International Film Bureau, Inc., Chicago. The entire series has been integrated into the German Bilingual Program curriculum of the Cincinnati Public Schools.

[6]We are currently using Ellen Blance and Ann Cook, *Monster-Hefte,* trans. by Christian Hünerhoff (Stuttgart: Klett, 1980 and 1981); Elizabeth Guilfoile, *Niemand hört auf Andreas,* trans. by Annette Haase (Chicago: Follett, 1961); and Esther K. Meeks, *Die neugierige Kuh,* trans. by Annette Haase (Chicago: Follett, 1961).

[7]Princeton, New Jersey: Educational Testing Service, 1965. Although dated, this test instrument was chosen over other more current materials because all four second-language skills are tested.

A Model Foreign Language Experience Program for the Elementary School

Patricia Davis Wiley

Achieving proficiency in a foreign language ordinarily requires from 4 to 6 years of study and should, therefore, be started in the elementary grades (*A Nation at Risk* 26).

An emerging consensus places the study of foreign languages and cultures alongside the five "basics" of English, mathematics, computer science, social studies, and the natural sciences as fundamental components of a sound education. (*Critical Needs in International Education* 2)

Foreign language instruction in the United States is indeed a critical issue. In a 1983 article in *Education Week*, Sheppard Ranbom reported that "only 15 percent of all high school students are enrolled in foreign language courses... and only one percent of all students are *ever* exposed to a foreign language in elementary school systems" (7). The ACTFL survey of "Foreign Language Enrollments in Public Secondary Schools, Fall 1982" reports 19% of all students in grades 7-12 and 22.6% in grades 9-12 taking a foreign language (611). At this writing, many states are reporting an increased enrollment in high school foreign language classes due to more rigorous high school graduation and college entrance requirements.[1] Reporting in *State Education Leader* on a survey undertaken by the Council of Chief State School Officers and the National Council on Foreign Language and International Studies, Rose Hayden notes that the chief state school officers considered foreign languages more important in 1983 than at any point since 1969 (4). It is noteworthy to compare these statistics with those following the passage of the National Defense Education Act (NDEA) of 1958, which precipitated renewed interest in second-language instruction in elementary and secondary schools across the United States.[2] This trend toward language study, commonly accepted as a component of European curricula, was responsible for the great popularity of foreign language study in the elementary schools (first known as FLES in 1953)[3]. A search of contemporary professional literature revealed that FLES was "offered by approximately 95 percent of large public school systems. . . 75 percent of

Patricia Davis Wiley is Associate Professor of Curriculum and Instruction at the University of Tennessee, Knoxville, where she chairs the program in Foreign Language Education.

51

the average systems. . . and by 50 percent of the small systems" ("Public School Programs" 113).

In this paper I will present a summary of research of the effects of early foreign language study, a brief overview of the foreign language education program at University of Tennessee, Knoxville (UTK), and a description of the organization, curricular content, methodology, and evaluation of Knoxville's unique foreign language experience (FLEX) program.

Effects of Early Foreign Language Instruction

Research has documented that the study of a second language during the elementary-school years may positively affect the young child's "general school achievement and linguistic progress" (Donoghue; Potts; Smith). It can also promote superior progress in high school language study and may result in a significantly higher gain in mental maturity compared to that realized by non-FLES students during the same period (Brega; Donoghue; Vovolo).

Learning a foreign language in elementary school also appears to promote language awareness. Robert J. DiPietro of the University of Delaware reports that "the study of foreign languages does indeed help children learn to read better in English" (Kindig 64-65). Other benefits of second-language study include greater critical-thinking ability, better mental discipline, and more refined levels of mental dexterity (Wiley), and higher measures of flexibility and creativity (Jarvis).

Foreign Language Education at UTK

The University of Tennessee at Knoxville is the only foreign language teacher-training institute in Tennessee with an established foreign language education program offering both undergraduate and graduate degrees specifically in foreign language education. The program serves those undergraduate and post-baccalaureate students seeking Tennessee secondary certification in one or more foreign language areas (including English as a Second Language) and graduate students seeking a Master of Science degree in foreign language education or a collateral area in the Ed.S., Ed.D., or Ph.D. programs.

The foreign language education program is unique in that its methods component includes three weeks of supervised experience instructing in public middle-school foreign language classes (in addition to regularly scheduled field experiences and student teaching). Graduate students have the opportunity to participate in FLEX in designated Knoxville elementary schools, teaching French, Spanish, or German in 30-minute sessions twice a week during the regular academic year. (Whereas the original FLEX acronym referred to a sampling of different languages offered to the same student population, the UTK FLEX program concentrates on a year-long foreign language experience in one language).

The Pilot FLEX Program

In response to requests from the community for elementary school language instruction, the foreign language education program in the department of curriculum and instruction at UTK developed in the spring of 1982 a FLEX program for the kindergarten and first grades at Pleasant Ridge Elementary School. Five graduate students from the foreign language education program and from the department of Romance languages were identified as instructors and given twice-weekly seminars immediately following each classroom experience at Pleasant Ridge. Thirty-minute Spanish instruction was offered twice a week to all K-1 students; graduate credit was awarded for this field experience to all FLEX instructors.

The school system's enthusiasm for the pilot FLEX program was so great that the program was expanded in 1982-83 to include grades K-5 at Pond Gap Elementary School. Due to the variety of language specialties of UTK graduate student instructors, French, German, and Spanish were offered to the students at Pond Gap. As the director and supervisor of the FLEX program, I have had the opportunity to observe the linguistic progress of the FLEX participants in the classroom and outside it, and I find that most children will spontaneously greet visitors, teachers, and one another in the second language studied and will attempt to engage others in conversation in the target language.

At this writing, the FLEX program has grown from a five-school operation to eight schools; in these schools, every third grader receives 30 minutes of language instruction twice weekly.[4] The program is supported through discretionary monies from the school system and through cooperative efforts of the department of curriculum and instruction at UTK. The FLEX teachers either hold advanced degrees in foreign language education or are pursuing a graduate degree in the program.

The FLEX Curriculum

The first-year FLEX curriculum was developed in 1982 and has remained constant. In addition to the topics listed, students are given some exposure to the culture (i.e., customs, geography, art, music, national holidays) of the people who speak the language studied.

First Quarter

Basic greetings: How are you? What is your name? Where do you live?

Common classroom objects: chair, table, desk, chalk, chalkboard, paper, pencil, book, door, window, and so forth

Miscellaneous objects: hat, box, bag, notebooks, and so forth

53

Parts of the body: head, mouth, eye(s), ear(s), hair, hand, foot, leg

Commands: stand up, sit down, touch, go, write, pick up, put/ place, give, show

Prepositions: at, toward, in, out, on, under, next to, in front of, behind

Colors: red, yellow, green, black, white, blue

Numbers: 1-20

Songs: "Are You Sleeping," "One Little, Two Little, Three Little Indians," Christmas songs

Second Quarter

Review of first quarter

Chain of three to five oral commands; teacher to student; student to teacher

Numbers: 25-100

Prepositional phrases (advanced, using known and new vocabulary)

Telling time

Weather expressions

Common foods, grouped according to meals

Articles of clothing

Additional body parts (e.g., fingers, toes, thumbs)

The calendar: days of the week

Third Quarter

Review of first and second quarters

The calendar: months of the year

Time expressions with appropriate activities

Weather expressions with clothing and sports vocabulary

Sports: nouns and verbs

Animals

Program Methodology

Since the primary emphasis is a meaningful and enjoyable experience with a second language, the total physical response method is used extensively in the FLEX Program. Aural-oral linguistic skills are easily taught using this technique, which stresses audio-motor coordination in learning. For example, in one of the first lessons dealing with common classroom objects, the teacher might say, "Je vais à la porte;" "Voy a la puerta;" "Ich gehe an die Tür;" [I am going to the door]. He/she would then go to the door. The instructor would then tell a student in the classroom "Allez à la porte;" "Vaya a la puerta;" "Geh an die Tür." [Go to the door]. The student would then quickly respond by performing the command requested. This technique is oriented toward the right hemisphere of the brain and is to be distinguished from instruction oriented toward the left hemisphere, in which foreign language students translate the foreign language into their native language before comprehension takes place. In other words, after receiving foreign language stimuli, the FLEX student performs the foreign language request, thereby internalizing and coding the message through audio input and motor output. This technique promotes a high retention span in long-term memory (see Asher).

FLEX classes are conducted as much as possible in the second language. A rich variety of props and pictures are used throughout the 30-minute lessons to maintain a high level of enthusiasm and to produce fast-paced, exciting activities. The regular classroom teachers frequently reinforce the second language in the classroom, e.g., with greetings, counting, songs, after the FLEX instructors have left.

A very popular activity in the FLEX classroom is what I call "foreign language rhythmics." A portable electric keyboard (e.g., a Casio model PT-1) with built-in rhythm, is used to produce musical patterns emulated by the students using the target language. Examples of foreign language utterances accompanying different electronically produced rhythms are *Beguine*: Comment allez-vous?; *Rock 1:* ¡Buenos Días!; *March:* Ca va?; Sehr gut; *4-Beat*: numbers; *Swing:* Guten Tag; Bonjour; *Samba*: ¡Donde vive usted?; Où habitez-vous? Yo vivo en la calle...; Wo wohnen Sie? *Rock 2:* verb conjugations.

Even though the emphasis is essentially on oral-aural skills in the FLEX classroom, tracing, modified cloze activities, and reproduction of the written foreign language are introduced in the middle of the academic year. By the end of the school year, students have a notebook, "cahier," "cuaderno," "Heft," filled with vocabulary, expressions, and songs in the language. Middle and end-of-the-year culminating activities may include five-minute individual oral reports on a particular foreign country, its people, geography, and customs; mini-skits in the target language; and language days, when parents and guests are invited to savor the customs and traditional foods of the countries studied in the FLEX classroom.

Response to the FLEX Program

Response to the FLEX Program has been positive and enthusiastic. Data collected from parents, teachers, and FLEX students since the program's inception in 1982 echo the desires of all concerned to continue the present program and expand it to other sites and grade levels. Solicited and unsolicited parental comments include the following:

My daughter . . . is extremely excited about participating in the pilot French program offered . . . this year. . . . Further monies need to be funded for the continuation of the program.

I was very pleased with both the teacher and the classroom participation, which I personally observed two days. With the upcoming curriculum change concerning a mandatory two years of a foreign language in high school before acceptance into a college or university,

55

this elementary program should be a big boost for these students. What an easier time learning foreign language they will have because of this fine program! . . . This, in my opinion, is a definitive step forward—for better schools in Tennessee. Keep up the good work!

Teacher comments echoed parents' enthusiasm.

I was excited before it [the FLEX program] began and I'm still excited about it; I hope it will continue next year.

I don't consider this time as "lost Language Arts time" This is "Language Development." The children are having the opportunity for oral expression and creative learning.

Student comments included these:

It's fun knowing two languages. You can talk something that other people don't.

It was fun, and it was easy to learn.

Most classroom teachers whose children are participating in the FLEX program consistently comment that their children have become more "language aware" than non-FLEX children. The same children who rarely volunteer responses in other subjects are those who appear to be more motivated and eager to volunteer in the FLEX classes. It appears that even the incidental copy-work the FLEX students perform in their foreign language class has a positive transference to other non-FLEX seat work. Consequently, FLEX time is a positive and meaningful learning experience for all those involved.

Summary

Even though the present one-year FLEX program in the Knoxville school system is successful as a pilot effort to offer an introduction of the language and culture of French-, German-, and Spanish-speaking peoples to selected elementary school children in the district, it must be articulated from the present third-grade level to other grades and expanded to other elementary schools in the district. So that it can become an integral and permanent component of the elementary curriculum, the FLEX program needs to be officially integrated into the Language Arts block of courses.

The major obstacles to the implementation of this plan appear to be: (1) appropriating adequate funding; (2) training additional FLEX instructors; (3) convincing the school system that the FLEX program is not a "curricular frill" to be offered to selected populations; and (4) documenting the FLEX program as an example to the state of an elementary foreign language model that could enhance present state-mandated basic skills modules, thereby strenghthening the Language Arts curriculum.

Notes

[1] High school foreign language enrollment in Tennessee has increased over 100 percent between fall 1984 and fall 1986 in response to a requirement effective in 1989 of two years of one foreign language in high school for admission to the University of Tennessee.

[2] More than $43 million was spent on improving second-language instruction between 1958 and 1960; foreign language enrollments grew 60.3 percent between 1960 and 1965 and an additional 10 percent between 1965 and 1968 (see Chastain).

[3] Kenneth Mildenberger, who in 1962 was assistant director of the foreign language program of the Modern Language Association of America, invented the term FLES to refer to foreign language instruction in the elementary schools (see "Language Structure at FLES Level: A Report by the FLES Committee of the American Association of Teachers of French," December 29, 1962).

[4] The Knoxville elementary schools participating in FLEX programs, 1985-88, are Bearden, Chilhowee, Fountain City, Pond Gap, Ridgedale, Rocky Hill, Sequoyah, and West Hills.

References

Asher, James A. *Learning Another Language through Actions: The Complete Teachers' Guidebook.* Los Gatos, Cal.: Sky Oaks Publications, 1979.

Brega, Evelyn, and John M. Newell. "High School Performance of FLES and Non-FLES Students." *Modern Language Journal* 51 (1967): 463-69.

———. "How Effective is FLES? A Study." *The DFL Bulletin* 4 (1965):6.

Chastain, Kenneth D. Second-Language Study: Historical Background and Current Status." *Learning a Second Language.* Ed. Frank M. Grittner. Chicago: Univ. of Chicago Press, 1980. 1-25.

Donoghue, Mildred R. "What Research Tells Us about the Effects of FLES." *Hispania* 45 (1965):555-58.

"Foreign Language Enrollments in Public Secondary Schools, Fall 1982." *Foreign Language Annals* 17 (1984):611-23.

Hayden, Rose. "Global Literacy Up, But Data Skimpy." *State Education Leader* 4.1 (1985):4-5.

Jarvis, Gilbert A. "The Value of Second-Language Learning." *Learning a Second Language.* Ed. Frank M. Grittner. Chicago: Univ. of Chicago Press, 1980. 26-43.

Kindig, Eileen, "Where Foreign Language Is Basic: The Akron Story." *Today's Education* 70 (1981):64-65.

National Advisory Board on International Education Programs. *Critical Needs in International Education: Recommendations for Action.* Washington, D.C.: GPO, 1983.

National Commission on Excellence in Education. *A Nation at Risk: An Open Letter to the American People.* Washington, D.C.: GPO, 1983.

Potts, Marion H. "The Effect of Second-Language Instruction on the Reading Proficiency and General School Achievement of Primary Grade Children." *American Educational Research Journal* 4 (1967):367-73.

President's Commission on Foreign Language and International Studies. *Strength through Wisdom: A Critique of U.S. Capability.* Washington, D.C.: GPO, 1979.

Public School Programs and Practices: Foreign Language Programs. *NEA Research Bulletin* 45(1967):113

Ranbom, Sheppard. "After an Era of Neglect, Traditional Humanities Are Being Revived." *Education Week.* 30 March 1983:7.

Smith, Wayne H. "Linguistic and Academic Achievement of Elementary Students Studying a Foreign Language." *Dissertation Abstracts* 27(1967):3882A

Vovolo, Joseph M. "The Effect of Foreign Language Study in Elementary School upon Achievement in the Same Foreign Language in High School." *Modern Language Journal* 51(1967):463-69.

Wiley, Patricia D. "High School Foreign Language Study and College Academic Performance." *Classical Outlook* 62(1984-1985):33-36.

The Public Loves Foreign Languages for Children

Gladys C. Lipton

Across the country there seems to be a resurgence of interest in early foreign language instruction of all types. FLES, FLEX, Exploratory, Immersion, Global Education, and so forth are today's superstars.

A decade ago, Anne Arundel county had a good education program, but foreign language study was delayed until ninth grade. After consulting with a number of educators, parents, students, counselors, and principals, I proposed a foreign language program for elementary school students. The goals of this program were limited: to provide an introduction to language and culture on a very limited scale, without costing the school district any money.

One major reason for starting foreign language instruction in the elementary schools was in response to a high school principal's suggestion to increase the number of students in language courses in the secondary schools, where too few students were enrolled. Although we offered only a limited foreign language experience (LEX) delivered by volunteers, the Board of Education did not immediately accept our proposal, fearing that even thirty minutes a week devoted to foreign language study might interfere with normally expected growth in language arts and mathematics, since this thirty-minute sequence would be included in the regular school day.

A pilot program was designed in one of the four elementary-school areas of the county. Twenty-one schools were involved in the project. When it came to staffing for the LEX program, there were few choices open to us at the time. Budgets were tight, and while there was enthusiasm for beginning a foreign language program for elementary school students, the thinking was geared toward funding positions for teachers in the basic skills of reading, mathematics, and science (subjects already firmly established in the elementary school curriculum). The area of foreign languages was first and foremost an additional subject, and the school district was not ready to fund teachers when there was not enough money for subjects that were considered essential. It should be noted that foreign languages in middle schools and high schools were considered a strong academic subject, and some of this support carried over to the elementary

59

Gladys Lipton was Program Coordinator of Foreign Languages in the Anne Arundel County, Maryland, Public Schools from 1977 to 1985. She is now Coordinator of Foreign Language Workshops in the Department of Modern Languages and Linguistics at the University of Maryland, Baltimore County.

school program. But as one educator reported, "It's hard to compete with the 'bread and butter' subjects."

In order to implement the program and in order to get a broad base of support, I suggested the use of non-professionals such as high school students, parents, and members of the community, as well as elementary school teachers and supervisors. Since the goals of the program were limited language awareness with an introduction and exposure to a foreign language and culture and since we suffered constraints of staff and time, it seemed a reasonable approach. Over the years, I have noted that with time and patience, funding for a stronger program with more ambitious goals can follow.

Although most foreign language educators would question the use of staff with "some" background in a foreign language and with a limited number of training sessions, one should consider the reasons for pursuing this approach. As noted in responses by some of the high school students and principals, the use of secondary students was particularly appealing as these students gained many benefits themselves while they were providing instruction for the elementary school students. One high school student remarked, "I really understand some of the things about French, now that I've been teaching it to elementary school students." Besides not costing the school district any money, the use of volunteers has united the community and helped instill in adolescents the need to make a contribution of oneself and one's talents for the good of the school and the community.

The volunteers received several training sessions in language, culture and teaching techniques. Curriculum materials were developed in French, German, and Spanish, with Latin added later. The research department developed a comprehensive evaluation design, which included questionnaires for elementary school students and teachers, adult volunteers, elementary and secondary principals, division directors, high school department heads—who trained the student volunteers—parents, and any other interested persons. At the end of a year's trial program in LEX, the research department randomly sampled student achievement and tabulated the results shown in the table.

	A Comparison of Results on the Iowa Tests of Basic Skills			
	LEX Participants		Nonparticipants	
	Number	Mean	Number	Mean
Grade 3				
Ability	276	110	587	106
Vocabulary	279	4.3	587	4.1
Reading Comprehension	275	4.5	587	4.1
Language Total	275	5.0	587	4.6
Grade 5				
Ability	349	111	308	108
Vocabulary	347	6.1	308	5.8
Reading Comprehension	347	6.1	308	5.8
Language Total	348	6.6	308	6.1

A comparable group of nonparticipants in LEX were tested, and the means between the participants and nonparticipants differed significantly at P < .01 level. As a result of the one-year pilot study, the Board of Education approved the optional teaching of foreign languages in the elementary schools where volunteers were available.

Was it worth the trouble? Definitely. The study gave us an opportunity to expand the pilot program to all four areas of the county, to increase the number of trained volunteers, to interest a number of elementary-school principals and parents. In 1984-85, we offered one of seven languages to 5,327 pupils in 42 elementary schools, using 294 high school students, 73 adult volunteers, 13 classroom teachers, and one media specialist. In 1985-86, my last year with the program, enrollments increased by an additional 1,000 students.

LEX is designed to give youngsters some pleasurable experiences in learning a foreign language as well as provide awareness of the people and the country or countries in which language is spoken. It is designed to develop the skills of careful listening and accurate pronunciation. Since it is an informal introduction to a foreign language, without regard for the formal aspects of sequential study, it should be an enjoyable experience for students, instructors, principals, and parents. It was hoped that the LEX program would establish a firm foundation and motivation for subsequent language study, and enrollments in the middle, junior high, and high schools confirm that expectation.

Training the Instructors

In the training session, many volunteers were eager to brush up on their foreign language skills; we also had a few native speakers. In order to give the volunteers adequate training in methodology, we had to overcome their own language training of too much grammar and too little enjoyment. We also trained the high school chairpersons who, in turn, could train their students. All training sessions dealt with language, methods of teaching songs and conversations, cultural-awareness activities, role playing, "make and take" sessions, and so forth. The greatest challenge in the training was to have the volunteers accept the philosophy of the joy of language learning. Most of them did, and their endorsement was apparent in their teaching.

Cost and Curriculum

The only way this program could be implemented was to provide instruction without any cost to the county. While the program did not and does not now include any specific budget requests, there are a few hidden costs. All instructors volunteer their time, except classroom teachers, one principal, and one media specialist.

The curriculum materials in French, German, Latin, and Spanish are very simple, with ample suggestions for free and easily accessible materials, such as posters, maps, experience charts, books, pictures,

61

flannel boards, records, cassettes, tapes, toys, food, greeting cards, transparencies, and other simple materials available to creative instructors. The topics include classroom objects, colors, numbers, family, clothing, greetings, time, weather, days of the week, months, and seasons.

The most pressing question we had to answer prior to launching the pilot study was "What are the reasons for beginning the introduction of a foreign language in the elementary school?" Some of our reasons were that children:

- enjoy learning a foreign language
- develop good habits of listening and pronouncing
- gain an understanding of how languages work
- become culturally aware of other peoples
- are interested in strange sounds and codes
- are not self-conscious about pronouncing new sounds
- like to mimic and do so very well

Special features and accomplishments of the program include:

- options open to principals in scheduling the foreign language sessions, such as mini-courses, informal instruction integrated throughout the day (often with language arts or social studies), a 30-minute period once a week, or 15 minutes twice a week, or before or after school.
- improvement in listening skills as a result of the foreign language lessons, as noted by many principals, teachers, and volunteer instructors.
- pleasure reported by high school students in their ability to use foreign language; many were impressed with the scope of the teaching process and reported that they loved working with young children while reinforcing their own foreign language skills.

What Does the Community Have to Say?

The Superintendent of Schools:

> I believe that the earlier we can have youngsters come in contact with a second language, the more they will learn, the more retention they will have. From my past experience, I know that the inclusion of a second language improves youngsters' overall performance on standardized tests, and the longer that they are involved in a second language, the better they do in all subjects. I think it opens another horizon for them.

President of the Board of Education (and parent):

> I think it is an excellent opportunity to expose children to what languages are about so they can make choices at later times in their lives. Both of my children have been involved in the LEX program and have had experiences in several languages.

Student member of the Board of Education (and a LEX instructor):

I enjoy working with children and by the end of the school year we all become great friends. I can see an immense value to the program. It benefits the elementary school children as well as the high school students who are interested in being teachers or working with children as a profession.

High school chairperson:

It has become quite a task to keep the program going, but I know in the end that we at the high school level are going to be the ones to benefit from it insofar as enrollment figures go over the next five, ten, fifteen or more years.

High school instructor:

I think it's fun so far and pretty successful. The kids don't catch on at first, but once you repeat lessons enough they catch on, and they're doing pretty well.

High school principal:

Our high school students are enthusiastic, and they really want to assist the elementary school students to learn about foreign languages. At the same time, they are involved in experiences that will be lifelong and will inspire and stimulate them to go further in the foreign language program.

Elementary school principal (also "instructor"):

I have always felt that learning a foreign language increases the students' understanding of a country and its culture. Giving the students an opportunity to hear, see, and speak another language develops a language foundation. As principal, I wanted to extend my interest in foreign languages, so I began to teach French, Spanish, and Latin. Now, every child in our school is having fun exploring a foreign language.

This picture of a foreign language experience program taught by volunteers is indeed very rosy. Are there any concerns or problems? Surprisingly, there are few. Some problems that have surfaced are the following:
- difficulty in transportation of high school instructors
- lack of sufficient volunteers to provide instruction to all students
- insufficient reference materials beyond those distributed at the training workshops
- lack of choice of language to be studied, as the choice depends on the language of the volunteer
- lack of continuity in the same language
- lack of conformity in scheduling the foreign language in all schools

Despite these concerns, there is almost universal approval of the

63

program. Since the goals are very limited, and we deliver what we promise can be accomplished, the LEX program is well received by all.

If you, the reader, want to establish an experience program with simple, realistic goals, consider the following suggestions:

- Assess the community and school interests and needs
- Organize an advisory committee
- Determine financial resources, availability of volunteers, language preferences, and existing secondary school language programs
- Formulate realistic goals
- Anticipate difficulties, problems, and opponents
- Investigate other successful programs
- Contact knowledgeable people for advice
- Prepare a detailed proposal for authorities and invite suggestions
- Plan to work on a pilot program with an evaluation design
- Develop curriculum materials to fulfill your realistic goals
- Develop a plan for recruiting volunteers
- Develop a plan for training programs
- Promote interest by speaking to parent, teacher, and principal groups
- Involve secondary foreign language teachers and invite their suggestions
- Evaluate; ask for input at all levels
- Be prepared for successes and failures
- Expect a pilot year and another of trial and error; then be prepared to enjoy the benefits of the program you have developed.

If the goals of the program are language exploration and awareness and are limited in scope, if the content is spelled out in detail, and if training sessions are provided along with pronunciation tapes, the program can achieve student, parent, and community support for early foreign language study.

Languages for Children at Tarrant County Junior College

Jane Harper

Northeast Campus is one of three campuses of the Tarrant County Junior College (TCJC) District in the Fort Worth, Texas, metropolitan area. Student enrollment in credit courses in the district is usually about 25,000 to 28,000, of which Northeast Campus generally enrolls from 10,000 to 11,000. The campus originally opened in 1968. During the ten-year period under consideration in this report, 1975-1985, the enrollment of the campus increased from 8,700 to 10,000 (14.9%) while the enrollment in the department of foreign languages grew from 559 to 1,475 (163.9%) in credit courses. During that same period, we also added non-credit offerings in languages which boosted department enrollment figures to 1,750. One component of these non-credit offerings is the program of languages for children.

Since this is a ten-year report, I shall describe the development of the program on a year-by-year basis. The first year, 1975, was one of initial study and decision-making. Several of our adult students in French and in Spanish had asked me as department chair to consider offering courses for their children. For a department of only four full-time faculty members offering three languages, the initial major hurdle (which would prove to be a continued constraint) was to locate instructors willing to spend the necessary time and energy who would have the creative abilities to plan, develop, and teach a new program. Two part-time faculty members agreed to work with me outside our regular hours and duties and without concern for remuneration.

We decided that our first requirement was to find out how much and what kinds of language instruction were available to the children of our community. We spent the rest of 1975 locating and visiting language classes for elementary children. There were not many in Tarrant County: two major, expensive private schools and a limited program in Spanish in a few schools in the Forth Worth Independent School District. There were no classes available in the suburban schools. The public school administrators explained that they could not offer languages, primarily due to budgetary constraints, commitment of time to other curricula, and lack of qualified faculty. If

65

Jane Harper is chairperson of the Foreign Language Department at Tarrant County Junior College, Hurst, Texas.

children in our community were to study languages, their instruction would have to be outside school hours, off school premises, with other personnel. The community college would be ideal: classroom space, lab facilities, media equipment, teaching materials, and faculty would be available during the afternoons and summers, the time least utilized by the college, yet prime time for elementary school children. We decided to develop a program.

In 1976 we planned the courses. Each course would consist of twelve classes of 50 minutes each, one per week during the fall and spring semesters, two per week during each summer term. Class size would be limited to fifteen students. We developed a course strategy based on our anticipated student population, one expected to be basically unpredictable. Since classes would be scheduled during after-school hours, they would necessarily compete with piano lessons, dance classes, sports, and scouts. A child might be able to enroll during the fall, but not in the spring, and might like to return for a summer term. Another might attend only during the spring or summer. At every age group we could expect first-time enrollees. After a year or two, we could also anticipate returning students in each class. After the initial offering, there would probably be a mixture of novices and returnees in every class. Therefore, we developed a non-sequential series of twelve lessons based on common topics, such as parts of the body, the family, rooms of a house, clothing, the beach, foods, pet animals, the circus, professions, and others. By rotating or re-grouping the topics, using five or six each semester, returning students would not be bored nor would new students be overwhelmed by the material. The emphasis would be listening comprehension of the spoken language and speech production of basic vocabulary and simple phrases.

After the design of the courses was completed, the actual materials for teaching each unit were developed in 1977. Acknowledging the short attention span of young children, we planned eight to twelve separate activities for each 50-minute class. Most activities required mediated instructional materials, with variety being important in capturing and holding student attention as well as in transmitting meaning and information. Most of the materials we created as slides, flash cards, flannel-board characters, large posters, puppets, toys, pictorial worksheets, and tapes. In addition, we selected and recorded songs and designed games to reinforce the vocabulary of each unit. We also created a "Parent Paper" for each unit to inform parents of the vocabulary, stories, and songs being taught and an accompanying cassette tape for home use.

By 1978 we were ready for students. During the summer we offered the first classes in Spanish, one for children in grades K–3 and one for children in grades 4–6.

The following summer, 1979, we added French to the summer program. We had three classes in Spanish and two in French. That fall and the next spring we offered both French and Spanish classes during the after-school hours for the first time. By the time the first French class was offered, the part-time instructor who had offered to work with the program had moved, and I did the teaching myself. The following year the Spanish teacher temporarily retired to have a baby, and the on-going search for teachers began.

By 1981 we had enough repeating students to require additional teaching units. Since our original twelve units were working well, we used the same format to create materials on ten more topics, such as a trip to the hospital, the kitchen, a toy store, a gift, transportation, and a city street. That year we added a second summer semester to our schedule of offerings for a total of nine classes during the summer. Our fall and spring semesters continued to enroll a total of three or four sections in French and Spanish.

In 1982 we added German to the curriculum. After an initial course taught by a full-time department faculty member, we added a part-time instructor, a German native and former TCJC student who had subsequently completed a graduate degree.

In the summer of 1983, we added courses for junior high school students in French, German, and Spanish. All three languages continued to be available for grades K-6 throughout the year, fall, spring, and two summer terms. After having sustained a stable but small enrollment in the after-school program since the fall of 1979, the enrollment jumped during 1983-84, with nine classes that fall, eleven that spring, and seventeen the following summer. During this period we also restricted one section to a special group of second-grade students from a private school who were bussed to campus during the school day two days a week for Spanish. Another new class served senior high school students who wanted extra conversation practice in French.

In the spring of 1985, we offered Italian for the first time. We now have four Spanish classes being taught "in-house" in the Children's Center on campus during regular school hours. We have our first off-campus Spanish class in a private school during the regular school day. At the senior high level, we have added Spanish and German to our conversation classes. We offer a total of eighteen sections, by far our largest number of classes in a single semester.

During these ten years of apparent progress, not all milestones have been achieved easily. The most difficult problem is the constant requirement for good teachers. Although four of the five current full-time faculty have taught at least one course in the program, with fifty to sixty sections offered annually, most of the instruction is provided by part-time faculty. As many as eight to ten different teachers are employed each semester for the children's program. Locating, recruiting, and training fluent, experienced, enthusiastic teachers is essential for the success of the program. Other major considerations are appropriate scheduling and coordination of classes, scheduling of equipment and materials, design of brochures and letters for publicity, and availability of a department spokesman for meetings with parent groups. Recruitment of students is also essential, particularly during the early years of a new program.

Over a period of ten years, the program of foreign languages for children at TCJC Northeast Campus has grown from an idea to a

67

project to an experiment to an established year-round program for 500 children, age 4-18, enrolled in four terms of French, German, Spanish, or Italian. Although the next few years are still in the idea stages, we are considering some additions to the program, such as workshops for teachers on materials development and use, summer courses in Latin for high school students, and extension of our off-campus offerings into other private elementary schools.

Perhaps with the new state requirement for the teaching of foreign languages "to the extent possible" in all Texas public high schools, a growing awareness by the public of the need for languages for younger children will develop and will create additional demands for language instruction at the elementary level. In that case, Tarrant County Junior College will have a faculty experienced in curriculum development, materials design, and instruction in languages for children to assist in the development of instruction for children in the public sector. Our ultimate goal is to be run out of the business of providing language courses for children by the universal offering of such programs in the public elementary schools of our community.

Launching Foreign Language Programs in Elementary Schools: Highpoints and Headaches

Ulrike Criminale

The Setting

Over the past six years, The Language School in Seattle, Washington, has established, conducted, and expanded extracurricular foreign language classes in thirty-one local elementary schools. All classes meet twice a week for 40-minute sessions on school premises immediately before or after the regular school day. Entirely tuition supported, the program organizes classes of ten to twelve students, grouped in age spans no greater than three grade levels.

Each school has a parent coordinator who sends out registration forms, collects tuition, stands by on the first day of class, observes the classes occasionally, and helps monitor the program during the school year. The coordinator also provides liaison among teachers, parents, the host-school administration, and The Language School. In 1984-85, tuition was $108 for twenty-four weeks (48 contact hours). Since 1985-86, tuition has been $104 for twenty weeks (40 contact hours).

The Language School aims to create an awareness of other cultures through contact with another language at an early age, and we strive to make that first contact an enjoyable experience in order to foster further language study. Using total physical response in the context of activities and games, we teach vocabulary and basic phrases. Although teachers do not need any teaching certification, all potential instructors should have experience working with children. The school conducts its own training in the total-physical-response method.

Highpoints

The Language School started serving the Seattle community in 1976, originally offering language classes for adults only. In 1979, after an initial experimental summer program for children, the first classes were offered at two elementary schools during the school year. For two years, the program grew slowly. After the appearance

69

Ulrike Criminale is Director of The Language School, Seattle, Washington.

of several commission reports that stressed the need for foreign language study (e.g., *A Nation at Risk* and *Excellence in Education*), the number of parental requests for classes for elementary school children jumped dramatically to 84 (in 1982-83) and then to 118 (in 1983-84). Simultaneously participating schools numbered as many as twenty-two, and enrollments have been as high as 911 students.

During the 1984-85 school year, enrollments tapered to 724 students in sixty-four classes. These classes were conducted in eighteen schools in six different school districts. We attribute this decline to three major factors. First, as of 1984-85, we required parents to commit themselves to a full year's program, paying full tuition in advance. Prior to fall 1984, parents had been able to enroll their children separately for two twelve-week semesters. Under that arrangement, however, second-semester classes were jeopardized by mid-year attrition. While ensuring continuity, the new policy of double payment required firmer commitment from parents. Second, we increased the minimum enrollment from eight to ten, and some classes thus failed to materialize. The third reason for decline actually demonstrates our success. The PTAs in several schools decided to set up and administer their own programs, a welcome development indicating increasing parental commitment to foreign language education for their children.

Headaches

Parents

Since unrealistic expectations abound for major accomplishments in a short period, it is extremely important to clearly state the program's objectives and make sure they are understood. Since these foreign language classes are tuition supported, they are subject to market forces, including supply and demand. If the parents are dissatisfied, or if the children grow bored or simply move on to other activities, e.g., music or sports, language classes are likely to be dropped.

Students

Quite frequently teachers are faced with students who become discipline problems. Often they are the brightest class members, who become bored if they are not constantly challenged. Sometimes it is evident that children have joined the class because of parental pressure; self-motivation is decidedly absent. Whatever the cause, discipline problems have to be handled immediately and firmly. A formal policy of discipline, known and accepted by all, will help resolve such problems.

Teachers

The teachers are the ones who define the success of the program. It is their enthusiasm and skill that hold the children's attention, their inventiveness in the choice of games and activities that enlivens the subject. Since they assure the program's success, they must be chosen with great care. Once selected, they will have to be given the best possible training in the chosen teaching method. If they are not experienced teachers, they also must be shown how to handle the inevitable discipline problems.

Since teachers often move on to more lucrative employment, program organizers must continually recruit staff.

The Organizers

Irrespective of their organizational base, program coordinators must devote special attention to several areas:
- Realistic objectives have to be established and clearly communicated with staff and parents. This is best done during a preliminary general meeting.
- Organizers, parents, parent coordinators, host schools, and teaching staff must communicate continually. If there is no central location, e.g., a teacher's lounge, communication must be by special meeting, phone, memo, newsletter, or a combination thereof.
- The product needs to be marketed to achieve and maintain a high level of interest. Foreign language week is a propitious time for such efforts.

71

Host Schools

The support of the administration and staff of the host school is quite important. If PTA pressure establishes a foreign language curriculum over the objections or indifference of a principal, the program tends to collapse, whereas the support of the principal will contribute to likely success. Finally, adequate facilities are needed to conduct good classes, and a principal's support will facilitate sharing desk space, chalkboards, and so forth.

Extracurricular programs such as this one have many potential headaches; the rewards of success, however, greatly compensate for the difficulties. We have noted these four signs of success: (1) the children are excited about the subject; (2) they go on to study foreign languages in junior or senior high school; (3) monolingual parents report that their children helped them communicate on a trip abroad; and (4) foreign language study is no longer seen as superfluous, but as a necessary part of education.

Assimilative Motivation and the Development of Second Languages in Children

C. Roy Graham

We who are involved in teaching a foreign language to children sometimes forget the origins of our discipline. Because our roots go back to the teaching of modern foreign languages to adults, and before that, to the teaching of classical languages such as Latin and Greek, we often conceive of language learning primarily as a cognitive activity. In spite of the research in child language acquisition in general and metalinguistic development in particular, we continue to organize our syllabi in neat grammatical sequences, being careful to introduce certain tenses first and going patiently through verb paradigms. We continue to treat language teaching as we would the teaching of any other school subject, such as math or social studies, by relegating it to a particular class period, by breaking it down into its component parts and teaching each of these parts in a systematic way, and by testing and grading students on their mastery of these parts.

What this conceptualization of language instruction ignores is that language is, in large part, a social phenomenon. More than just a set of sentence patterns that one has to learn, it is one of the primary means by which we form close social ties as well as the means by which we establish our own social identity. When we speak a particular language and, especially, a particular dialect of a language, we proclaim to all the world who our closest associates are; we betray our social group membership. Smith has called this function of language the integrative function, which he contrasts with the communicative function or the process of communicating referential meaning.

Associated with this integrative function of language is a motivation which I have elsewhere called assimilative motivation. When we ignore this function of language, no matter how technically well conceived our program, it is destined to be not as effective as it might.

In order to evaluate the effects of this motivation on the acquisition of language in children, let us examine some studies of bilingual development in natural contexts. One of the earliest of such studies is by the Kenyeres, who kept a diary of the French and Hungarian language development of their daughter Eva. Until the age of seven

C. Roy Graham is Professor of Linguistics at Brigham Young University.

when their family moved to Geneva, Eva spoke only Hungarian. Thrust into a second language environment, Eva first refused to learn French. Soon, however, she developed friendships with French-speaking peers and within six months no longer wished to speak Hungarian, even when her parents addressed her in that language. After two years of living in Geneva, the family returned to Budapest. Here, Eva went through another adjustment period. Within a few months her parents reported that she was embarrassed to speak French with them unless no one else was around.

In 1949 Tits published a similar study of a Spanish refugee girl who lived with a Belgian family. When the girl was six years old, she attended a school where her peers spoke French. She advanced very rapidly in learning French and within months she claimed that she could no longer speak Spanish, in spite of attempts on the part of her foster parents to maintain her Spanish-speaking ability at home.

Perhaps the best known and most carefully documented study of early bilingual development is Leopold's four-volume study of his daughter Hildegard's learning of German and English in an English-speaking environment. He spoke only German to her from birth while his wife spoke only English. By the end of her fourth year, Hildegard's language was decidedly English with occasional intrusions of German words. At the end of her fifth year, the Leopolds moved to Germany for about seven months. By the end of a month, she had become "completely fluent" in German while in English she was "unable to say more than a few very simple...sentences... ." ("A Child's Learning of Two Languages" 26-27). On the Leopolds' return to the United States, her adjustment process was reversed. Within a few weeks, she had regained her fluency in English.

These and similar studies demonstrate the tremendous influence of assimilative motivation on the acquisition of native-like speech during childhood. This influence can also be seen when the social reference group speaks a dialect or language other than that of the majority. Under such conditions learners will typically acquire the dialect of the reference group. Benton, for example, has reported that Maori children in New Zealand acquire the English dialect of their own ethnic group rather than the standard New Zealand dialect of the Caucasian teachers and children in their schools. This he attributes to their close social identification with those who are most like themselves. I have personally observed that Mexican immigrant children settling in black neighborhoods in Los Angeles typically learn the English of their peers rathers than that of their standard English-speaking teachers.

In second language immersion classes, this peer group influence can also be very powerful. Cohen has observed in the Culver City immersion program that "...where there are several native speakers of the second language in the class..., they too may begin to use certain of these [non-native] interlanguage forms" (105).

To further appreciate the effects of socialization on language learning, it is instructive to examine situations in which assimilative motivation is weak or nonexistent. In many bilingual communities in

73

the Southwest where the majority of the students speak Spanish and where Spanish is used during certain periods of the day for instruction, monolingual Spanish-speaking children typically become fluent in English while monolingual anglophone children learn very little Spanish. Edelsky and Hudelson have studied just such a community in Arizona and have reported that during the entire nine-month period in which they observed the children in both experimental sessions and natural interaction "...Spanish was not used by any [Spanish speakers] on a one-to-one basis with any of the Anglo children" (38). On the other hand, English was used consistently by the Anglos to address the Chicano children. They concluded that the English-speaking children failed to use and learn Spanish largely because of the social status of the two languages. The children had internalized the attitudes of the larger community toward the two languages and "...neither ethnic group showed any evidence of expecting that the Anglos would learn the marked language" (41).

Thus we can see that attitudes toward a language can so affect the inclination of children to socialize in that language that the normally expected acquisition process does not take place, even when they have the opportunity to immerse themselves in that language. This, of course, is only the opposite side of the acquisition coin mentioned above. The Maori children mentioned by Benton acquired the dialect of their own ethnic group but, at the same time, failed to acquire the standard dialect of the dominant group. The Mexican immigrant children acquired the black English of their neighborhood but failed to acquire the standard dialect of their teachers. The same situation exists with many language minority groups in the United States. In my visits to the Navajo reservations of southern Utah and northern Arizona, I have observed the same phenomenon.

In these circumstances, I have often been asked by teachers what can be done about teaching a standard English dialect to children when their peers and their families speak non-standard dialects. It appears to me that the solution does not lie in doing more language drills and learning more grammatical rules. If we want children to learn a particular language or dialect, we should take advantage of their normal inclinations to pursue certain learning strategies.

In a nine-month study of children's language acquisition, Wong Fillmore observed the interaction of five monolingual Spanish-speaking first graders learning English in a bilingual classroom. Analyzing her notes, she divided the children's development into stages based on their learning strategies. She observed that "...the first stage [was] characterized by a general concern, not so much for communicating as for getting a handle on the language and establishing a social relationship with speakers of the language" (659). During this period the children often sacrificed their need to communicate in favor of their desire to interact socially. During the second stage, the children were primarily concerned with communicating. "The goal [was] to get the point across, one way or another" (662). The children learned many "formulaic expressions" that they used as wholes and applied in whatever situations they could. Only during the third stage did the children become concerned with grammatical correctness. During this stage they began working on the larger units first and gradually began refining the grammar to conform to native norms. This they did with no direct instruction in sentence structure. The primary motivation for this refinement appears to have been efficiency of communication and social integration.

These three stages unfold naturally in children in the reverse order in which they frequently are assumed to occur in foreign language classrooms. That is, teachers are concerned first with developing correct sentence patterns, second with communication, and then, if ever, with social interaction. Yet if we want the full range of second language skills to develop in our children, we must pay much more attention to their socialization in that language. That such a course is effective is indicated by a number of studies in which parents persisted in socializing their children in a foreign language even though the children lived in a monolingual environment. Saunders reports on raising his two children in German and English in Australia, where they had little access outside the family to people who spoke German. He reports the difficulties encountered when his children began trying to speak to him in English rather than in German. By persisting in his insistence that they speak to him in German, he was eventually able to help them overcome the social barriers and feel comfortable speaking German.

Another such study is that of Fantini, who raised his son Mario to be bilingual in Spanish and English. Again, it was through the parents' persistence in speaking Spanish in the home that Mario developed both languages.

If the teacher is the only proficient second language model the children have, then the teacher must concentrate on getting the children to identify emotionally and socially with him or her and with the target language and its people.

Some possible suggestions for achieving this identification in a foreign language teaching context are (1) create situations through stories, games, songs, parties, discussions, and so on for genuine social interaction in the language; (2) take the emphasis off producing grammatically correct utterances and place it on verbal participation in the kinds of activities mentioned above; (3) create a special esprit de corps in the classroom by giving children names in the language, by having contests to see if they can function for full class periods without speaking English, and by talking very positively about the peoples of the countries where the target language is spoken; (4) plan field trips, fairs, language bowls, and show movies to create an enthusiasm for the language and an appreciation for the culture; (5) take every opportunity to point out the value of speaking a second language; (6) establish a personal relationship with the children that will make them feel appreciated and valued; and (7) establish language clubs whose purpose is to promote the use of the foreign language at times other than the classroom period.

In English as a second language or standard English as a second

75

dialect situations, the following suggestions may be helpful: (1) Accept the children's first language or dialect. Do not force them to choose between the teacher's way of speaking and that of their peers. (2) Make the children proud of their ethnic heritage but at the same time encourage identification with the teacher's culture, thereby inspiring the children to become bi-dialectal or to develop another register in their speech. (3) Create exciting communication activities through which new forms of the language are introduced. If the children are introduced to new vocabulary and new forms of the language, they will have to learn it in the teacher's dialect because it will be unavailable in the dialect of their peers. (4) Increase the emphasis on literacy. Most instructional material is written in a formal register and as children become more literate, they naturally develop a more standard dialect. (5) If possible, conduct learning activities so that speakers of the non-standard dialect socialize with speakers of the standard.

The activities suggested above represent a few examples of what might be done to encourage greater emphasis on socialization in the acquisition of a second or foreign language. The reader can undoubtedly add many others to the list. The main objective of these suggestions is to encourage teachers to permit the natural language acquisition strategies of children to work for them rather than against them.

References

Benton, Richard. *Research into the English Language Difficulties of Maori School Children.* Wellington, New Zealand: Maori Education Foundation, 1964.

Cohen, Andrew D. "Researching the Linguistic Outcomes of Bilingual Programs." *The Bilingual Review* 9.2(1982):97-108.

Edelsky, Carole, and Sarah Hudelson. "Acquiring a Second Language When You're Not the Underdog." *Research in Second Language Acquisition: Selected Papers of the Los Angeles Second Language Acquisition Research Forum.* Ed. Robin Scarcella and Stephen Krashen. Rowley, Mass.: Newbury House, 1981. 36-42.

Fantini, Alvino E. *Language Acquisition of a Bilingual Child: A Sociolinguistic Perspective.* Brattleboro, Vermont: The Experiment Press, 1974.

Graham, C. Ray. "Beyond Integrative Motivation: The Development and Influence of Assimilative Motivation." *On TESOL '84.* Ed. Penny Larson, E. Judd, and D. Messerschmitt. Washington, D.C.: TESOL, 1985. 75-87.

Kenyeres, Adele. "Comment une Petite Hongroise de sept ans apprend le français." *Archives de Psychologie* 26(1938):321-66.

Leopold, Werner F. *Speech Development of a Bilingual Child: A Linguist's Record.* 4 vols. Evanston, Ill.: Northwestern Univ. Press, 1939, 1947, 1949, 1949.

———. "A Child's Learning of Two Languages." *Report of the Fifth Annual Roundtable Meeting on Language and Language Teaching.* Ed. Hugo J. Mueller. Monograph Series in Language and Linguistics. Washington, D.C.: Georgetown Univ. Press, 1954.

Saunders, George. "Adding a Second Native Language in the Home." *Journal of Multilingual and Multicultural Development* 1.2(1980):113-44.

Smith, David M. "Some Implications for the Social Status of Pidgin Languages." *Socio-linguistics in Cross-Cultural Analysis,* Ed. David M. Smith and Roger Shuy. Washington, D.C.: Georgetown Univ. Press, 1972. 47-56.

Fillmore, Lily Wong. *The Second Time Around: Cognitive and Social Strategies in Second Language Acquisition.* Diss. Stanford Univ., 1976.

Should We Teach Children Grammar?

Mervin R. Barnes

In a 1973 article in *Language Learning* as well as in a 1974 article in *TESOL Quarterly*, Dulay and Burt pose a very interesting question for foreign language acquisition: "Should we teach children syntax?" They determine that children learning English as a second language acquire certain structures of English in a fixed sequence and that "the learning order of these structures is controlled by processing strategies, in the sense that the child must be cognitively 'ready' in order to acquire any one of them." Moreover, they suggest, "No one has fould a way to accelerate the child's progress through the steps in the acquisition of syntax.... At this point, our knowledge of the language acquisition process tells us that exposing the child to a natural communication situation is sufficient to activate his language learning processes" (256). Thus the answer to the question, "Should we teach children syntax?" is "No". Although the second language (L2) teacher "should continue to *diagnose* children's L2 syntax," Dulay and Burt suggest that "We should leave the learning to the children and redirect our teaching efforts to other aspects of language" (257).

Actually, Dulay and Burt's conclusions are not new to the literature; even a superficial glimpse at past methodological literature reveals that the direct method was based on the learning of language through usage rather than through the explicit teaching of grammar. The Berlitz Language Schools have become internationally famous by using a method based on the assumption that "You learn to *speak* a language *by speaking it*—and in no other way, (*The Berlitz Self-Teacher*, v). Even some of the behaviorist methodologists discourage the teaching of grammar. The Rehder and Twaddell series of high school language texts, for example, completely ignores grammar, and the entire learning experience is based on the learning of situational dialogues and expansion through pattern drills.[1] The main significance of Dulay and Burt is that they supplied for the first time an empirical basis for the thesis.

Ellis has conducted a more recent experiment on the relationship between formal grammar teaching and language acquisition, and his results seem to confirm the conclusions of Dulay and Burt. Ellis at-

Mervin R. Barnes is Professor of Modern Languages, Literatures, and Linguistics at the University of Oklahoma.

tempted to test the relative validity of the interface position, which claims that formal grammar knowledge can be converted to linguistic performance, and the non-interface position, which claims that it cannot. He describes an experiment in which children learning English as a second language received formal instruction on the WH interrogative in English. The children were tested both before and after the formal instruction in order to determine whether the explicit presentation of grammatical description followed by practice with grammar exercises would contribute to the development of WH questions. Although he finds no such evidence, he pointed out that his study does not disprove the thesis either, since "the instruction provided may have been of the wrong type, in insufficient quantities, at the wrong time, etc." (151). It becomes immediately apparent that the "interface" thesis, which states that formal grammar knowledge can be converted to linguistic performance, cannot be disproved in the general case. One can always claim that we simply used the wrong approach and that another approach to the material might have yielded different results. This problem illustrates quite clearly one of the major weaknesses in much of the theoretical work in L2 acquisition today, as well as the experimental work based on theory.

If the evidence for child L2 acquisition predominantly contests the interface position, the evidence concerning L2 acquisiton in adults is quite different. Seliger, Krashen, and Hartnett find a strong correlation between proficiency and the time spent in formal instruction among a group of students at the Queens College English Language Institute in New York. There was no such correlation between proficiency and practice time. Krashen and Seliger and Krashen, Zelinski, Jones, and Usprich also present evidence in favor of formal instruction for adults. For adults, at least, the evidence would appear to support the concept of formal grammar instruction.

But if the interface thesis holds for adults, then why not for children? After all, children must learn some rules of grammar in order to use the language; otherwise, they could never learn to combine words into sentences, and they would be restricted to the use of memorized patterns and routines. But if children must learn the grammar anyway, then are we not suggesting by not teaching the grammar that they not only have to learn the rules, but also have to figure out first what they are? Would it not be better to aid their acquisition of proficiency by showing them the rules that they must learn? To Ellis' question whether the instruction might be wrong, I would add another, perhaps more important question: Is it possible that the problem lies not in the instruction but in the *grammar* that we teach?

One of the curious things about current theoretical models is that they say little about the details of language acquisition and language teaching. Ellis decided to use the audio-lingual approach for teaching the WH interrogatives not because theoretical grounds or his original hypothesis dictated the choice, but because "Any formal language work that normally took place was of the audio-lingual type. There was little in the way of grammatical explanation, probably because this was considered difficult for this kind of child to grasp" (141 f).

79

Nor do Seliger, Krashen, and Hartnett define what "formal instruction" consists of.[2] Thus it might include the audio-lingual approach or even grammar translation. Krashen and Terrell do describe a theory of acquisition that makes some fairly specific requirements of a methodology. In "Accounting for Child-Adult Differences in Second Language Rate and Attainment" (Krashen, Scarcella, and Long 202-26), Krashen even evaluates several teaching approaches in the light of what the theory says about language acquisition, but these theoretical requirements do not always develop naturally out of the basic theory, and as Taylor points out in his review of Krashen and Terrell, the authors sometimes draw conclusions that are not completely justified on the basis of the literature cited. It is precisely this lack of theoretical definition that underlies Ellis' inconclusive results.

In the remainder of this paper I will examine some of the theoretical aspects of L2 acquistion. Specifically I will try to show that one of the problems associated with the teaching of grammar to children involves the nature of the grammar rules taught as well as the instructional methodology.

Child-Adult Differences in L2 Learning

The question whether we should teach grammar to children stems partially from the problem of child-adult differences in language learning. The belief that children acquire language faster than adults is well established and Snow is probably right when she suggests that a large part of this belief may be due to parents' inability to judge their children's proficiency in a foreign language, or to children's expertise at leading adults to believe that they know more than they really do. It seems quite likely that children do become very proficient with the foreign language within a restricted context, and that they simply are not required to operate beyond that context and thus reveal their real weaknesses in the language. Certainly there is a tendency to assume that the appearance of native proficiency within a limited context often leads one to assume that the speaker has native or near-native proficiency on a global level as well. Anyone who has become fluent in the use of a few phrases or sentences in a foreign language can attest to the problems that can arise when a native speaker misjudges one's proficiency in the language. Misleading hints as to a speaker's proficiency need not be restricted to one's fluency in speaking as is apparent in Snow's example of the child who was scolded for disobeying the teacher when, in actuality, she simply had not understood the teacher's request. The child had done such a good job of acting that the teacher had assumed that she spoke Dutch when she didn't. (148-49).

Recent research, however, has indicated that the assumption that children learn languages faster than adults is, to a large extent, a myth; in fact, on a short-term basis, adults have the advantage when it comes to language learning.[3] It is only on a long-term basis that children show an advantage. Explanations for this long-term advantage attributed to children are variable, ranging from Lenneberg's thesis of lateralization of the brain at puberty to Krashen's association of adult learning with affective factors and the onset of Piaget's stage of formal operations ("Accounting for Child-Adult Differences") to Genesee's suggestion that children are better simply because they have more years to learn the language.[4]

Some of the evidence showing that older children and adults are superior language learners is very misleading, however, in the sense that they are tested on precisely those aspects of language over which adults appear to have the greatest control. Snow and Hoefnagel-Höhle, for example, tested the speakers by having them repeat word lists which were then evaluated for pronunciation by native speakers. On the basis of these tests, they concluded that older speakers gained control of Dutch pronunciation more rapidly than children. This type of discrete item test, however, does not really evaluate a speaker's ability to use the language or even to produce the correct sounds *in speech*. Rather such exercises test the speaker's knowledge about the language and his ability to imitate sounds in isolation. As a linguist I can reproduce most language sounds with very little difficulty, but under the pressure of speech in a foreign language, that ability sometimes disappears and English pronunciation habits slip in, even in German, a language which I speak rather fluently.[5]

Snow and Hoefnagel-Höhle confirm precisely this aspect of language learning in an article whose data actually contradict the conclusions of the authors. Snow and Hoefnagel-Höhle tested a group of English speakers who were learning Dutch. The tests covered several aspects of language, including pronunciation, auditory discrimination, morphology, sentence repetition, sentence translation, sentence judgment, and the Peabody Picture Vocabulary Test. On all of these tests, the adults and adolescents outscored the children, thus apparently supporting the author's conclusion that

> the 3- to 5-year-olds scored consistently worse than the older groups on all the tests and that the 12- to 15-year-olds showed the most rapid acquisition of all the skills tested. These findings are basis for rejecting the hypothesis that the period 2 to 12 years constitutes an optimal time for language acquisition (103).

But the above test measurements are all discrete item tests which the authors themselves feel might be oriented toward the adults (103). The most interesting data, however, come from the story comprehension test and the storytelling task. Here the results differed noticeably from the other tests.

In the storytelling task, the subjects were asked to tell a story on the basis of a set of pictures. A fluency score was calculated by taking the ratio of number of words to seconds talking. In the story comprehension test, they were asked to listen to a story in Dutch and retell it either in Dutch or in English. Comprehension was scored on the basis of mentioning 30 key points in the story. In both of these tasks, the 3- to 10-year-olds started far behind the adults and adolescents on the first trial. By the third trial, however, the 6-7-year-olds actual-

81

ly outperformed all other groups, including not only the adults but also the 12- to 15-year-olds, who were the top performers on all of the other tests. In the storytelling task, the adults finished last, even behind the 3- to 5-year-olds. Snow and Hoefnagel-Höhle seem to confirm this evaluation with their statement that "All the 6- to 15-year-old subjects had achieved sufficient control of Dutch by the third test session to be described as good bilinguals," although they also add that the subjects differed considerably in the degree to which they achieved control of the individual skills, i.e., the grammar (109).

The evidence from Snow and Hoefnagel-Höhle, then, seems to indicate that the child does surpass the older learner in one specific and very important area—fluency. In other words, the child is able to outperform the adult in Krashen's sense of acquisition, whereas the adult appears to have the advantage in controlling the learned monitor rules. If this is a valid perception, then the data support Krashen's association of puberty and Piaget's stage of formal operations with the child's access to the ability to monitor his speech.

Monitors and Language Acquisition

Krashen's Monitor Model is far too well-known to require more than a brief description of the major points that are important for the discussion in this paper.[6] Krashen suggests that there are two types of rules active in language: "learned" rules and "acquired" rules. The learned rules are the result of conscious learning, i.e., the rules as they are presented in the formal classroom. The acquired rules are those the child *subconsciously* learns in the acquisition of his first language. The acquired rules are used to produce speech whereas learned rules are used primarily to monitor and evaluate the product of the acquired rules.[7]

In natural language acquisition, both children and adults tend to acquire language subconsciously. But at the age of puberty, children develop a conscious grammar that corresponds to the increased meta-awareness of language more typical of adults. "Adults (not all) are better *learners*, they can talk about rules like subject-verb agreement,…" (Krashen, "Accounting" 209). This access to the monitor allows adults to get a faster start in learning a second language, because the adult performers "simply utilize the surface structure of their first language, and then employ the conscious grammar as a Monitor to make alterations to bring the L1 surface structure into conformity with their idea of the surface structure of the second language" (210). Thus the monitor theory predicts not only the more rapid short-term learning of the adult, but also the long-term superiority of the child. Because adults learn only the learned rules of the monitor and not the subconscious rules that are necessary in speech, they soon reach an impasse, unless they also acquire the subconscious equivalent of the learned rules. In other words, as long as the performance pressures of time and knowledge are limited, adults can use the monitor to help produce accurate speech. But as proficiency increases, so do the performance pressures, so that speakers eventually hit a ceiling in terms of the functions they can perform in the language.

One should notice at this point how well the monitor hypothesis explains the data in Snow and Hoefnagel-Höhle. The children, unfettered by the need to monitor, perform well in the story-retelling task because they have acquired their language, rather than learning it. Their acquired speech also allows them to process the narration faster in the comprehension test, thus understanding more details than the adults, who are slowed down by the need to use their monitoring systems.

Thus the monitor hypothesis makes a specific prediction about language learning for children;

> For younger children almost all language skills must be acquired direct-ly from natural language acquisition experiences. Learning exercises will be used only for older students, and then in a judicious manner since acquisition activities are more important even in the case of adults (Krashen and Terrell 61).

Careful attention to the preceding discussion reveals one of the major flaws in Krashen's monitor: it consists not of one model, but rather of two. Krashen refers to the "monitor hypothesis" (Krashen "Accounting"; Krashen and Terrell) and the "Monitor Model *for second-language acquisition*" (my emphasis), but in reality the monitor itself has little or nothing to do with language acquisition. It is rather a model for language *production* or *performance*. Krashen refers to the monitor as an acquisition model, but whenever he ac-tually applies the model, it is only to a *performance* situation. Con-sider his statement that adults "can talk about rules like subject-verb agreement..." or his claim that adults can "employ the conscious grammar as a Monitor to make alterations to bring the L1 surface structure into conformity with their idea of the surface structure of the second language." He is actually speaking much more about the speech act than he is about the acquisition of the rules, yet he says lit-tle or nothing about this aspect of the grammar.

The role of the monitor and acquisition rules as a performance model is especially visible in the data of Snow and Hoefnagel-Höhle. The model does not explain how the children and adults *acquired* their Dutch; it only explains their speech in a given task at a given time. It says absolutely nothing about what happened to the speakers' grammars between the testing sessions, except through the *unsupported assumption* that they acquired the rules subconscious-ly. Certainly the acquisition rules appear to be subconscious at the time of the tests, in the sense that the speakers cannot formulate the rules that they are using. In any case they must differ from the monitor rules in some significant way, but that difference exists regardless of the manner in which the rules were learned by the speakers. When one considers the evidence on routines and patterns in Hakuta and in Fillmore, one has to wonder just how subconscious the acquisition of the production rules could possibly be. And Hakuta and Fillmore are not the only scholars who record the use of patterns and routines in L2 acquisition. Wagner-Gough and Itoh and Hatch mention similar learning strategies.

Krashen reveals a somewhat casual attitude toward the role of routines and patterns in L2 acquisition, claiming that "the creative construction process is independent of routines and patterns."[8] In any case their presence seems to be far too pervasive to simply cast them aside without an extensive investigation of how they are used, especially when the biggest problem seems to be simply that they do not fit into the theory. If patterns do play a significant role in L2 acquisition, particularly with acquisition of grammar, then we can safely reject subconscious learning as a major factor in L2 acquisition.

Krashen also presents other hypotheses about major factors in L2 acquisition, including the input hypothesis and the affective filter hypothesis, but a discussion of these topics is irrelevant to the main thesis of this paper.

Competence vs. Performance

The basic concept of the monitor is really not new to linguistic theory. This bipartite model can be traced back through the Chomskyan division of competence and performance to de Saussure's *langue* and *langage*. In Chomskyan terms a speaker's linguistic competence is his knowledge about the language; his performance is his actual production. Those are precisely the concepts that occur in the monitor model where the acquisition rules correspond to performance rules and the monitor corresponds to the competence rules.

But there is another opposition in linguistic theory that is appropriate here, and that is the old contrast between the semantics-based model and the syntax-based model. The semantics-based model attempts to map an underlying semantic structure into a syntactic surface structure; the syntax-based model begins with a syntactic structure to which one applies linguistic rules to obtain a surface structure which is then "interpretable" by the semantic component of the model.

These two syntactic models correspond once again to elements in the monitor model. Monitor rules focus on form; so do syntax-based rules. Acquisition rules focus on meaning; so do semantics-based rules. Perceived in this way, the monitor model sheds new light on the problem. It takes the acquisition rules out of the mysterious and makes them more accessible to the linguists and the L2 methodologists. Instead of being subconscious and undefinable, they become simply a different kind of rule, one that converts meaning directly into a syntactic structure. By investigating and carefully defining such rules as they function in the speech act, we can simultaneously examine the communicative situation and redefine it more precisely. Such a redefinition allows us to understand more clearly how children learn grammar rules and how to teach these grammar rules. Perhaps most important, it brings out the fact that grammar is meaning! If we want to teach grammar, we cannot separate it from the meaning it is intended to represent!

Consider first some easy rules, the inflectional rules. A standard pattern drill for learning inflection is to simply substitute a new subject. I take my examples here from German, an inflected language:

(1)   Ich gehe in die Stadt   [I'm going to town]
        Du
        Du gehst in die Stadt   [You are going to town]
        Er
        Er geht in die Stadt   [He is going to town]

This type of drill focused around the grammar structure relies completely on the interpretative semantic model and does not require the speaker to understand what he is saying. According to the semantics-based model, however, the pronouns are not replacing words, but rather they refer directly to meaning. Think how much more effective that same drill could be if we restructure it into a drill in which we asked questions about pictures, questions which require the student to use precisely the pronouns we want to drill. The student would be focusing on meaning, but he would be required to learn grammar. He would be acquiring production rules.[9]

This perspective on the acquisition rules also reveals quite clearly what problems are implicit in pattern drill and why pattern practice does not always lead to oral proficiency. Pattern practice is based on reaction to a stimulus. But when does one ever have the occasion in speech to react to a stimulus in the manner suggested by the pattern in (1)? Consider, however, the following type drill:

(2) John and Ed are going to town. What is Ed doing?
        He is going to town.
     Bill and I are eating soup. What am I doing?
        You are eating soup.

Such an exercise does two things: (1) It requires students to respond to a question in a natural manner that would parallel what happens in natural conversation, and (2) It requires students to understand the question and the answer before they can respond correctly. They are practicing acquisition rules. But these rules operate at a more abstract level of grammar than those that work with pictures, because they function strictly at the linguistic level and not at the reference level.

There is one exercise I use in my beginning language classes that closely simulates the semantic model. I go around the class asking each person a question, e.g.

(3)   Wie heißen Sie?   [What's your name?]

After asking several people the question, I change the question without warning.

(4)   Wie heiße ich?   [What is my name?]

The drill has a very specific purpose, and that is to enforce on the students the fact that they have to listen for *meaning*. A slight variation shows the importance of recognizing the inflectional endings.

(5)   Wie heißt Sie?   [What is her name?]

Grammar is meaning. It takes a good ear to catch it, but the question in (5) in conjunction with the question in (3) clearly emphasizes the

85

relationship between grammar and meaning and forces the student to pay attention to form as a part of meaning.

The same grammar rules can be taught as well as drilled using similar procedures. If I teach the class a sentence like (6):

(6)   Ich heiße Schmidt.   [My name is Schmidt.]

and follow that up with the question *"Wie heißt er?"* then one can supply the answer, *"Er heißt Schmidt."* In doing so, one is teaching grammar, but the rules are the acquisition rules, the rules used in actual speech, rules which the right kind of practice can make subconscious.

Should We Teach Grammar to Children?

The model that I have described in this paper is basically a variation of the monitor model but with some major changes, primarily in the perception of the acquisition rules. Learning to speak is learning to use grammar, and to avoid the teaching of it may well be a significant disservice to the learner, whether adult or child. The crucial problem is to determine what form the rules should take. That is where the theoretical approach that I have focused on in this paper can be useful. It can help us guide our search for appropriate exercises.

One thing should be made quite clear. The few drills and exercises that I mentioned in this paper are not necessarily new. I have no doubt that many readers have used similar exercises before. What I have tried to show is that we can establish a set of theoretical guidelines to help us devise new patterns and evaluate the exercises and methodologies that we have available already. Consider for example Ellis' experiment with the WH interrogatives. I point out that Ellis presented no theoretical basis for choosing the audio-lingual approach to teach the WH interrogatives. He articulated no basis for rejecting the approach either. The model discussed here, however, which I have dubbed elsewhere the Focus Grammar or the Focus Hypothesis ("The Focus Hypothesis and the Teaching of Grammar"), predicts precisely that the audio-lingual approach as it is normally defined would probably make little difference in the development of WH questions in children. In fact, it even suggests how the pattern drills can be adjusted in order to achieve some success: alter the drills so that the questions themselves are derived directly from a semantic stimulus. That is one of the major advantages of the focus model of grammar. Although the model itself may turn out to be wrong in detail, it indicates a direction that theoretical models must take. They must treat production rules not as some mysterious element of the subconscious but rather as well-defined equations approximating real processes and accessible to linguistic analysis. Only then can we hope to make real progress in understanding language acquisition.

Notes

[1]Rehder, et al. This is not to suggest any similarity in method between Dulay and Burt and Rehder and Twaddell. In fact Dulay and Burt explicitly reject the use of the audio-lingual method that the Rehder and Twaddell series is based on. Compare this series with the basic MLA text, *Modern Spanish*, which also uses extensive pattern drills, but drills that are based primarily on specific grammar points discussed in the text.

[2]In all fairness to Seliger, et al., one could hardly have expected them to distinguish between different methods in a questionnaire for students. It does, however, illustrate the problem involved.

[3]It would be pointless to try to list the extensive published research on this topic. Several articles have been collected by Krashen, Scarcella, and Long, and the references in those articles can lead to a dozen or so more. McLaughlin has a review of the literature with a bibliography (ch. 3).

[4]Snow is probably right, however, in rejecting neurolinguistic explanations such as Lenneberg's (145).

[5]There may be another potential problem in the data on pronunciation. Snow and Hoefnagel-Höhle had three native speakers judge the subjects' pronunciation; however, they did not judge entire words but rather sounds within the words, so that there is the possibility that the evaluation of a given sound might have been influenced by its proximity to other sounds that were pronounced incorrectly. The authors appear to have neutralized outside interference to a large extent, however, in the careful manner in which they had the judges meet together and standardize their criteria (86).

[6]I use the term Monitor Model to refer to Krashen's theoretical model partially because the monitor aspect of the theory is the most salient and of greatest importance to the thesis proposed in this article. Although Krashen himself speaks of the "Monitor Model" in his earlier works, e.g., "The Monitor Model for Second-Language Acquisition," in his more recent works the "Monitor Hypothesis" has become only one part of a more general theory that he refers to as "the theoretical model" or "second language acquisition theory" (Krashen and Terrell 23). More detailed accounts are available in "The Monitor Model," Krashen, Scarcella, and Long, Krashen and Terrell, and Dulay, Burt, and Krashen, as well as in various other general publications by Krashen.

[7]Although Krashen distinguishes carefully between "acquired" rules and "learned" rules, Dulay, Burt, and Krashen use the words more or less as synonymous terms.

[8]Krashen, Scarcella, and Long (99). See also Krashen and Terrell (423-43, 460). Dulay, Burt, and Krashen reveal a much more receptive attitude toward routines and patterns (235-42).

[9]In "Kommunikation, Bilder und die grammatische Übung" I discuss the use of pictures to teach pronouns.

References

Barnes, Mervin R. "Teaching German Tenses". *Die Unterrichtspraxis* 7.1 (1974):77-81.

_____. "What Is a Linguistic Rule?" *The Sixth LACUS Forum 1979.* Columbia, S.C.: Hornbeam Press, 1980. 21-29.

_____. "Kommunikation, Bilder und die grammatische Übung." Paper read at the VII. Internationaler Deutschlehrertagung, Budapest, 1-5 August 1983.

_____. "The Focus Hypothesis and the Teaching of Grammar." Paper read at the Seventh World Congress of Applied Linguistics, Brussels, August 1984.

_____. "Focus Grammar and Language Acquisition Rules." *The Eleventh LACUS Forum 1984*. Columbia, S.C.: Hornbeam Press, 1985. 492-97.

The Berlitz Self-Teacher: German. New York: Grosset and Dunlap, 1950.

Dulay, Heidi, and Marina K. Burt. "Should We Teach Children Sytax?" *Language Learning* 23.2(1973):245-58.

_____. "Errors and Strategies in Child Second Language Acquisition." *TESOL* Quarterly 8.2(1974):129-36.

_____. "Natural Sequences in Child Second Language Acquisition." *Language Learning* 24.1(1974):37-53.

_____, and Stephen D. Krashen. *Language Two*. New York: Oxford Press, 1982.

Ellis, Rod. "Can Syntax Be Taught? A Study of the Effects of Formal Instruction on the Acquistion of WH Questions by Children." *Applied Linguistics* 5.2(1984):138-55.

Fillmore, Lily Wong. "The Second Time Around: Cognitive and Social Strategies in Second Language Acquisition." Diss. Stanford Univ., 1976.

Hakuta, Kenji. "Prefabricated Patterns and the Emergence of Structure in Second Language Acquisition." *Language Learning* 24.2(1974):287-97.

Hatch, Evelyn Marcussen. *Second Language Acquisition: A Book of Readings*. Rowley, Mass.: Newbury House, 1978.

Higgs, Theodore V., and Ray T. Clifford. "The Push toward Communication." *Curriculum, Competence, and the Foreign Language Teacher*. ACTFL Foreign Language Education Series. Ed. Theodore V. Higgs. Lincolnwood, Ill.: National Textbook, 1982. 57-79.

James, Dorothy. "Toward Realistic Objectives in Foreign Language Teaching *Profession 84*. New York: MLA, 1984. 33-36.

Krashen, Stephen. "The Monitor Model for Second-Language Acquisition." *Second-Language Acquisition and Foreign Language Teaching*. Ed. Rosario C. Gingras. Arlington, Va: Center for Applied Linguistics, 1978. 1-26.

Krashen, Stephen, Carl M. Jones, Stanley J. Zelinski III, and Celia Usprich. "How Important Is Instruction?" *English Language Teaching Journal* 32(1978):257-61.

Krashen, Stephen, and Herbert Seliger. "The Rose of Formal and Informal Environments in Second Language Learning: A Pilot Study." *International Journal of Psycholinguistics* 3(1976):15-21.

Krashen, Stephen, Robin C. Scarcella, and Michael H. Long, eds. *Child-Adult Differences in Second Language Acquisition*. Rowley, Mass.: Newbury House, 1982.

Krashen, Stephen, and Tracy D. Terrell. *The Natural Approach: Language Acquisition in the Classroom*. Oxford: Pergamon Press, 1983.

McLaughlin, Barry. *Second-Language Acquisition in Childhood*. Vol. 1 *Pre-school Children*. 2nd Edition. Hillsdale, N.J.: Lawrence Erlbaum Associates, 1984.

Rehder, Helmut, Ursula Thomas, W. Freeman Twaddell, and Patricia O'Connor. *Deutsch: Verstehen und Sprechen.*Teacher's Edition. New York: Holt, Rinehart, and Winston, 1962.

Seliger, Herbert, Stephen D. Krashen, and Dayle Hartnett. "Two Studies in Adult Second Language Learning." *Kritikon Litterarum* 2.3 (1974):220-28.

Snow, Catherine E. "Age Differences in Second Language Acquisition:

Research Findings and Folk Psychology." *Second Language Acquisition Studies.* Ed. Kathleen M. Bailey, Michael H. Long and Sabrina Peck. Rowley, Mass.: Newbury House, 1983. 141-150.

_____, and Marian Hoefnagel-Höhle. "Age Differences in the Pronunciation of Foreign Sounds." *Language and Speech.* 20(1977):357-65. Rpt. in Krashen, Scarcella, and Long, 84-92. Citations are from the rpt.

_____. "The Critical Period for Language Acquisition: Evidence from Second Language Learning." *Child Development* 49(1978):1114-28. Rpt. in Krashen, Scarcella, and Long.

Taylor, Gray. "Empirical or Intuitive?" Rev. of *The Natural Approach: Language Acquisition in the Classroom*, by Stephen D. Krashen and Tracy D. Terrell. *Language Learning* 34.4(1984):97-105.

The Pappenheimers: Multimedia German Program for Children

Christian P. Stehr and Tamara D. Stehr

In 1976, in cooperation with the Goethe Institute and Inter Nationes, West Germany, Oregon Public Broadcasting produced sixty 30-minute television programs for college German. These programs incorporated the well-known film series *Guten Tag* and *Guten Tag, Wie Geht's*, selected cultural segments from the *Deutschlandspiegel*, German folksongs, and instructional modules teaching pronunciation and grammar.

Oregon residents greeted the broadcast of this language series with such enthusiasm that Oregon Public Broadcasting decided to distribute the series nationally. During the following four years, the Oregon German series was transmitted via satellite to over 140 member stations of the Public Broadcasting System (PBS), from New York to Hawaii, and found a reception unprecedented in the history of televised foreign language instruction in the United States.

The experience gained in these first efforts encouraged the establishment of the much more complex and ambitious co-production project: Westdeutscher Rundfunk, TransTel Cologne, and Oregon Public Broadcasting cooperated with the Goethe Institute, Munich, in producing *The Pappenheimers*, a German language and cultural appreciation television series for children.[1]

To lay the foundation for this PBS children's series, the Goethe Institute sponsored a conference in Portland, Oregon, June 5-12, 1979. The participants discussed production techniques, format, and instructional goals, with an eye toward production of a pilot in the following year. The conference was attended by representatives from all levels of instruction, including early childhood development specialists. Joining television experts from West Germany were U.S. consultants from three major network children's series currently on the air: *Children's Television Workshop, Mr. Roger's Neighborhood,* and *Studio See.*

First the group viewed general children's television programs from all over the world which had been obtained from the organizers of *Prix Jeunesse,* an international competition for children's television programs held bi-annually in Munich, West Germany. The members of the workshop critiqued this film material and during this evaluation

Christian P. Stehr is Associate Professor of German at Oregon State University. Tamara D. Stehr is Associate Director for International Programs of Oregon Public Broadcasting.

drafted an extensive list of "dos" and "don'ts." The interchange of ideas on format and production technique was extensive and productive.

The conference participants agreed that the format of the television series would be a magazine approach with strong emphasis on learning modules consisting of on-location, real-life German scenes (background information on Germany, situational use of German), studio transitions (a host figure, music repetition, and other continuity techniques), and animation segments (in the target language for reinforcement and review). The conference participants agreed on the educational goals and decided that the primary target audience would be English speaking. However, by producing the modules on location in Germany with a strictly German soundtrack, the German language and cultural appreciation series could be utilized in any country by providing a voice-over narration in the appropriate language.

The conferees also decided that German writers would be best suited to produce the television scripts for the series. The Goethe Institute, Munich, subsequently contracted with three well-known German children's book writers for a first treatment of the pilot episode. They were asked to develop a highly entertaining story line, using a maximum of twenty selected German words, and incorporating locale and culture, both traditional and contemporary. The script was to be a half-hour program, with a logical division at mid-point so that the programs could be used as 15-minute broadcasts if desired. Finally, the story and situation had to be linked to the host-moderator in the Oregon studio who would do the opening and closing, make the transitions from module to module, as well as narrate the German filmed scenes. Of the three scripts submitted, all parties agreed on the work of the author team of Peter Lustig and Elfie Donnelly. Their treatment incorporated the desired cultural and language appreciation elements in the outlined international format and created what was to become the series title and its most recognizable element: host-moderator Charley Pappenheimer.

The series' host was described as a central figure with whom one can identify: a friendly, likeable, curious, inquiring and grandfatherly individual. He sings and plays the piano, activities which are linked to his rather unique residence: an extraordinary Volkswagen bus. A distinguishing feature characterizing all Pappenheimers, including Charley, the American representative of the clan, is the small, wire-rimmed glasses they wear.

Critical to the project's success at the next stage was the ability of Oregon Public Broadcasting to come up with a Charley Pappenheimer who would rise to the challenge of script writers Lustig and Donnelly. In February of 1980, the veteran Hollywood actor Dallas McKennon was invited for an audition for the role of Charley Pappenheimer, which he donned as if it were second nature. McKennon played Cincin Natis in the popular *Daniel Boone* television series; he did voice characterizations for Walter Lantz Cartoon Studios, including roles on the *Archie* series and the *Woody*

91

Woodpecker series, and for Walt Disney Studio productions, *101 Dalmations* and *Lady and the Tramp*. He has a great many character voices at his disposal, a talent which is exploited in the *Pappenheimer* series. McKennon's audition was sent to the German production partners, and their enthusiastic approval of his selection as host-moderator was immediate.

Follow-up meetings in New York and Cologne reunited the members of the first planning conference. They met to review the draft script. Few changes had to be made, and the central character, Charley Pappenheimer, was heartily endorsed. Fred Garbers of Locomo Productions in New York, an animator highly acclaimed for his work for CTW's *Sesame Street* and other major children's TV productions, was commissioned to produce the animated segments.

On June 21, 1980, the final version of the half-hour pilot for the *Pappenheimer* series was edited with desired logical division in the middle, providing integrated 15-minute segments, each utilizing the three types of modules: location film, studio-based locale, and animation.

A third conference was held in Cologne in August 1980, for consultations with the script writers about the overall concept and goals of the series. Results of a preview were also presented at this conference: *The Pappenheimers* pilot had been shown to a group of 50 first to fourth-grade children, predominantly boys, at a New York YMCA. The attention rate had been over 75%, and virtually all viewers volunteered their favorable reactions afterwards. Enthusiastic and approving comments were made about every feature of the show: Charley Pappenheimer and his bus, the animated portions, and the action scenes filmed in Germany.

Following approval of the pilot, production of the full series was begun. Lustig and Donnelly produced 12 successive scripts, each focusing on a different branch of the Pappenheimer family in various West German locales and representing vaious life styles. The 13 half-hour episodes presented a vocabulary of over 400 words.

The completed series was first introduced to the PBS market in the fall of 1983, at which time the initial ancillary materials also became available. In September 1983, Langenscheidt Publishers issued illustrated dialogues in German, English, and phonetic transcription for each of the 26 animated cartoons in the series; an alphabetized listing of every German word occurring in the series (with English equivalents); and suggestions for individual and classroom use. An accompanying audio cassette offered the complete soundtrack from each of the 26 cartoons.[2] By special arrangement with Langenscheidt, it was agreed that the price of these materials would be minimized to ensure that as many viewers and schools as possible would be able to take advantage of their availability.

The first full broadcast of the series took place on the Oregon Public Broadcasting system beginning in January 1984. The programs were aired in a prime-time family viewing slot, Sunday evenings at 7:00 pm. Each episode was repeated the following Saturday morning at 9:00 am. The viewer response was even better than had been hoped, with hundreds of letters and book requests coming in and viewers unanimously proclaiming the series a welcome and charming addition to public television's educational programming and to children's fare. While many parents wrote to obtain the ancillary materials for their children, almost as many adults purchased them for their own use.

While some public television stations and schools began utilizing *The Pappenheimers* at nearly the same time it had its maiden run on Oregon Public Broadcasting, the first full-scale utilization began in the fall of 1984, when the series was fed to stations via Westar satellite and after directors and coordinators of instructional television had had a chance to include it in long-term programming plans. Thus far the series has been adopted by numerous state departments of education and public television stations.[3]

In addition to broadcast, *The Pappenheimers* is being used by numerous colleges and schools that have purchased the series on videotape for in-house use.[4] Although it was conceived as an educational series for K-6 target audience, educators at higher levels, too, are finding that this unique series provides valuable supplementary material even at higher levels.

Because *The Pappenheimers* is not only a German language series, but primarily a cultural appreciation series, it was intended from its inception that it would be utilized even by teachers without previous German skills. This aim is emphasized in the ancillary materials and reinforced by a pilot program presently underway in Corvallis, Oregon. The Corvallis school district is developing guides that will be made available to all interested educators wishing to adopt the series for use in their school, district, or state. This pilot program has enrolled some 95 students in six classes of 15 to 20 students each. The children are grouped according to grade level, with kindergarten and first-graders, for example, meeting together, and fourth and fifth-graders meeting together. All students who enrolled in these classes (held at two different grade schools) did so voluntarily. They represent a cross-section of skills and intellect, as it was stressed at the beginning that this was not a program aimed at only talented and gifted students.

Each week the teacher shows one of the 15-minute *Pappenheimer* programs using a Beta VCR and monitor in the classroom (each 30-minute episode has been edited into two 15-minute halves for use in just such a setting) and then discusses the contents with the children and works with them on vocabulary acquisition. Sometimes a class session is spent reviewing just the cartoon segments (which provide a condensed format for most of the vocabulary), working on maps showing the varous West German locations presented in the episodes, or singing Charley's German songs. Student and parent reaction to these *Pappenheimer* classes has been enthusiastic. Many more pupils requested to take part in the classes than could be accommodated by the volunteer instructor, and many of the children who did enroll have already made plans to take regular German classes as soon as they get to middle school.

While the *Pappenheimer* reputation is spreading in the United States and utilization is growing rapidly, the series is also finding success in other parts of the world. The Charley Pappenheimer American English version was broadcast in West Germany by WDR (West German Broadcasting) for English-speaking viewers and received a most favorable response. WDR also produced a Turkish-German version in which Charley's host segments were replaced by Turkish host segments for broadcast to the numerous Turkish-speaking children in West Germany (children of the "guest-workers") as a way of sharing with them in a motivational format German language and culture. Finally, a Spanish-German version is presently in production in which Charley's host segments and off-voice narration are dubbed in Spanish. This version will be broadcast primarily in Latin America.

In conclusion, the multimillion dollar international coproduction effort which produced *The Pappenheimers* appears to have succeeded in its aim to create a successful children's German culture and language appreciation program. Not only has it been successful in its own right, daily finding new fans and utilization in new settings, but it has demonstrated both that foreign language video materials are appropriate for children, and that foreign language video materials for children are needed and wanted.

Notes

[1]Information on *The Pappenheimers* and pilot videotapes (please specify format) are available from the Oregon Public Broadcasting Distribution Center, 230 Kidder Hall/OSU, Corvallis, OR 97331, telephone (503) 754-2147.

[2]Tamara D. Stehr, *The Pappenheimers: An Animation and Vocabulary Guide* (New York: Langenscheidt Publishers, 1983), 128 pp.; *Accompanying Audio Cassette with Sound Track from the Animation Segments.*

[3]Television stations broadcasting the series include: KAWE-TV, Bemidji, Minn. (whose signal introduced Canadian viewers to *The Pappenheimers*); KOOD-TV, Topeka, Kans.; KUHT-TV, Houston, Tex.; WLAE-TV, New Orleans; WPSX-TV, University Park, Pa.; WVPT, Harrisonburg, Va.; WYCC-TV, Chicago, Ill.; WXXI-TV, Rochester, N.Y.; Arkansas Public TV Network; Manitoba Educational TV; North Dakota Prairie School Television; Tennessee Public TV Network, Vancouver, Wash., School District Instructional TV; and Wisconsin Public Television.

[4]Schools and school systems adopting the series include Appleton, Wis., School District; East Allen County Schools, Inc.; Fariview Bilingual School, Cincinnati; Hanover, N.H., High School; Hastings, Minn., Public Schools; Huntsville, Ala., City Schools; Kingman, Ariz., High School; Nebraska Dept. of Education; Portland, Ore., Public Schools; Round Rock, Tex., High School; South Dakota Dept. of Education; Utah Dept. of Education; and West View Schools, Topeka, Ind.

Colleges and universities subscribing to the series include Angelo State Univ.; Biola Univ.; Drew Univ.; Univ. of Kentucky; Pepperdine Univ.; and Wichita State Univ.

Other institutions include the Goethe Institutes of Boston, Los Angeles, Toronto, and Vancouver (Can.) and the Saturday School Association of Vancouver, Canada.

94

Speak It, Read It: Simultaneous Acquisition of Language and Reading Skills

Lucille R. Guckes and Barbara Kandaras

When and how do we teach the preliterate second language student to read? Does the second language student need to acquire oral mastery of the target language before beginning reading instruction? Should students be taught to read (decode visual symbols) in their first language before learning to read a second language or is it possible to work on oral language acquisition and beginning reading simultaneously?

In *Second Language Acquisition and Second Language Learning*, Stephen Krashen postulates that language acquisition, even the acquisition of a second language, differs from language learning. He sees acquisition as an assimilative process, a process of developing the necessary tools for communication. The learner acquires grammatical structures by understanding messages, not by focusing on the form of the input or by analyzing the message. Krashen also believes that an order exists in the acquisition of language, that grammatical structures are acquired in a predictable order as the learner is involved in listening and speaking.

What about learning to read? Like language acquisition, reading begins as a listening and speaking process as children add this new print communication tool to their repertoire. Furthermore, the sequential stages through which the learners move as they acquire the ability to read appear to parallel the stages of language acquisition.

The first stage in both language acquisition and reading instruction is the silent stage when students receive input through listening, through looking and through actions (Holdaway). Then, as students develop confidence, they begin to express their ideas, to communicate through actions, representations and imitation. The Total Physical Response activities suggested by James Asher and by Bertha Segal are valuable components in the learning program during this stage. These activities provide productive learning time but, at the same time, allow the beginning student to feel comfortable.

The second stage in reading and in language acquisition, the oral production and pre-reading stage (Clay), establishes the foundation for the students' initial speaking and reading experiences as the

95

Lucille Guckes is Professor of Language Development at the College of Education, University of Nevada, Reno. Barbara Kandaras is Principal of Grace Warner School, Washoe County School District, Reno, Nevada.

teacher speaks and writes the students' own communications from words, gestures and other representations the individuals use to express their thoughts (Stauffer). These familiar materials are then used for many activities enabling students to assimilate the structure of the language as well as the sounds and symbols that represent their own ideas (Van Allen; Hall).

A second important activity during this pre-reading stage is shared listening and reading of carefully prepared and selected materials. Pictures and words are used to extend the vocabulary input beyond the immediate environment, and repeated activities that add new patterns extend the students' syntax (Holdaway; Melser).

The third stage in learning to read is the analytical or early reader stage. During this stage, still carefully guided by the teacher, the students use recalled words and phrases to formulate their message, whether in verbal or visual form. The next step is developing the ability to note similarities in sentences and words, thereby acquiring the use of syntax and word recognition skills.

In the fourth stage, the reader becomes semi-independent. Now the teacher stresses the use of the student's second language reading and writing as communication skills and guides the student's exploration of new ideas and experiences through their application.

Reviewing the stages of both reading and language acquisition, it becomes apparent that listening and reading, as receptive processes, move through similar stages and can provide support for each other. As Goodman stated, students "can sometimes comprehend what they cannot express" (56). Thus, as teachers stress comprehension of input, this input provides a foundation for language acquisition and learning to read simultaneously.

Silent Language and Pre-Reading Stage

Research on language acquisition confirms that second language students undergo a silent period extending from several hours to as much as ten weeks (Asher; Krashen). Although the students may not be speaking, they are actively learning as they experience this first encounter with the second language; thus it is most important not to rush this period. One of the most crucial skills for students to develop during this period is listening comprehension (Krashen, *Principles and Practices in Second Language Acquisition*). Language acquirers must be allowed the "silent period" so they gain the necessary exposure to the new language's phonemes and rhythm. Basic skills in listening comprehension must be developed before language production and reading instruction can proceed.

Listening Comprehension and Oral Responses

Since we do not wish to force students to produce utterances in the target language until they have had an opportunity for the acquisition process to begin, the "silent period" must be devoted to activities in which the students receive comprehensible input using all forms of communication so they are able to participate in a language activity without having to respond in the target language. Particularly effective during this period are the techniques developed by James Asher that form the basis for his Total Physical Response Approach. This technique has been further expanded and adapted by Bertha Segal and by Stephen Krashen and Tracy Terrell to reinforce listening comprehension while the students listen to, observe and act out directions given by the teacher. Since the students are not forced to produce responses in the target language, they are able to focus their entire attention on comprehension of what is said.

In the beginning, using the Total Physical Response technique, the teacher does all the talking. The teacher undertakes an action and describes it, e.g., "I am jumping," "I am walking," or, "I am sitting." The students will perform the actions simultaneously, as the teacher demonstrates and repeats the statement. Parts of the body as well as body actions can be taught through TPR: "Wave your hand. Put your hand on your head. Touch the desk with your hand," and so forth. Total Physical Response is an active technique using the whole body.

As listening vocabulary is acquired during the TPR activities, the students are asked to respond, first, by using gestures and movements, then by giving names of other students and "yes" and "no" answers. The next step integrates the use of either-or questions where the response word has just been pronounced by the teacher. From the either-or format it is an easy step to the identification of items or actions that have been previously introduced using questions and statements such as: "What am I doing?" (walking). "What color is this?" (blue). "This is a _____." (ball). This early language production moves through the above steps from "yes-no" responses, to "either-or," and then to identification by first using concrete items and actions to accompany the oral input. The same sequence of response patterns is then used with pictures for combined oral-visual input. Students then progress from single-word responses, through nuclear sentences, to meaningful phrases, and finally to simple sentences using the structure of their new language (Taeschner).

This early language production still focuses on an immediate context and is carefully guided, first using concrete items and actions and then pictures, as students acquire the ability to use natural conversation. Free conversation fails for the beginning student because the vocabulary goes far beyond the students' capabilities of comprehension. That is the reason these structured activities of the classroom are of utmost importance; they provide information and communication at a level that allows for success (Parreren).

The students' first reading is linked to the short exchanges and dialogues described above as an extension to the listening activities and the students' beginning production of language. This early reading can be accomplished by placing labels (e.g., "This is the door.") around the classroom and using TPR dialogues with oral and printed directions presented simultaneously, accompanied or followed by the appropriate actions. Thus, as students first encounter reading, the stress is on comprehension of the message, using familiar activities and vocabulary.

The dialogues begin with a short oral and printed command such as, "Open the door." After this oral and printed statement is mastered, it is recombined and expanded to produce descriptive statements and questions such as, "The door is open. The door is green. The door is wide. This is the door. Where is the door?" during succeeding lessons. The teacher conducts the activity by presenting the printed statement, pointing to each word as it is read aloud. The student then repeats the statement and finally carries out the action as the statement is reiterated. Additional repetitive practice is provided, using appropriately posted classroom labels. These printed labels repeat a selected statement format, varied only with the label for the item; example, "This is the door. This is the window. This is the clock." To provide further practice and clues, the label portion of each statement, "door, window, clock," is printed in a different color with separate vocabulary cards colored to match each label. This material can then be used to provide students with independent, self-checked practice. Just as in the acquisition of oral language, students then move to reading, as well as hearing, known sentences with a missing word, using their comprehension of the sentence structure and content to select the appropriate word from among the words they are learning. For example, "This is the _____" is shown as the teacher points to the door and the student has the cards "door, clock" available. Thus, as students move through these beginning steps in reading, the lessons reinforce and expand the activities used to guide the students in their initial production of oral language.

Story Listening

During this silent period, students are also introduced to the sounds of the language, using picture stories with carefully controlled language. At first students hear only the rhythm and the flow of the language, but they soon progress to hearing intonation and distinguishing phonemes. While reading the story, the teacher points to each word to help students hear and see the word units, and to distinguish the oral and visual signals of word breaks, simultaneously. This word pointing helps the students understand and identify the correspondence between the spoken word and the written word. At the same time, the illustrations are used to develop the meanings of words and to provide comprehensible input for the language heard. Thus students are learning to use context to provide meaning to both words and sentences. As the teacher repeats the story frequently, the students are encouraged to join in until they can readily reproduce each phrase or statement after the teacher.

Since the flow of comprehension is carried by the illustrations in these first experiences with books, the stories and the illustrations should be relevant for the students. The illustrations provide an essential function in these books, and the effectiveness of the comprehension flow of the pictures is a key dimension governing the selection of books. Other essential factors in book selection are the repetition of syntax patterns as well as vocabulary and the use of natural language patterns that foster the transfer of the classroom learning to the students' daily lives.

Language Production and Early/Beginning Reading Stage

As students move from the silent stage of the pre-reader to the production stage of the beginning/early reader, the total physical response approach, the early language production activities, and the picture story reading techniques are continued and extended.

Group Story Approach

At this point, the teacher helps students create group stories to share ideas and to enhance listening and reading instruction. Since students express recent, common experiences, these stories provide comprehensible input of the highest level.

The use of group stories is adapted from the Language Experience Approach (Van Allen; Stauffer) developed to introduce native speakers to the written form of their own language. The Group Story Method provides an immediate, concrete experience for the group and uses the knowledge of the students. The teacher stimulates the students to use their newly acquired language as they talk about the experience, then guides and extends the students' contributions by repeating, reaffirming, and expanding the language produced by each student or providing the language when necessary. For example, after a walk around the school, the teacher asks, "What did we see?" One student answers, "We see a boy." The teacher reaffirms the answer ("Yes, we saw a boy.") seemingly without deliberate correction. When another student responds, "Tree," the teacher expands the production by reaffirming ("Yes, we saw a tree.") This pre-composition stage also introduces new vocabulary as students seek the word needed to express their ideas. Students are guided through an extensive discussion about the experience until each one has made several contributions and has been reinforced and guided to expand ideas to sentence form.

After this discussion with oral production and abundant reinforcement of the students' ideas, the teacher suggests students record their observations to share with others. Together, the students and the teacher decide how the story is to be organized, and then the group or individuals suggest the content of each statement. Students and teacher then orally combine, edit, and revise ideas until they have composed a statement that expresses what the students wish to say. Each sentence can be developed by one student (or by several), based on the desires and competence of the students and the purposes of the teacher. Using this oral expansion to practice syntax, the group story builds on the syntactic input provided during "teacher talk," early language production, and picture-story reading, enabling acquirers to produce the syntax as well as the vocabulary of the new

99

language. Since these materials are to be used extensively for follow-up activities and reading over an extended period, the use of correct syntax from the beginning avoids the confusion built by repeated learning of incorrect second language patterns. After the final form of the statement is determined, the students repeat the sentence to build memory and to guide the teacher's writing. Simultaneously, they are performing language pattern practice with comprehensible materials from their own experiences. As each word is printed on the chart, the students and the teacher read the word and note the space used to signal each word.

After the group story is completed, the teacher reads the entire story, pointing to each word, as was done with the picture-story reading, and emphasizing the appropriate word sequencing (e.g., left-to-right for English) of the language. Next, the entire group of students rereads the story in unison several times. Following this preparation, individuals are supported by the teacher as they read any part of the story, one word, a sentence, or the whole story.

The utility of the group story does not end after the teacher and the students have read it several times. These stories become important resources for the development of reading comprehension skills, new concepts and vocabulary, and discrimination and word recognition skills. Hall, Veatch, and others have described a wealth of such activities using group stories as reading practice.

As students become skilled in composing group stories, familiar books can become models for different kinds of stories. Visual stimuli can be used to stimulate discussion for a story topic. As individuals develop skills in composing sentences, they can dictate their individual sentences or complete stories. This activity leads naturally into free writing using "invented spelling" as suggested by Donald Graves. However, the group story technique is not abandoned as students start to write independently. The group story is an important tool for introducing new grammatical structures, such as compound sentences or quotations, in a natural situation without tension or failure. It is also enjoyable with any age group to cooperate in creating a story about an experience or a topic.

The above use of familiar materials for shared-book and group-story activities facilitates the extensive reading practice Krashen (*Second Language Acquisition*) found essential for the acquisition of a second language. Other studies done in the Fiji islands, by Elley and Mangubhai, which revealed a direct correlation between students' second language comprehension, speech acquisition and extensive reading of high-interest stories, emphasize the importance of this reading connection for language acquisition.

Vocabulary and Concept Development

The preparation of group stories and charts can be an important tool in the content areas to guide thinking and expression. Group stories based on field experiences, models, study prints, and films can introduce background, develop concepts and vocabulary, and raise questions about a topic. They also provide an excellent means for cooperative reporting and sharing of information gathered in investigating a question.

As students produce words, and later read them, it is essential that the underlying concepts of each word be developed and extended. A selected word can become the topic of a group story or a total integrated unit to build students' knowledge of their environment as they extend the meaning of the word. The teacher selects a concrete noun from a story being read, from sentences being used, from an environmental need, or from a student's inquiry. First, the object is presented using a picture, an overhead transparency, or other visual stimulus. Then, a discussion of the object leads to notes, written statements about the object, and a variety of follow-up activities appropriate to the students' level of language development.

For example, the concept "soap" is selected for development. At the pre-reading stage only one aspect of soap, its use, is included in the activity. After discussing, demonstrating, and showing pictures of the use of soap, a group story is written such as,

SOAP
I can wash myself with soap.
I can wash the dishes with soap.
I can wash the car with soap.

After the oral activities associated with the group story are completed, the students—individually or collectively—can make a soap picture collage by cutting and pasting magazine pictures of soap and its related use on chart paper.

As they progress to the beginning/early reader or the semi-independent reader stages, students can work with more than one aspect of the word, based on the students' language competence and experiences, e.g., uses, synonyms, origins, and adjectives for describing the object. The use of a map (Figure 1) to organize students' and teacher's contributions provides an effective visual tool for this discussion.

101

Figure 1. Mapping a Concept

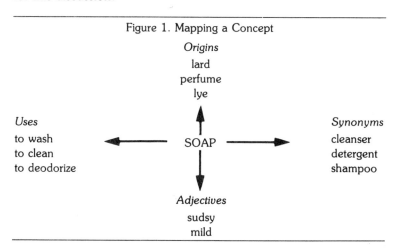

Origins
lard
perfume
lye

Uses
to wash
to clean
to deodorize

SOAP

Synonyms
cleanser
detergent
shampoo

Adjectives
sudsy
mild

Following the discussion and this introduction to note-taking and organization, students can prepare a group story with the teacher or work independently on individual stories, using the words and ideas developed during the group interaction. As students acquire more language and can deal with these more abstract language forms, this same technique can be used to develop concepts of verbs and modifiers.

Early Reader Stage

During the pre-reading stages, development of oral and visual vocabulary and related comprehension skills provides the foundation for the transition to beginning reading. While students are mastering these language and comprehension skills, the teacher is also guiding their development of many language concepts essential for reading. These concepts are first encountered during oral language activities and are further assimilated during both oral and visual practice. Using the activities described, the teacher incorporates language concepts, such as the ability to distinguish between statements and questions and the appropriate use of the following forms:

- past, present, and future forms of verbs
- singular and plural forms of nouns
- prepositional phrases
- descriptive adjectives (color, number, size)
- terms for time and place (today, yesterday, tomorrow, at home, at school)
- subject pronouns (I, he, she, you)
- object pronouns (me, him, her)
- possessive pronouns and adjectives

Although the Total Physical Response activities are no longer the foundation for the beginning reader's learning, they are not abandoned. Unfamiliar concepts, whether lingual, mathematical, or subject-related, still need to be introduced using actions and concrete manipulation whenever possible. The shared-book activities are still included, and group stories play a major role in the introduction and practice of new speaking, reading, and writing skills, using previous knowledge.

Integrating Language Learning

The integration of various language activities is vital in guiding successful language acquisition and the development of reading proficiency (Chastain). It is important that each lesson period include:

Daily Lesson Schedule
1. (5-10 minutes) *Shared-book activities* for listening to the sounds and rhythms of the language (includes listening to stories and choral reading and reciting).
2. (10-15 minutes) *Language pattern practice* using:
   a. Total Physical Response
   b. Student responses, first to oral input, then to combined visual and oral

input and, as students develop beginning reading skills,

 c. Activities for the introduction and practice of second language word-recognition skills.

3. (10-25 minutes) *Group-story activities* based on students' interests, classroom experiences, or a topic for concept development. These activities will include:

 a. Discussing the topic and experiences
 b. Composing the story
 c. Reading the story
 d. Using the story as a foundation for other oral activities.

All the activities involved in producing and using a group story are not necessarily included in each day's lesson. On some occasions, such as a birthday, a new snowfall, or even the birth of a new brother, it will be important to prepare and read the story in one session. On other days, however, this time will be used to do a variety of activities, using stories already prepared. To feel compelled to prepare a new story every day can become just as odious a chore as any other activity that is done repetitively without a true purpose.

4. (10-20 minutes) *Independent learning activities* are an essential component of the lesson. These activities reinforce and extend the skills introduced and guided by the teacher until the student has reached a moderate level of competence. These independent activities should be based on, and grow out of, the activities used during the rest of the lesson. Examples include:

 a. Listening posts for the shared books and group stories
 b. Language mastery activities using dialogue and exchanges from the language pattern practice
 c. Independent reading of group stories, shared books, and other picture-story books related to the previous topics.
 d. Preparation of word banks for known vocabulary.
 e. Matching, sorting, classifying, and composing activities with cards and sentence strips using pictures, words, and sentences from students' word banks and previous lessons.
 f. Art activities related to present or past group stories, shared books, and language pattern practice.
 g. Dramatization based on previous activities.

Each of the language acquisition activities is based on the concept of compreshensible input, i.e. language that is meaningful to the student.

Conclusion

As second language learning begins, listening comprehension is developed by using the concrete environment, movements, and visual resources for input followed by students' physical responses. As students become comfortable responding orally, first with words, then with sentences, printed symbols—word cards and sentences strips, picture-story books, and group stories—are added to the concrete and oral input.

During the pre-reading and beginning-reading stages, printed symbols are used simultaneously with oral language and concrete input to provide an additional mode of learning and to enable the

103

students to experience language functions as they manipulate words both verbally and visually. Only after they have acquired the vocabulary and the basic language concepts described do students learn formal decoding skills for reading. Thus, after extensive involvement with group stories and shared books, children develop listening comprehension skills, oral language patterns, and the symbolic background necessary to start formal reading instruction.

References

Asher, James J. *Learning Another Language through Actions.* Los Gatos, Cal.: Sky Oaks Productions, 1982.

Chastain, Kenneth. *Developing Second-Language Skills: Theory to Practice.* Boston: Houghton Mifflin, 1976.

Clay, Marie. *Reading: The Patterning of Complex Behavior.* Exeter, New Hampshire: Heinemann, 1979.

Elley, Warwick B., and Francis Mangubhai. "The Impact of Reading on Second Language Learning." *Reading Research* Quarterly 19. 11 (1983): 53-67.

Graves, Donald H. *Writing: Teachers and Children at Work.* Exeter, New Hampshire: Heinemann, 1983.

Hall, MaryAnne. *Teaching Reading as a Language Experience.* Columbus Charles E. Merrill, 1981.

Holdaway, Don. *The Foundations of Literacy.* Sydney: Ashton Scholastic, 1979.

Krashen, Stephen D. *Principles and Practices in Second Language Acquisition.* New York: Pergamon, 1982.

_____. *Second Language Acquisition and Second Language Learning.* New York: Pergamon, 1981.

_____, and Tracy D. Terrell. *The Natural Approach: Language Acquisition in the Classroom.* New York: Pergamon, 1983.

Parreren, C.F. van, and J.A.M. Carpay. "First and Second Language Learning Compared." *The Context of Foreign Language Learning.* Ed A.J. van Essen and J.P. Menting. Essen, Netherlands: Van Gorcum & Company, 1983.

Melser, June. *The Story Box Teachers' Book: No Failing!* Auckland, New Zealand: Shortland Publications, 1983.

Segal, Bertha. *Teaching English through Actions.* Brea, Cal.: Bertha Segal Inc., 1980.

Stauffer, Russell G. *Directing the Reading-Thinking Process.* New York Harper and Row, 1976.

Taeschner, T. *The Sun is Feminine.* Berlin: Springer Verlag, 1983.

Van Allen, Roach. *Language Experiences in Communication.* New York Houghton Mifflin, 1976.

Veatch, Jeannette, et al. *Key Words to Reading.* Columbus: Charles E Merrill, 1979.

To Read You Must Write: Language Acquisition among Limited-English-Proficient Children

Curtis W. Hayes,
Robert Bahruth, and
Carolyn Kessler

James Asher has convincingly demonstrated that we can teach a second language and our students will learn it if our classroom activities are meaningful, if they touch our students' lives and mirror their experiences. Through our attitude, we must also create an atmosphere in which students will feel secure. Smith labels this attitude "sensitivity," and Asher writes: "If students are presented with no-risk learning experiences, if they feel comfortable and secure, then they can learn." Pointing to the alarming statistic that only four percent of those who enroll in second language courses remain until they are proficient, Asher suggests that sensitivity is lacking in many second language classrooms.

Judging by the calls for educational reform and a "return to the basics," the failure rate in learning to read and write must also be high. Asher's reasoning, as well as Smith's, suggests that the risk of failure in language classrooms may be too high for learning to take place. Therefore we need to foster a classroom environment that propitiates learning vocabulary and acquiring grammatical structures, in short, that develops language competence.

Our students, fifth graders with ages ranging from 10 through 16, were second language learners of English. Dominant in Spanish, all had been categorized as limited in English-language proficiency (LEP). All were, in fact, reading and writing at least three grades below the norm. Some could not read at all. They lived in a rural area, all sons or daughters of Mexican-American migrant farm laborers, most of whom were themselves illiterate. The children's academic self-concept was so low that each perceived learning as an assortment of impossible tasks. Moreover, they had actually come to believe that they were the source of their problems. When we met them at the beginning of the school year, they were failures and were looking forward to the time when they could leave school and follow the path of the migrant farm laborer, earning just enough to place

Curtis W. Hayes and Carolyn Kessler are Professors of Linguistics and of English as a Second Language at the University of Texas at San Antonio. Robert Bahruth is an Instructor at Austin Community College and formerly taught in the Pearsall, Texas, Independent School District.

them at the subsistence level of income. There seemed to be no alternative; not one had goals or aspirations beyond a future in the fields

Their parents were honorable, good people. All worked hard and
long in the heat of summer, traveling from one agricultural region to
another, planting, cultivating, and harvesting for others. Except for
cars that were constantly in need of repair and the clothes they took
with them, they owned very little. They returned from the fields in
August and September, worked in menial jobs during the fall and
winter, and left again in April and May, before school was out. When
they returned, they enrolled their children in school. Just as there exists a cycle of planting, cultivating, growing, and harvesting, there is
also a cycle of school tasks. Yet for most of our children, the harvest
yielded failure. They had failed to learn to read and write sufficiently
well to ensure success in higher grades.

Why they could not read and write, even after five years of school
is a subject for another paper. Suffice it to point out that these
migrant children do not do well in school. As we surveyed the curricula of their previous school experiences, one cause for failure
became apparent: these children had had little opportunity to read
and write. Krashen notes that reading is an activity of increasing
returns: the more you read the better you become. Good readers enjoy and read books for pleasure and seek additional opportunities for
reading (even "under the covers with a flashlight"). We found that
poor readers read less when they should be reading more. If they are
identified as having reading difficulties, if they are "problem" readers
as our children were, they are placed in remedial classes and re-
taught the skills of reading. But as Goodman, Goodman, and Flores
point out, to "re-teach" is exactly the wrong approach to follow:

> It is simply not possible to treat literacy as an isolated set of skills and
> expect children to learn. In too many programs for bilingual children,
> there is too much concern for form without function, too much tradi-
> tion and too little relevance, too much focus on skill and not enough
> on comprehension, too much making kids adapt to the curriculum
> rather than adapting the curriculum to the kids. That is not good for
> any learners: for bilinguals it can be tragic. (36)

Yet it had been that way for our children.

We began the school year in August by giving our children many
opportunities and much time to read and to write. We read them
stories of their experiences and the experiences of children their age.
In short, we began to adapt the curriculum to our children. During
those first few weeks of school, contrary to the traditional procedure
we did not have an obligatory oral reading period, with students in
groups reading to us. By reading to them, we were increasing their
awareness of how stories fit together (story grammars), how prose is
organized, especially the narrative structures of many of the stories
written for children of their age. In addition, by spending a great deal
of time reading to them, we demonstrated that reading, unlike what
many of them had assumed, was interesting and stimulating. We
gathered books from the school library, from the public library, from

used-book shops, from generous friends. Our classroom eventually became filled with books. We encouraged our children to take books home. Each day we would read the first few pages of a couple of stories, stopping at a crucial juncture in each, and then inquire: "Would anyone like to finish this story at home?" We always had more hands than we could accommodate. Our ultimate purpose was to get them "hooked on books"—and we did.

During these first few weeks, we also introduced our students to the dialogue journal (DJ). The DJ is not new but for us it was a catalyst, changing our non-writing students into writers as well as reinvolving us in the writing process. We first asked our students to write three lines about a topic of their choice, about anything they could and would write about from their experiences in school, at home, in the fields, or in their day-to-day activities with their families. They provided the context, the focus. We set aside fifteen minutes a day for journal writing. We responded to their writing with at least three lines of our own. Occasionally we might write longer responses but never shorter ones. There were some restrictions: we never edited or corrected mistakes; and we always responded to their focus. More important, perhaps, we always attempted to convey our responses in clear, understandable language. In effect, we provided them with "comprehensible input" from which they could extract meaning and structure (Krashen and Terrell).

Although we gave class time for writing in the journals, we wrote our responses at home. Early in the school year most students wrote only three lines, the minimal requirement. It took us approximately one-half hour to respond to the set of short entries. Later, as their fluency increased and their entries became longer, it took us about two hours to respond. The strength of the DJ is that fluency increases with the amount of time devoted to the journal. As our students wrote, they became better writers. As their entries grew longer, their spelling, punctuation, legibility, and organization improved, and their papers began to look better.

The DJ was a powerful instrument in our teaching strategy. Why did the DJ work? First, let us look at our goals:

1. We wanted to convey to our students that writing (and reading) can be important in their own lives. We read to them, to ourselves, and we wrote. Our students saw us participating in and enjoying these two activities.
2. We wanted to develop fluency, to turn fearful writers into bold ones. One way we could do this was to give them time to write in class.
3. We wanted to desensitize them to errors, to show them that errors are an integral part of the process of learning. All our children did not initially participate with enthusiasm, a circumstance that reflected their past failures. For instance, Larry, who tested at the first-grade level in August, turned in a blank piece of paper on which we wrote, "How can we answer you if you don't write to us?" Larry wrote a few disjointed words the following day; we asked him in our reply, "What problems bother you

about writing?" He answered, "Well, I can't not spell right that's what's bother me about writing." As the year progressed, Larry became one of our better writers and readers, an eager participant, not only in his journal writing but also in the other classroom reading and writing tasks.

The use of the journals reaped far greater rewards than we had anticipated. We found that they provided a natural language exchange. Our children's English was still developing, and we provided developed English in our responses. The journal writing was primarily narrative in style: students told us about going on picnics, helping their families in the fields, taking care of younger brothers and sisters, working on cars, traveling from one region to another, experiencing deaths in their families, and other events central to their lives. Early in the year, some children began to write expositorily. Children would comment on what they were reading, or on what we had read to them. One student began a journal entry with a generalization— "The story I like best"—followed by details supporting his opinion and ending with a conclusion.

The journals also provided a sense of audience. Our children wrote to an audience who read their entries and responded. They were eager the next day to read our replies. As we addressed their interests without criticizing them, the exercise fostered a positive self-image. The DJ improved our relationships with our children and theirs with us as it provided a private conversation between us and our children, through which we learned from each other.

As they continued to write, the children developed a sense of success, a "can-do" attitude. They found that they could write understandable and interesting messages to someone who appreciated their efforts. Since each student was at a different level of development and proficiency, we addressed individual needs by providing information they could understand. We also provided a reading lesson each day, as the children had to read what we had written in order to respond.

Just as Larry was worried about his spelling, some teachers are concerned with correcting errors in student journals. Errors do occur in spelling, punctuation, and sentence structure. We found that the journal entries improved as the students became more fluent and competent in English and more aware of standard editorial practice. While most of the errors that occurred in their entries eventually were resolved without our correction, others did not and were a cause for concern. Acknowledging that our students were still sensitive to spelling, punctuation, and structure, in our responses, we modeled correct usage. "Modr sikle" was spelled correctly in our response, and the child spelled it correctly in a later journal entry. Some students asked us to correct their spelling (Larry's anxieties were shared by others). As we were interested in meaning, we were reluctant to turn journal writing into "form" lessons. We did ask them to underline words they were unsure of, and we would use those words, correctly spelled, in our reply. Later in the year, we began to underline in our replies words that they had misspelled. By following this practice, spelling anxieties seemed to lessen; the children became increasingly sensitive to additional editorial considerations, as they improved their writing proficiency.

Reading, by children and to children, continued to comprise a large portion of the school day. As the year progressed, we looked toward social studies, science, and mathematics for sources of writing ideas. As in the past, our children would be required to write academic, expository essays in these subjects. The shift in subject matter dove-tailed nicely with the classroom reading and writing activities that had already become routine. The final drafts were laminated and published as "books." At the end of the school year, the class had published twenty-one books, beginning with narratives and gradually introducing other subjects. We shall not give examples from each of the twenty-one books; we will share with you, as we continue, an early essay, a mid-year essay, and finally an essay that was written for the "farewell" volume.

For each book, we would first discuss themes suggested by students. Once a topic was selected, e.g., "Everything You Always Wanted to Know about Aliens but Were Afraid to Ask," we would then discuss the kinds of information that would go into the essays. We divided the class into groups of approximately six students. Each student prepared a first draft, read it to the group, and responded to questions from the group concerning clarity ("What do you mean, when you say…") and cohesion ("I don't know how the aliens got to Earth"). Each child was expected to suggest revisions to other members of the group. Students incorporated the suggestions into a second draft, which was also read to the group. During the reading of the second draft, children could still ask questions and share impressions. After this reading, the children prepared a third draft that was to be edited. We organized an editing team to help the children spell correctly, punctuate appropriately, and provide a pleasant format for their papers. The editing team pasted up the volume, providing cover, table of contents, dedication, title page, and bibliography, if appropriate.

One of the first volumes collected love letters to mothers and fathers. Inasmuch as early in the year many students had limited vocabularies, we suggested that if they did not know a word, they could depict it. Some of their rebuses are transparent, while others are obscure and require their full context in order to be understood.

For many of our children the "love letter" assignment was the first writing assignment they had completed successfully. By observing our students as they wrote and revised, we knew that they were enjoying writing. At the same time they recognized writing as an intellectual activity. They published their letters in a volume they titled "Love Letters" (see figure 2 in the appendix).

These love letters provided us with impetus for more extended writing. In mid-year we published our first science report, "Small Wonders and Magic Machines." We recognized the evolution of our

109

children's writing skills from one report to the next. In our second science volume, published in May, just before our children left for the fields, their expression is clearer, spelling has improved (even "scissors" is spelled correctly), and the format is clearer and neater (figure 3).

One of our final efforts was on biography. We discussed the kinds of information biographers included. Then the children started on their own and collected them in a volume that we called "Autobiographies of Not Yet Famous People." Patricia's autobiography illustrates that effort. Certain misspellings remain. She still does not have the "there/their" distinction. The influence of Spanish prevails in certain constructions, e.g., "I have 12 years" (figure 4).

Even though the papers still contain mistakes, we can notice remarkable improvement from the efforts of August and September, when the children were reading below grade level or not reading at all. By the end of the year, all our children were reading and writing freely, fluently, and purposefully—reading texts that interested them and reading others for information for various reports. During the year, we covered all the curriculum, including science, math, and social studies. Our children had increased their reading proficiency and their written production. For our final text, consisting of a potpourri of their best, some children revised a previous paper, while others contributed an original. We called it "Odds and Ends," a title that reflects what we had read and written during the year. On the title page we listed all the texts we had published that year (figure 5).

What were the results of our efforts, and what could account for these results? We worked with theories of language acquisition that paved the way for practices. Our children averaged three years' growth in reading proficiency, as measured by two reading tests, one developed by the Economy Company, the other by the school district. We did not need to test to see improvement, however. We compared their August efforts with those of May and knew that dramatic improvements had taken place.

In August, our children had been failures. They thought of themselves as failures, and they anticipated failing in our class. From the outset we attempted to make them believe that they could and would succeed, that reading was interesting, that they could be trusted in what they selected to read, and that writing (providing reading for others) was a powerful intellectual tool that they could master. They convinced themselves. Their self-image improved. In the volume on future careers, which they called "Great Expectations," we learned that they wanted to become doctors, teachers (four in the class), or nurses, or to enter other careers that would entail higher education. One girl listed "orange grove grower" as a future possibility. We asked whether she wanted to work in the groves; she replied she wanted to own them.

Along the way from August to May, they also acquired more English-language skills. They were second language learners of English. They employed English in our classroom; they spoke Spanish at home at play. They enjoyed language and the prestige of being bilingual. Our classroom was where the day's activities could be discussed, opinions sought and shared, journals written, books prepared. The atmosphere of our classroom encouraged them to communicate with their classmates, allowing active use of language input. The language they acquired during the course of the year was meaningful and useful.

Finally, they demonstrated to themselves more than to us that they could perform well, whether doing math, science, or social studies and language arts. They could handle school subjects. As they left us, they were confident students, anticipating the beginnings of school in August and looking forward to a successful sixth year.

References

Asher, James J. "Motivating Children to Acquire Another Language." Presentation at the International Conference on Second/Foreign Language Acquisition by Children. Oklahoma City, 30 March 1985.

Goodman, Kenneth, Yetta Goodman, and Barbara Flores. *Reading in the Bilingual Classroom: Literacy and Biliteracy.* Rosslyn, Va.: National Clearinghouse for Bilingual Education, 1979.

Krashen, Stephen D. "The power of reading." Plenary address at TESOL Nineteenth Annual Convention. New York City, April 1985.

_____, and Tracy D. Terrell. *The Natural Approach: Language Acquisition in the Classroom.* Hayward, Cal.: The Alemany Press, 1983.

Smith, Frank. "Demonstrations, Engagement and Sensitivity: A Revised Approach to Language Learning." *Language Arts* 58.1 (1981):103-112.

Figure 1

I like to read because I can move to other book like
I was in Curbstone Dragon and I move the book
Mustard Seed magic.

Do you enjoy the stories in those books or are there
other books you enjoy more? You have to read these books
because they will help you to be able to read any book you
want to later on.

The storie I like in all of the stories of all
the one I like was the Mystery of the
Moving Snowman if I read all the stories in
Mustard Seed magic maybe I can pick a other
Storie that can be more good then the storie
Of the Mystery of the Moving Snowman. But
this Book is the best of all the books I ever
read in my hole years. Because I like the
storie of the mystery of the moving Snowman
because who a boy or a girl find know the
Snowman muvid to house and house.
How ever Knowes th anwer wines a
sled. And a boy and a girl saw the snow
snowman on there yard. They were wd
working together and they win the
sled. Thates Why I like that Storie and
I thing thates the stonie I like Best
Of all the storeies I ever read in all
the book I ever read in all my
yeares is mustaRD SEED maGic.

Figure 2

Francisco Garza

Mom

Yester day we ☐ the ☰. In the ☐.

With a △ and with a ◖ and we need the ☼

To see the ☰. And we ╱ in the ☐.

About the ☰ and the △ and

The ◖ and the ☼ and we go back

To the ☐☐☐☐ and we have a good

Time. for do that out side.

I

YOU
MOM

113

Figure 3

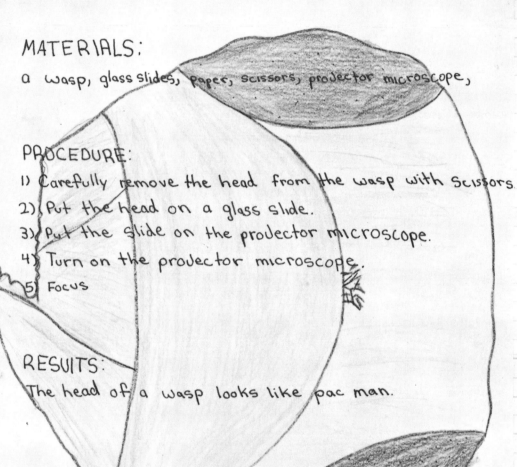

May 21, 1984   Science Report Apolinar Garcia.

The wasp Head.

MATERIALS:
a wasp, glass slides, paper, scissors, projector microscope,

PROCEDURE:
1) Carefully remove the head from the wasp with scissors.
2) Put the head on a glass slide.
3) Put the slide on the projector microscope.
4) Turn on the projector microscope.
5) Focus

RESULTS:
The head of a wasp looks like pac man.

16

114

Figure 4

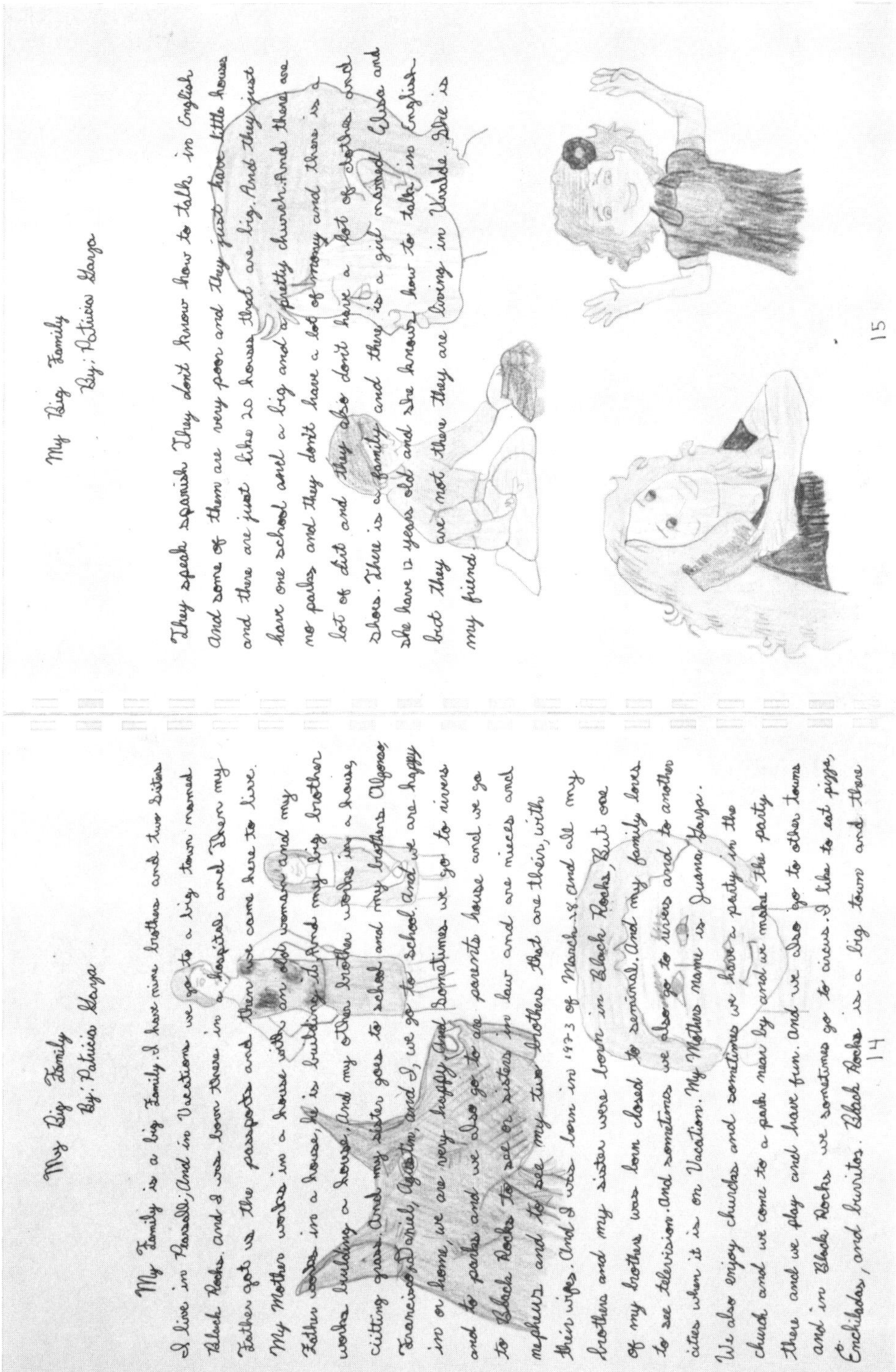

My Big Family
By: Patricia Llarga

My family is a big family. I have nine brothers and two sisters. I live in Peralta. And in vacations we go to a big town named Black Rock. And I was born there in chapital and there my father get up the passports and there we came here to live. My mother works in a house with my dad unmarried and my father works in a house. It is building. And my other brother works in a house, building a house. And my other sister goes to school and my brothers Olganey, Francisco, Daniel, Agustin and I, we go to the school. And we are happy in our home. We are very happy. And sometimes we go to rivers and to parks and we also go to our favorite house and we go to Black Rock. To see the sisters in law and our nieces and nephews and to see my two brothers that are Thien, with their wifes. And I was born in 1973 of March 15 and all my brothers and my sisters were born in Black Rock. But one of my brothers was born closed to seminole. And my family loves to see television. And sometimes we also go to rivers and to another cities when it is in vacation. My mother name is Juana Llarga. We also enjoy churches and sometimes we have a party in the church and we come to a park near by and we make the party there and we play and have fun. And we also go to other towns and in Black Rock we sometimes go to circus. I like to eat pizza, enchiladas, and burritos. Black Rock is a big town and there

14

My Big Family
By: Patricia Llarga

They speak spanish. They don't know how to talk in English. And some of them are very poor and they just have little house and there are just like 20 house that are big. And they just have one school and a pretty church. And there are no pools and they don't have a lot of money and there is a lot of dirt and they also don't have a lot of clothes and shoes. There is a family and they is a girl named Elisa and she have 12 years old and she knows how to talk in English but they are not there they are living in Uvalde. She is my friend.

15

Figure 5

Odds and Ends
    Mr. Bahruth's 5th Grade Class

Other books in print by the same authors:

Abecedario
Limited Edition
Love Letters
Autumn Leaves
The I Dare You Cookbook of Weird Recipes
Everything You Always Wanted to Know About Aliens...
    ...but were afraid to ask.
Our Favorites
International Alphabet Soup
Small Wonders and Magic Machines (Science Reports)
Uncle Sam's Biography
Great Expectations
Mother Nature's Tiny Wonders (Science Reports)
The New Improved I Dare You Cookbook of Weird Recipes
Conversation Pieces
The ABC Bestiary
Make-Believe Bestiary
The What Did U Say? Handbook of Idioms
Autobiographies of Not Yet Famous People
Our Outing
Dreamland

Copyright © May 24, 1984   The Farewell Edition
Printed in Texas "The Lone Star State" by:
López y Villarreal Publishers, Inc.
New York, London, Paris, Madrid, Pearsall.

Cover Layout and Design by Lisa Wills and Florencia Medrano

Testing in Beginning FLES: Listening

Loren Alexander

As we become more involved in a growing program for Foreign Languages in Elementary Schools (FLES), it becomes more important to establish reasonable goals and to measure the degree to which those goals are attained. This paper discusses procedures for testing listening skills in a FLES program in the early stages of instruction, for example, in the third grade at the end of 10-20 hours of instruction.

Listening comprehension is generally accepted as the most basic among the primary skills of listening, speaking, reading, and writing (James). Most modern methods for older learners allow an extended period of listening skills' acquisition before developing the other three skills (Asher; Dodson; Lozanov). In fact, the currently popular techinques of total physical response developed by Asher are an expansion and careful organization of activities that can focus on listening over a long period of time and can introduce almost all aspects of grammar and vocabulary. Both secondary and FLES teachers have found this age-old technique a very valuable tool, especially in the form promoted by Asher. Of course, we are speaking here of listening as an element of communication. If we wish to help learners become communicators in the foreign language, we must create courses that encourage the teacher to use the foreign language "as a means of communication in the classroom" (Rivers).

If we wish to devote a lengthy portion of the school year to listening skills as an element of communication, it becomes necessary to develop a testing program that correlates closely with the instruction and that functions within the limited time-slot allotted to FLES. Ideas focusing mainly on secondary school or adult learners can often inspire us, but often do not prove usefull in FLES. For example, Jerry Larson's suggestions for testing speaking ability in the classroom rely on the use of a language laboratory. Few if any FLES programs have access to such equipment, nor would they find it efficient with young learners. We can most likely adapt Larson's ideas to FLES, but adapt them we must!

We also need to test with procedures that call for minimal interference from other skills in the attempt to perceive the learners' level of comprehension. As Gunter Nold shows in his analysis of

117

Loren Alexander is Associate Professor of Curriculum and Instruction and of Modern Languages at Kansas State University.

discourse in elementary school foreign language learners' transactions with their teacher,

> the two functions of classroom discourse, informing and eliciting, are both focused in this transaction. They in turn aim at different pedagogical objectives: the transmission of information and the use of correct forms of the second language. And yet, both functions are combined in one transaction (56).

Thus we begin to understand the complexities of discourse and the difficulty of separating one element, listening, for evaluation. Of course, we shall probably never be able to apprehend fully the internal, intellectual response of the listener; we must rely on some external indicator of the quality of comprehension of messages in the foreign language. The simpler the task of responding in a non-linguistic manner (physical actions) or a manner that requires only minimal linguistic skill ("yes" or "no"), the better we shall be able to judge the quality of comprehension of the message without relying on the complexities of the full spoken utterance.

Examples of our strong focus on speaking, to the neglect of listening, can be found easily in curricula for FLES. The excellent set of materials and guidelines for K-3 FLES produced by Jones et al., lists ten objectives for the first lesson, of which three use the mother tongue to elicit information, and seven rely on a spoken response. None calls for a listening-only response.

My own observations lend support to the assumption that the skill of listening is rarely tested in isolation; rather, there is normally a mix of listening and speaking, or listening and speaking, or listening and writing. The listening portions of many nationally standarized exams that treat this evaluation procedure properly present pictures accompanied by several oral comments, in response to which the learner merely marks A, B, C, or D on an answer sheet. But how many of us have developed similar tests for our day-to-day teaching? The time demands to develop such test items, to say nothing of the sophisticated procedures involved in writing the item-response options, preclude such skill measurement in the average curriculum.

We now are beginning to reap the rewards of current efforts to develop a set of refined guidelines for oral proficiency testing. Heilenman and Kaplan's chart of various aspects of a curriculum for novice-level French illustrates the detailed information that will assist the testing and teaching processes at a specific level.

Heilenman and Kaplan list three content areas: (1) functions—making lists, memorizing materials, and so forth; (2) routine activities and topics from daily life: e.g., objects, places, colors, dates, and numbers; (3) accuracy, e.g., basic word order. In addition, they describe the functional control required for specific levels of language relative to the four basic skills. The skill of listening, like the other categories, can be broken down into three levels of control: full, partial, and conceptual. Full control for listening implies "Understanding memorized material; Operating in situations aided by context"

(64-65). It is this type of detailed explanation of proficiency that helps the teachers construct appropriate test items for their beginning FLES learners.

Teachers can develop their own chart of language skills and discourse functions that coincide with their own goals and setting. If this skill delineation is perceived as a process rather than as a fixed set of demands, one can use such a chart to great advantage as a springboard for testing and for subsequent curriculum planning and material preparation. Analyzing an example of a teacher's self-developed testing procedure, Alexander and John point out the innovation of testing four learners at once with the assistance of a native speaker from the local community. Innovative ideas can stimulate all of us to carry out our own testing program in a manner consonant with our setting.

Recalling such groundwork and recognizing that testing procedures influence content and the clarification of goals, let us turn to the kinds of testing that measure achievement in listening, to the exclusion or near exclusion of the other language skills.

There are at least three types of test item response for the listening skill: (1) action response; (2) evaluation response; and (3) communication response.

Action Response

In an action response one hears a command and physically carries out the command: "Stand up!" "Put the big green book under the little red book!" "Draw ears on the dog and color them brown!" There is no demand for linguistic utterance in the response. The teacher can check more than one child at a time, in the interest of the efficiency demanded by most FLES programs. Three or four students can carry out the body-movement commands; the teacher can observe who responds without hesitation, who responds correctly but haltingly, and who responds incorrectly. The items can be weighted accordingly; for example, 2 points for immediate and correct response; 1 point for response with hesitation; and 0 points for incorrect response, even if the correct response quickly follows. In most instances, the learners will be able to give a response of some kind, if only in imitation of other learners who give a quick response. All can feel some satisfaction, and this is to be encouraged. Evaluation can perhaps best serve the purpose of informing teachers how well they are teaching, rather than precisely determining the full range of achievement that the individual learners have attained.

Flashcards with items on any topic can be placed around the room; the teacher refers in some manner to one of the cards, and students point to the appropriate card. It is very easy to see who points readily to the correct card, who hesitates, and who shows confusion. This use of flashcards should initially accompany the regular lessons, thereby introducing nothing new in content or procedure for the learners when testing time arrives. Such prior work with the testing procedure in daily instruction promotes a comfortable, low-anxiety setting for testing.

Action responses also include procedures other than those mentioned here. One can ask the learner to check the appropriate picture in a series of three or four on a sheet of paper. The physical action involved is minimal, and the response does not involve a linguistic utterance. To some degree, such action responses measure the skill of listening, but to no degree the skill of speaking. The required interpretation of a set of pictures does, however, entail an aspect of testing that has little if anything to do with the accurate comprehension of the teacher's utterance in the test item. To the degree that an interpretation of the picture is involved, the item measures something other than listening.

The complexity and the degree of familiarity of the teacher's utterance can become factors in the determination of scores. For example, the item "Put the big green book under the little red book" is more demanding in a situation with five colors of books and three sizes of each than the situation in which one has only one big green book, one little red book, and one little green book. And, if the colors involved are the tenth and eleventh colors introduced to the class, one can anticipate that these will sometimes be less well learned by testing time than the first two that were learned. One could then give more weight to either set, depending on the information one wishes to discover: Are the learners retaining language learned early in the course? Have the learners acquired comprehension of recently introduced utterances?

Of course, the focus here has been on only one element of this test item, the terms for colors. One can and should also judge the quality of response to the part of the utterance having to do with the verb, i.e., what to do with the properly selected books.

Evaluation Response

An evaluation response calls for the learners to indicate whether an utterance accurately portrays reality or to choose the correct response from a set. For example, the learner can be asked to indicate whether a statement is true or false by nodding or shaking the head, circling a letter or symbol, using minimal language skill by saying "yes" or "no", and so forth. One can narrate a well-known story, one that was a part of the regular lessons, and make misstatements, e.g., "The three bears poured their soup on the floor." At this point, we wish merely to receive confirmation of the veracity or accuracy of the statement. At another level of language acquisition, we could ask the learner to narrate what actually happened in the story at this point, and we would then be checking speaking skill.

Other evaluation response items call for students to discern whether items are the same or different, good or bad, or to discriminate among other easily designated dichotomies. Multiple choice items are possible but too easily become bogged down in judgments that are difficult to measure for accuracy. For instance, one could have the learners look at a picture of the three bears and present an item asking them to indicate which bear is small, which bear is larger than the small bear, and which bear is largest. The possibilities for misinterpretation of the cue by the learners for non-linguistic reasons, e.g., the quality of the drawing, make responses to this kind of item more difficult to interpret accurately.

We could spend much time deriving many dichotomous situations before we would need to develop multiple choices. The answers to a long list of dichotomies can give us much information in a brief time, thus increasing the validity of the test. Such items can also be checked by action and response with linguistic utterances. These latter would, however, be asking for more than an indication of comprehension; they involve judgment according to a common standard: What is "high" and when does "low" become an accurate response? Evaluation response items demand a higher level of cognitive skill and should be treated as such when they are compared to or used in conjunction with action response items.

Communication Response

Communication response items call for any suitable utterance on the part of the learner. Any of an infinite variety of utterances will be accurate, because any one will indicate that the learner has comprehended the teacher's utterance. The question "What do you like to eat?" can be answered in various ways, with various linguistic constructions, all of which indicate that the learner understands the question.

This type of response incorporates more complexity than we might wish. The spoken response to the test item creates a set of discourse functions that become difficult to interpret properly. One finds many possibilities for response, each of which is difficult to analyze and explain clearly. The learner's utterance involves not only his perception of the teacher's message but also its intent and the formulation of an appropriate response with well chosen linguistic structures. On the other hand, the communication response can be accurate over a wide range of possible utterances. And if the judgment of the accuracy of the response involves only the determination of whether the learner comprehended the message, the questions of correct form, terminology, and pronunciation will play no role beyond the teacher's ability to comprehend the learner's intent.

The communication response is, of course, a significant step toward full verbal communication and two steps beyond the action response. The importance of including this type of item is counterbalanced by the difficulty of maintaining focus on the listening skill. In testing listening comprehension one could limit such items and then emphasize them in a speaking test.

It is important to acknowledge that these ideas are a tentative exploration of a vastly complex and, to some degree, virgin territory. As John Clark writes, "In the absence or near absence of comprehensive conceptual guidelines for the test development process, it

121

is suggested that the most appropriate procedure for instrument development would be to submit to empirical tryout a large number of potentially useful assessment formats..." (16). Each of us can learn to develop evaluation procedures and test items that reflect the state of the art and can learn to discuss such problems with appropriate terminology that is a tool for enlightened teaching.

Summary

Much testing in foreign language instruction neglects the listening skill or involves listening-writing or listening-speaking combinations rather than giving full attention to a response uncontaminated by other skills. Total Physical Response focuses our attention on a situation that calls for no linguistic utterance in the learner's response. Using this procedure as a standard, we can advance to other techniques that parallel the physical response to an oral command.

Three types of response, action, evaluation, and communication response, can be evaluated for the listening (comprehension) skill without resorting to the other language skills (speaking, reading, writing) or with only minimal use of simple utterances that make little or no demand on the speaking skill. Scoring schemes are the prerogative of the teacher, who best knows what kind of information should be gleaned from the test and what kind of situation is involved, i.e., the setting, the characteristics of the learners, the instructional objects, and the teacher's aims.

Teachers are encouraged to experiment with various testing procedures, evaluation criteria, and scoring schemes, and to report the results in the journals of our expanding field of foreign language teaching and learning. We begin best at the beginning: FLES in the first few weeks of instruction with emphasis on the primary language skill—listening.

References

Alexander, Loren, and Maria John. "Testing Oral Skills in a FLES Short Course" *Foreign Language Annals* 18.3 (1985): 235-38.

Asher, James J. *Learning Another Language through Actions*. Los Gatos, Cal.: Sky Oaks Productions, 1977.

Clark, John L. D. "Testing a Common Measure of Speaking Proficiency." *Measuring Spoken Language Proficiency*. Ed. James R. Frith. Washington, D.C.: Georgetown Univ. Press, 1980. 15-26.

Dodson, C. J. *Language Teaching and the Bilingual Method*. London: Pitman, 1974.

Heilenman, Laura K., and Isabelle M. Kaplan. "Proficiency in Practice: The Foreign Language Curriculum." *Foreign Language Proficiency in the Classroom and Beyond*. Ed. Charles J. James. Lincolnwood, Ill: National Textbook Co., 1985. 55-78.

James, Charles J., ed. *Foreign Language Proficiency in the Classroom and Beyond*. The ACTFL Review of Foreign Language Education Series, vol. 16. Lincolnwood, Ill.: National Textbook Co., 1985.

Jones, Joanne, Sherry Eggers, and Ruth Ann Martin. *Introducing Young*

Children to German: Kindergarten through Third Grade. Oklahoma City: Central Printing, 1982.

Larson, Jerry W. "Testing Speaking Ability in the Classroom: The Semi-direct Alternative." *Foreign Language Annals* 17.5 (1984): 499-507.

Lozanov, Georgi. *Suggestology and Outlines of Suggestopedy.* Transl. M. Hall-Pzharlieva and K. Pashmakova. New York: Gordon and Breach, 1978.

Nold, Gunter. *Children's Use of a Second Language in the Classroom: A Contrastive Analysis of Discourse.* Louisville, Ky.: Interdisciplinary Program in Linguistics, 1978. ED 172 552.

Rivers, Wilga M. "A New Curriculum for New Purposes." *Foreign Language Annals* 18.1 (1985): 37-43.

Individual Differences in Second Language Learning among Korean Immigrant Children

Heesoon Jun-Aust

Second language learning has undergone five major phases since 1900. The "direct" method, applied as a medium of instruction from approximately 1900 to 1925, assumed that direct exposure to the target language was the only efficient way to learn a second language. The "grammar-translation" and "audiolingual" methods followed. These three methods presupposed that individuals were affected identically by a particular medium of instruction. Gardner and Lambert's 1959 article pioneered research on the influence of learner variables on second language learning. Attitudinal, motivational, intellectual variables, and the effects of their interaction were popular topics studied by many researchers during this fourth phase (Anisfield and Lambert; Brown; Chastain; Christiansen and Livermore; Gardner; Gardner, Ginsberg, and Smyth; Gardner and Lambert; Gardner and Smythe; Hamayan, Genesee, and Tucker; Hickey; Kittell; Lambert, Gardner, Barik, and Tunstall; Lambert, Tucker, and d'Anglejan).

Sociolinguistic aspects of second language learning were popular topics of study in the fifth phase (Ervin-Tripp; Fishman; Fishman, Cooper and Ma; Gumperz; Holmes; Hymes; Lambert; Oller, Baca, and Vigil; Oller, Hudson, and Liu; Schumann; Tucker, Hamayan, and Genesee; Zampogna.)

The results of second language learning research seem to be contradictory—partly because of vaguely defined variables, poor methodology, poor assessment tools, and poor understanding of the particular second language group's cultural and language idiosyncracies (Alderson; Chastain; Dieterich, Freeman, and Crandall; Robinett; Roca). Better controlled studies (Fillmore; Genesee and Hamayan) which investigated individual differences in second language learning revealed that intellegence and desire to be accepted by English-speaking peers were major determinants for second language learning.

Although Fillmore's 1976 study revealed that peer interaction in social situations and children's desire to be accepted by American children were important variables to facilitate second language learning, an important concern not addressed was whether the peer-

Heesoon Jun-Aust is a member of the faculty of psychology at Centralia College.

124

pairing effect would be the same in a normal classroom situation. Her five subjects *played* with their paired peers in a room containing many attractive toys, and it was not clear whether the toys were instrumental to peer interaction or if having peers present was adequate for peer interaction. If the toys were instrumental, then classroom implementation of peer-pairing would have little value. In addition, Fillmore used a *correlational* technique to examine the effects of peer-pairing, and the present study used an *experimental* design to investigate the effects of peer-pairing on second language learning.

Another consideration was to compare the effects of motivation and the effects of peer-pairing on children's second language learning. This study was unique in that it attempted to define integrative motivation by multiple measures from both the learner and the learner's teacher. Four measures of integrative motivation were used: two from the subjects and two from the subjects' teachers. Furthermore, in an attempt to obtain a valid measure of integrative motivation, one of the measures from each subject and each teacher used a standardized scale. The reviewed literature (Carroll; Chastain; Crone and Marlow; Fillmore; Hamayan, Genesee, and Tucker; Rubin; Schumann; Stern; Swain and Burnaby) claimed that motivation and personality characteristics enhance or retard second language learning. Detailed review concerning motivation and personality characteristics indicated that there was an overlap between the two definitions. For example, individuals with extroverted personalities also showed strong motivation to be liked by members of the target language group and would try to make friends with them (Fillmore; Rubin). Therefore, both personality characteristics, such as popularity and lack of inhibition, and motivational characteristics, such as desire to be accepted by others, desire to be like the speakers of the second language, and desire to learn the second language, were included in the definition of integrative motivation.

Of equal concern in this study was construction of appropriate language tests for the subjects. A substantial number of studies that were reviewed used test items that are inappropriate to a particular ethnic group or societal setting. For instance, the variables that were found to be significant in Canadian research were, without evidence, assumed by some researchers (Oller, Baca, and Vigil; Oller, Hudson, and Liu; Schumann; and Spolsky) to be significant in the United States. Likewise, the variables that were found to be significant with one ethnic group were also assumed to be significant for *all ethnic* groups (Pierson et al.) The present study avoided the above limitations by constructing test items around the tradition and the culture of the subjects.

The purpose of this study is to examine factors influencing individual differences in second language learning. The effects investigated were (a) peer-pairing with American children of second language learner's choice, and (b) integrative motivation.

Three hypotheses of the study were (a) subjects who are peer-paired will have significantly higher scores on both formal language

125

performance and the actual language behavior than subjects who are not peer-paired, (b) subjects who score high on integrative motivation will have significantly higher scores on both formal language performance and the actual language behavior than students who score low on integrative motivation, and (c) subjects who are peer-paired and score high on integrative motivation will have significantly higher scores on both formal language performance and actual language behavior than students who either are peer-paired with lower scores on integrative motivation or are not peer-paired with higher scores on integrative motivation.

Method

Subjects

Limited-English-speaking Korean children in two elementary schools in the Tacoma, Washington, Public School District were selected as subjects. The two elementary schools, about seven blocks apart, had a "pullout" bilingual program conducted by English-speaking Korean teachers. Children were placed in the bilingual program on the basis of their performance on the district's language proficiency test (Peabody Picture Vocabulary Test). These children's English proficiency was reassessed by their bilingual teachers at the beginning of the study. Only those children whose performance level was 20% or lower on both assessments were identified as limited-English speakers and were included in the study. All the subjects were recent immigrants (of less than six months) whose language at home was Korean. In other words, they had similar cultural and linguistic environments, even though their age range was wide (grade 1 to 6). These children came from 19 different classes (9 from one school and 24 from another school).

To divide the children into a control group and an experimental group, the classes were randomly assigned to one of the treatment conditions, resulting in an unequal sample size (15 in the control group and 18 in the experimental group). Random assignment of subjects was not used in order to avoid placing children from the same class into the control and the experimental groups. Because some children's families relocated, only data pertaining to 14 children from the control group and 16 children from the experimental group were analyzed.

Predictor Variables

There were two predictor variables: peer-pairing and subject's integrative motivation. Peer-pairing versus non-peer-pairing was experimentally manipulated on a longitudinal basis (4½ months) and the integrative motivation was examined correlationally.

1. *Peer-pairing versus non-peer-pairing.* The Korean children in the peer-pairing condition were asked to name an English-speaking child

126

Table 1

Number of Subjects by Grade, Sex, and Treatment Conditions

	Boys		Girls	
Grade	Peer-Pair	Non-Peer-Pair	Peer-Pair	Non-Peer-Pair
1	0	1	1	1
2	0	0	0	0
3	1	0	3	1
4	1	1	2	0
5	4	0	2	6
6	0	3	0	3
Total	6	5	8	11

from their classes with whom they would like to work. The chosen peers were seated with the subjects by their classroom teachers. In addition, the teachers asked the American peers to "help" their Korean friends "learn English by explaining to them, answering their questions, or just by being friends." The teachers were informed that the crucial variable of the study was the effect of peer-pairing on English language learning. In the non-peer-pairing condition, there were no special seating arrangements.

2. *Subjects' integrative motivation.* The integrative motivation of the subjects was determined by the child's report and the teacher's rating. Two sets of attitude measures were administered to each subject and each subject's teacher. One was a structured interview with a questionnaire format, and the other was a standardized scale—The Piers-Harris Children's Self-Concept Scale, for the children, and The Devereux Elementary School Behavior Rating Scale, for the teachers.

Since the literature indicated that desire to be liked by others is the best measure of integrative motivation, only those items of the Piers-Harris Children's Self-Concept Scale that pertain to cluster scores of popularity were used as a partial measure of integrative motivation. Only those items of the Devereux Elementary School Behavior Rating Scale pertaining to integrative motivation were analyzed.

Items for questionnaires (see Appendices A and B) were based on the literature reviewed, which suggested variables that appeared to have significant effects on second language learning (Carroll; Fillmore; Gardner and Lambert; Genessee and Hamayan; Rubin; Stern). Only those items pertaining to motivation and personality characteristics were analyzed for the study since other items were included to minimize the response set. The internal consistency reliability coefficient of the subject's questionnaire was alpha = .71 and that of the teacher's questionnaire was alpha = .63. The scores of the four scales were converted into Z scores and then averaged for the subject's overall score for integrative motivation.

Criterion Variables

1. *Listening comprehension.* During an individual interview, each subject was asked to listen to a tape and answer either in English or Korean. The tape was made by a monolingual English speaker, and question items were composed of basic English required for daily functioning and Korean cultural items (see Appendix C).

2. *Oral production test.* During an individual interview, each subject was asked to tell a story in English about two pictures. The subject's response was tape recorded and was rated by six college students on a five-point scale. Intraclassificatory reliability (r = .96) among the six ratings was established.

3. *Actual language behavior.* To investigate how much English interaction there was with peers and teachers, time sampling of actual language behavior of the subjects in the ordinary school setting was collected at the mid-point of the study. There were four kinds of actual language behavior: (a) the subject is addressed by peer, (b) the subject talked to peer, (c) the subject is addressed by the teacher, and (d) the subject talked to the teacher.

Procedures

1. *Data from subjects.* The subject's interview format questionnaire, the Piers-Harris Children's Self Concept Scale, listening comprehension pretest, and oral pretest were individually administered at the beginning of the study. The three tests were administered to all subjects in the following order: (a) the interview format questionnaire and (b) the Piers-Harris Children's Self-Concept Scale. The interview format questionnaire, which consisted mainly of demographic information, was administered first in an attempt to diminish apprehension with the test situation. All tests were administered by a trained bilingual interviewer during the "pullout" bilingual period. Each subject was asked to come to a resource room, which in each school was located close to the bilingual classroom.

The interviewer began by visiting with the subjects to establish rapport; all test instructions were given in Korean. If it appeared that the instructions were not clear to the subject, the interviewer used other Korean words or sentences until the subject understood the questions. The subjects were asked to describe what they had to do in a given test. In responding during the interview, the subjects were encouraged to ask questions concerning any particular item about which they were unsure.

For the oral production and listening comprehension pretest, the subjects were randomly assigned to the order of test taking. Half the subjects were administered the listening comprehension test first. In this test the subjects listened to an English monolingual female speaker talking at a normal speed; the subjects were asked to answer in either Korean or English. The tape played only once for all subjects and for all questions. For the oral production test, the subjects were shown two pages of a storybook, one of the most famous and well-known Korean folk tales, and asked to make a story about the pictures in English. When the subjects indicated that they understood the instructions, they were given as much time as needed to tell a story, which was recorded.

Identical oral production and listening comprehension post-tests were administered to the subjects about four and a half months later. Listening comprehension tests were scored individually by counting the total number of correct responses made by each subject (maximum correct responses = 15). Each subject's oral production tests were recorded on an individual tape. A number ranging from one to 63 was randomly assigned to the 63 tapes, which were rated on a five-point scale by three male and three female college sophomores. When ratings were completed, the tapes were regrouped by pre- and post-tests with the subjects' coding numbers. Each child's pretest score was obtained by adding the points assigned by all 6 raters, resulting in a maximum of 30 points per subject. The same procedure was used for the post-test.

At the mid-point of the study, two female observers came to watch each subject in the classroom and during recess. Each observer charted the subject's language behavior at the tone of a beep introduced at 10-second intervals during each three-minute time sampling per situation. A recording chart was prepared for each observer. The observer, who looked at the subject when the beep sounded, would place a check mark (ν) in an appropriate column indicating to whom the subject was talking or by whom the subject was addressed. Each subject was observed during four different situations (class observation and recess observation by both observers). Therefore, there were 18 possible check marks per situation; the maximum possible for a subject in all four situations was 72 (see Appendices D and E). Random assignment was used to decide which school should be observed first; then the class and recess observations were made at the convenience of the teachers. Children in the same class were randomly assigned for the observations within a particular class. The two observers did not simultaneously observe the same subject.

129

Before the actual observation period, inter-rater reliability was established. The two observers rated two subjects for the same length of time. When the records were compared, both raters had identical check marks for each of the two subjects.

2. Data from the teachers. Prior to the experiment, a letter explaining the experiment and a consent request were sent to teachers who had subjects in their classes. A teacher conference with the investigator was set up by each of the school principals. The teachers were informed that the study was to investigate factors involved in second language learning by Korean immigrant children and the purpose of using the teacher questionnaire and the Devereux Elementary School Behavior Rating Scale was explained. The questionnaires and self-addressed envelopes were distributed.

Those teachers who had peer-paired subjects were asked to remain for further instruction. They were informed of the operational definition of peer-pairing and were asked to make seating arrangements so that peer-paired subjects would be seated near their chosen peers. In addition, the teachers were asked to tell the American peers that the teachers wanted them to "help" their Korean friends "learn English by explaining to them, answering their questions, or just being friends."

Results

The Pearson Product Moment Correlation Coefficient analysis revealed that there were statistically significant correlations among oral pretest, oral post-test, listening pretest, and listening post-test, regardless of group membership. There was also significant correlation between "talk to peer" and "addressed by peer," regardless of group membership. Overall, however, there were more variables that indicated significance in the peer-paired group (42 variables) compared to those of the non-peer-paired group (22 variables).

Best Predictors for Formal Language Learning

The oral production post-test and listening comprehension post-test were used as dependent variables to measure formal language learning. Stepwise multiple regression analyses revealed that the oral production pretest was the best predictor for both oral production and listening comprehension performance. The listening comprehension pretest and the group membership (peer-paired or non-peer-paired) were also significant predictors for listening comprehension.

130

Best Predictors for the Actual Language Behavior

To find the best predictors for the actual language behavior, "talking to peer" and "addressed by peer" were used as dependent measures. Stepwise regression analyses indicated peer-pairing and interaction between peer-pairing and integrative motivation were significant variables.

Peer-pairing and integrative motivation had significant effects on subjects' actual language behavior. Table 2 presents mean, standard deviation, and "F value" of ten variables by group membership and high and low integrative motivation. Integrative motivation alone did not predict either actual language behavior or formal language performance. It played a significant role, however, when it interacted with peer-pairing: a group of subjects who had high integrative motivation but were not peer-paired had lower mean scores (x = 7.4 for "talk to peer" and x = 3.4 for "addressed by peer") than the group of subjects who had high integrative motivation and were peer-paired (x = 16.8 for "talk to peer" and x = 15.5 for "addressed by peer"). It was also noteworthy that the oral production and listening comprehension pretests, which were selected as the best predictors of formal language learning, were not significant predictors for the actual language behavior.

Discussion and Conclusions

Hypothesis 1 was partially confirmed by the study. The effects of peer-pairing were significant for actual language behavior and listening comprehension. However, the peer-pairing was not a significant factor in oral production. The fact that the effects of peer-pairing were important factors in actual language behavior was indicated by Fillmore's longitudinal study. The current study confirms the hypothesis that peer-pairing increases actual language behavior in the normal classroom situation.

Hypothesis 2 was also partially confirmed. Integrative motivation was a significant variable in the actual language behavior but was not a significant predictor for formal language learning.

The motivational variable (integrative motivation), which was extensively reviewed in the literature, did not seem to be a crucial factor in formal language learning—at least it was not with Korean immigrant children in this particular area. The results of the study cause one to question whether a global generalization about effects of motivation on second-language learning can be made. The results of this study indicate that there may be distinctively different factors involved in actual language behavior and formal language performance of second-language learning. For example, motivation did not appear to be a major factor in determining how well children per-

Table 2

Mean, Standard Deviation, and *F* Value of Formal Language Learning and Actual Behavior Measurement by Group with High and Low Integrative Motivation

| | Low Integrative Motivation | | | | High Integrative Motivation | | | | F |
| | Peer-Pair | | Non-Peer-Pair | | Peer-Pair | | Non-Peer-Pair | | |
	Mean	S D	Mean	S D	Mean	S D	Mean	S D	
LISPRE	2.1	3.9	4.4	7.2	7.6	4.0	8.7	4.0	6.2*
LISTPOST	7.3	2.9	5.9	1.9	10.6	2.9	9.4	1.8	16.7**
TPEER	11.2	4.3	3.3	2.9	16.8	8.9	7.4	6.9	4.8*
APEER	7.7	4.0	2.4	1.8	15.5	5.6	3.4	2.9	5.8*
TTEACH	0.5	0.8	0.2	0.4	1.6	1.7	1.6	2.9	4.5*
ATEACH	0	0	0	0	0.9	1.1	1	2.6	3.6
OPPRE	13.3	6.7	9.6	4.6	18.3	5	18	8.4	10*
OPPOST	17.5	5.6	14.2	5.7	24	5.9	21.3	6.8	10.9*
LISDIF	5.2	2.7	1.4	5.9	3	1.9	0.71	2.7	0.47
OPPDIF	4.2	5.4	4.7	4.3	5.8	2.8	3.3	2.7	0

Note: LISDIF: Difference Between Listening Pre- and Posttest   *p < .05
          OPPDIF: Difference Between Oral Pre- and Posttest   **p < .001

formed on the formal language tests, although its effect was statistically significant in predicting actual language behavior when it was paired with the treatment conditon (peer-pairing). Likewise, prior linguistic knowledge, which was powerful for formal language learning, failed to be significant in predicting actual language behavior.

Hypothesis 3 was confirmed by the study. The subjects who were peer-paired and scored high on integrative motivation had higher scores on both formal language tests and actual language behavior than the subjects who either were peer-paired and had lower scores on integrative motivation or were not peer-paired and had higher scores on integrative motivation.

Integrative motivation alone was not as strong a predictor as peer-pairing in Korean children's second-language learning. Even for the actual language behavior ("talking to peer"), only 2% of the variance was accounted for and failed to show statistical significance, while 35% was explained by peer-pairing. Therefore, it seems reasonable to conclude that peer-pairing was instrumental to demonstrated interaction between peer-pairing and integrative motivation. This finding is in support of Fillmore's contention that proper input through social interaction leads a learner to develop appropriate learning strategies to facilitate second-language learning.

The brief study period (4½ months), formal language tests of Korean cultural orientation, and the restricted population limit the extent of generalization.

An ad-hoc stepwise multiple regression analysis was used in an attempt to examine which variable was the most significant predictor of how well children talked. The variable "addressed by peer" emerged a great deal more important than "talking to peer" in predicting oral language performance. "Addressed by peer" was the second-best predictor after the oral production pretest. The variable "talking to peer" was the sixth best predictor; thus, an insignificant percentage of variation was explained by this variable.

According to this study, merely practicing talking with the target language group does not necessarily increase a second language learner's oral performance. Rather, the opportunity to be addressed by the target language speakers is a crucial factor. The classroom teacher's encouragement to the American pupil provided the opportunity to be addressed by the target language speakers.

The practical implications of this study in the classroom are simple and easy to apply. The peer-pairing is cost effective; finding a peer of the second language learner's choice, making seating arrangements and encouraging the American peer to be altruistic to the second language learner are the only necessary conditions for the peer-pairing. The peer-pairing provides the second language learners with a sense of personal importance and acceptance. The American peers also gain satisfaction because of the teacher's request for their assistance and because of their altruistic behavior. The teacher profits because the second language learners better comprehend and speak English. Thus, the peer-pairing is a positive practice for all involved.

Appendix A.
Questionnaire for Subject

Code_____

Sex: _____M _____F
Age: 5 6 7 8 9 10 11 12

No. younger siblings: 1 2 3 4 5 6
Age of younger siblings: 1 2 3 4 5 6 7 8 9 10 11
No. of older siblings: 1 2 3 4 5 6 7
Age of older siblings: 1 2 3 4 5 6 7 8 9 10 11 12 13 14 15 16 17 18 19
                20 21 22 23 24

Place of birth: 1. Korea   2. America   3. Other _____(Please specify)

A. PEERS

1.   Your friends are very important to you   yes ( )   no ( )

2.   You enjoy talking to your friends more than to adults   yes ( )   no ( )

3.   You most like to play with your:

       a. English speaking friends.

       b. Korean speaking friends.   a ( )   b ( )

4.   You like to play most with:

       a. Dramatic play (house, school, doctor/nurse, etc.)
          with English speaking friends.   a ( )

       b. Dramatic play with Korean speaking friends.   b ( )

       c. Alone with toys, games or books.   c ( )   **133**

B. ADULTS

1.   You enjoy talking to adults more than to your friends   yes ( )   no ( )

2.   You like your teacher very much.   yes ( )   no ( )

C. LANGUAGE

1.   You like to practice new English words that you hear.   yes ( )   no ( )

2.   You do not like to speak English because you are afraid
       you will make a mistake.   yes ( )   no ( )

3.   When your teacher asks you a question in English you
       are happy to answer in English.   yes ( )   no ( )

4.   You learn English most from:

       a. Parents   a ( )

       b. T.V.   b ( )

       c. Friends   c ( )

       d. Teachers   d ( )

       e. Books   e ( )

5.   Your parents encourage you to study English.   yes ( )   no ( )

6.   You have had the opportunity to hear English spoken
       with friends of the family.   yes ( )   no ( )

7. The language you speak most at home with your sisters/brothers is:

    a. Korean   a ( )

    b. English   b ( )

    c. Other   c ( )

8. Two people you play with the most after school are:

_____ _____

9. You speak: a. Korean b. English with them.   a ( )   b ( )

D. COUNTRY

1. Do you wish you were still in Korea?   yes ( )   no ( )
2. Are you glad that you are in America?   yes ( )   no ( )

Appendix B.
Questionnaire for Teacher

Please answer as directed by the instructions. DO NOT PUT DOWN YOUR NAME, as personal data will be kept confidential. Thank you very much for your cooperation.

Code_____

Your Sex: _____M _____F

Please put a check in the "yes" or "no," or the letter that indicates the appropriate answer.

1.	The student is very outgoing	yes ( )	no ( )
2.	The student is shy.	yes ( )	no ( )
3.	The student enjoys talking to English-speaking peers more than to English-speaking adults.	yes ( )	no ( )
4.	The student engages in solitary play during free time	yes ( )	no ( )
5.	The student enjoys talking to English monolingual adults (i.e., teachers) more than to English monolingual peers.	yes ( )	no ( )
6.	The student enjoys practicing new English words without hesitation.	yes ( )	no ( )
7.	The student hesitates to speak English.	yes ( )	no ( )
8.	The student is quick to give answers to questions.	yes ( )	no ( )
9.	The student spends time before he or she responds.	yes ( )	no ( )
10.	The student has a positive attitude about adjusting to new culture and language.	yes ( )	no ( )
11.	The student's parents are very cooperative with the school.	yes ( )	no ( )
12.	The student plays most with:		
	a. Monolingual English-speaking peers.	a ( )	
	b. Limited-English-speaking peers.	b ( )	
	c. Bilingual peers.	c ( )	
13.	The student uses free time with games that require verbalization.	yes ( )	no ( )
	If yes,		
	a. The student plays with monolingual English-speaking peers.	a ( )	
	b. The student plays with limited-English-speaking Koreans	b ( )	
	c. The student plays with bilingual peers.	c ( )	

135

COMMENTS:

Appendix C.
Listening Comprehension Test

Code_____

Listen carefully to the tape and answer questions either in English or Korean.

1. This is Korea's main vegetable dish. It is usually made of cabbage, garlic, green onion, and red pepper. It is hot and spicy. Can you tell me what it is?

    _____

2. This is a Korean holiday. Koreans usually dress up in Korean clothes and bow to parents and relatives. The parents and relatives give children money for bowing. Can you tell me the name of this holiday?

    _____

3. A traditional Korean meal always includes this dish. It is served with almost every meal. What is this food called?

    _____

4. Instead of a fork, Koreans and other orientals use two long, thin sticks to eat with. What are these sticks called?

    _____

5. We are now in a room that is used less often than most of the other rooms in the house. But it has a very important function in the social life of the family. Guests are received here, and there are chairs, a sofa, pictures, lamps, tables, and reading material for their comfort and enjoyment. Where are we?

    _____

6. This machine removes dust and dirt from floors, carpet, furniture, and window sills. Its motor blows air and creates a strong suction. It makes a loud noise when it is on. There are two types: an upright and a canister model. What is it?

    _____

7. Listen carefully and tell me the story in Korean.
    Mrs. Park: What type of house are you looking for?
    Mr. Jones: I would like a small place with three bedrooms and a bath.
    Mrs. Jones: I would like a big old house with a fireplace in the living room.
    Mrs. Park: Is there anything that you would both like?
    The Joneses: Yes, someone who likes what I like!

8. Do you like to learn English?   yes ( )   no ( )

9. What do you do to help your mother or father at home? _____

    _____

10. What do you like to do when you are alone? _____

    _____

11. How do you get to school? _____

Appendix D.
Sample of Observation Charts

Peer Pair

School   Grade   Room Number
Teacher's Name   Observer's Number: 1   Situation: Class

Subject's Code Number	Talking to:			Addressed to from		
	Paired Peer	Another Peer	Teacher	Paired Peer	Another Peer	Teacher
01P						
02P						
03P						

Peer Pair

School   Grade   Room Number
Teacher's Name   Observer's Number: 1   Situation: Class

Subject's Code Number	Talking to:		Addressed to from	
	Peer	Teacher	Peer	Teacher
01P				
02P				
03P				

Note: Maximum number of check marks for each subject is 18

Appendix E.
Actual Language Behavior by Treatment Groups

Table 1.

Peer Pair (N=14)

	Talking to						Addressed to/from					
	Paired Peer		Another Peer		Teacher		Paired Peer		Another Peer		Teacher	
	Class	Recess	Class	Recess	Class	Recess	Class	Recess	Class	Recess	Class	Recess
Name	A B	A B	A B	A B	A B	A B	A B	A B	A B	A B	A B	A B
01P	1 0	2 0	2 3	1 3	0 0	0 0	3 1	1 0	2 1	2 1	0 0	0 0
02P	3 4	5 6	5 4	5 2	0 1	0 0	3 3	3 4	1 1	3 3	0 2	0 0
03P	0 1	3 2	1 0	5 4	0 0	0 0	0 0	1 0	0 0	2 2	0 0	0 0
04P	2 0	1 0	2 1	0 0	0 0	0 0	2 1	0 0	1 0	0 0	0 0	0 0
05P	4 4	0 2	0 1	2 2	1 0	0 0	3 2	2 3	0 1	2 1	0 0	0 0
06P	0 0	0 1	1 1	3 2	0 0	0 0	0 0	0 0	1 1	0 2	0 0	0 0
07P	5 0	3 4	0 5	3 0	1 0	0 0	4 4	6 3	0 0	0 4	0 0	0 0
08P	1 1	0 1	2 2	4 3	1 1	0 0	1 1	0 0	1 1	2 3	0 0	0 0
09P	0 0	2 3	0 0	0 2	0 0	0 0	0 0	1 2	0 0	4 3	0 0	0 0
10P	0 0	6 3	1 0	0 0	1 1	0 0	0 0	3 2	4 3	1 0	1 0	0 0
11P	2 0	2 1	0 1	4 6	1 2	0 0	0 0	2 3	0 1	5 3	0 3	0 0
12P	0 0	2 3	0 1	3 2	3 2	0 0	0 0	2 4	0 0	1 3	1 0	0 0
13P	2 1	5 3	5 3	3 2	1 0	0 0	3 3	3 2	1 4	4 4	0 0	0 0
14P	0 0	0 2	0 0	3 3	0 0	0 0	0 0	2 2	0 0	2 4	0 0	0 0
	20 11	31 31	19 22	36 31	9 7	0 0	19 15	26 25	11 13	28 33	2 5	0 0
	201				16		170				7	

Note: Actual language behavior of each subject=talking to teacher and addressed from peer and addressed to subject from teacher. Maximum score of actual language behavior for each subject =72.
A=Observer 1; B=Observer 2.

138

Table 2.

Peer Pair (N=16)

	Talking to				Addressed to/from			
	Peer		Teacher		Peer		Teacher	
	Class	Recess	Class	Recess	Class	Recess	Class	Recess
Name	A B	A B	A B	A B	A B	A B	A B	A B
01NP	6 9	2 4	1 0	0 0	0 3	2 3	0 0	0 0
02NP	1 0	0 0	1 0	0 0	0 0	0 0	0 0	0 0
03NP	2 1	3 3	0 0	0 0	1 2	0 2	0 0	0 0
04NP	0 0	0 0	0 0	0 0	0 0	0 0	0 0	0 0
05NP	2 1	0 0	0 0	0 0	0 0	0 0	0 0	0 0
06NP	1 0	2 2	0 0	0 0	0 1	0 3	0 0	0 0
07NP	1 1	0 0	1 0	0 0	1 0	0 0	0 0	0 0
08NP	0 0	4 6	0 1	0 0	0 0	0 1	0 0	0 0
09NP	0 0	1 4	3 5	0 0	0 1	1 3	2 5	0 0
10NP	0 0	0 3	0 0	0 0	0 0	0 2	0 0	0 0
11NP	0 0	3 6	0 0	0 0	0 0	3 2	0 0	0 0
12NP	0 0	0 0	0 0	0 0	0 0	1 1	0 0	0 0
13NP	0 0	1 1	0 0	0 0	0 0	2 3	0 0	0 0
14NP	0 0	0 2	0 0	0 0	0 0	0 2	0 0	0 0
15NP	0 0	2 1	0 0	0 0	1 0	0 2	0 0	0 0
16NP	2 3	2 0	0 1	0 0	0 0	2 1	0 0	0 0
	15 15	20 32	6 7	0 0	3 7	11 25	2 5	0 0
	82		13		21		7	

Note: Actual language behavior of each subject=talking to peer and talking to teacher and addressed from peer and addressed to subject from teacher. Maximum score of actual language behavior for each subject =72. A=Observer 1; B=Observer 2.

References

Alderson, J. Charles. "The Cloze Procedure and Proficiency in English as a Foreign Language." *TESOL Quarterly* 13.2(1979):219-27.

Anisfield, Moshe, and Wallace E. Lambert. "Social and Psychological Variables in Learning Hebrew." *Journal of Abnormal and Social Psychology* 63(1961):524-29.

Brown, H. Douglas. "Affective Variables in Second Language Acquisition." *Language Learning* 23.2(1973):231-44.

Carroll, John B. "Characteristics of Successful Second Language Learners." *Viewpoints on English as a Second Language.* Ed. Marina K. Burt, Heidi Dulay, and Mary Finocchiaro. New York: Regents, 1977.

Chastain, Kenneth D. "Affective and Ability Factors in Second-Language Acquisition." *Language Learning* 25.1(1975):153-61.

_____. "Testing Listening Comprehension Tests." *TESOL Quarterly* 13.1 (1979):81-88.

Christiansen, Ted, and Gary Livermore. "A Comparison of Anglo-American and Spanish-American Children on the WISC [Wechsler Intelligence Scale for Children]." *Journal of Social Psychology* 81(1970):9-14.

Crowne, Douglas P., and David Marlowe. *The Approval of Motive: Studies in Evaluative Dependence.* New York: Wiley, 1964.

Dieterich, Thomas G., Cecilia Freeman, and Jo Ann Crandall. "A Linguistic Analysis of Some English Proficiency Tests." *TESOL Quarterly* 13.4(1979):535-50.

Ervin-Tripp, Susan. "An Analysis of the Interaction of Language, Topic and Listener." *The Ethnography of Communication. American Anthropologist* 66.6, Part 2(1964):86-102. Special Publication. Ed. John J. Gumperz and Dell H. Hymes.

Fillmore, Lily Wong. "The Second Time Around: Cognitive and Social Strategies in Second Language Acquisition." Diss. Stanford Univ., 1976.

Fishman, Joshua A. "Bilingualism with and without Diglossia: Diglossia with and without Bilingualism." *Journal of Social Issues* 23.2(1967):29-38.

_____. "Sociolinguistic Perspective on the Study of Bilingualism." *Linguistics* 39(1968):20-48.

Gardner, Robert C. "Motivational Variables in Second Language Acquisition." *Attitudes and Motivation.* Ed. Robert C. Gardner and Wallace E. Lambert. Rowley, Mass.: Newbury House, 1972. 199-216.

_____. "On the Validity of Affective Variables in Second Language Acquisition: Conceptual, Contextual, and Statistical Considerations." *Language Learning* 30.2(1980):255-70.

_____, R.E. Ginsberg, and P.C. Smythe. "Attitude and Motivation in Second Language Learning: Course-Related Changes." *Canadian Modern Language Review* 32.3(1976):243-66.

Gardner, Robert C., and Wallace E. Lambert. "Motivational Variables in Second Language Acquisition." *Canadian Journal of Psychology* 13(1959):266-72.

_____. "Language Aptitude, Intelligence and Second Language Achievement." *Journal of Educational Psychology* 56(1965):191-99.

_____. *Attitude and Motivation in Second Language Learning.* Rowley, Mass.: Newbury House, 1972.

Gardner, Robert C., and P.C. Smythe. "Motivation and Second Language Acquisition." *Canadian Modern Language Review* 31.3(1975):218-30.

_____, R. Clément, and L. Gliksman. "Second Language Learning: A

Social Psychological Perspective." *Canadian Modern Language Review* 32.3(1976):198-213.

Genesee, Fred, and Else Hamayan. "Individual Differences in Second Language Learning." *Applied Psycholinguistics* 1(1980):95-110.

Gumperz, John J. "On the Linguistic Markers of Bilingual Communication." *Journal of Social Issues* 23.2(1967):48-57.

Hamayan, Else, Fred Genesee, and G. Richard Tucker. "Affective Factors and Language Exposure in Second Language Learning." *Language Learning* 27.2(1977):225-40.

Hickey, Tim. "Bilingualism and the Measurement of Intelligence and Verbal Learning Ability." *Exceptional Children* 39.1(1972):24-28.

Holmes, J. "Sociolinguistic Competence in the Classroom." *Understanding Second and Foreign Language Learning.* Ed. Jack C. Richards. Rowley, Mass.: Newbury House, 1978. 134-62.

Hymes, Dell. "Models of the Interaction of Language and Social Setting." *Journal of Social Issues.* 23.2(1967):8-28.

Kittell, Jack E. "Intelligence Test Performance of Children from Bilingual Environments." *Elementary School Journal* 64(1963):76-83.

Lado, Robert. *Language Testing: The Construction and Use of Foreign Language Tests.* New York: McGraw-Hill, 1961.

Lambert, Wallace E. "Psychological Approach to the Study of Language, Part 1. On Second Language Learning and Bilingualism." *Modern Language Journal* 47.3(1963):51-62.

_____. "A Social Psychology of Bilingualism." *Journal of Social Issues* 23.2(1967):91-109.

_____, R[obert] C. Gardner, H[enri] C. Barik, and K. Tunstall. "Attitudinal and Cognitive Aspects of Intensive Study of a Second Language." *Journal of Abnormal and Social Psychology* 66.4(1963):358-68.

Lambert, Wallace E., G. Richard Tucker, and Alison d'Anglejan. "Cognitive and Attitudinal Consequences of Bilingual Schooling: The St. Lambert Project through Grade Five." *Journal of Educational Psychology* 65.2(1973):141-59.

Oller, John W., Jr., Lori L. Baca, and Alfredo Vigil. "Attitudes and Attained Proficiency in ESL: A Sociolinguistic Study of Mexican-Americans in the Southwest." *TESOL Quarterly* 11.2(1977):173-83.

Oller, John W., Jr., Alan J. Hudson, and Phyllis Fei Liu. "Attitudes and Attained Proficiency in ESL: A Sociolinguistic Study of Native Speakers of Chinese in the United States." *Language Learning* 27.1(1977):1-27.

Pierson, Herbert D., Gail S. Fu, and Sik-yum Lee. "An Analysis of the Relationship between Language Attitudes and English Attainment of Secondary Students in Hong Kong." *Language Learning* 30.2(1980):289-316.

Raven, J. *The Coloured Progressive Matrices,* Sets A, Ab, B. London: Lewis and Co., 1962.

Robinett, Betty W. *Teaching English to Speakers of Other Languages: Substance and Technique.* New York: McGraw-Hill, 1978.

Roca, Pablo. "Problems of Adapting Intelligence Scales from One Culture to Another." *High School Journal* 38(1955):124-31.

Rubin, Joan. "What the 'Good Language Learner' Can Teach Us." *TESOL Quarterly* 9.1(1975):41-51.

Schumann, John H. "Affective Factors and the Problem of Age in Second Language Acquisition." *Language Learning* 25.2(1975):209-35.

_____. "Social Distance as a Factor in Second Language Acquisition." *Language Learning* 26.1(1976):135-43.

_____. "Social and Psychological Factors in Second Language Acquisition." *Understanding Second and Foreign Language Learning.* Ed. Jack C. Richards. Rowley, Mass.: Newbury House, 1978. 163-78.

Scovel, Thomas. "The Effect of Affect on Foreign Language Learning: A Review of the Anxiety Research." *Language Learning* 28.1 (1978):129-42.

Seliger, Herbert W. "Does Practice Make Perfect? A Study of Interaction Patterns and L2 Competence." *Language Learning* 27.2(1977):263-76.

Spivack, G., and M. Swift. *Devereux Elementary School Behavior Rating Scale.* Devon, Penn.: The Devereux Foundation, 1967.

Spolsky, Bernard. "Attitudinal Aspects of Second Language Learning." *Language Learning* 19.3-4(1969):271-83.

Stern, H.H. "What Can We Learn from the Good Language Learner?" *Canadian Modern Language Review* 31(1975):304-18.

Swain, M[errill], and B. Burnaby. "Personality Characteristics and Second Language Learning in Young Children: A Pilot Study." *Working Papers on Bilingualism* 11(1976):115-28.

Tucker, G. Richard, Else Hamayan, and Fred Genesee. "Affective, Cognitive, and Social Factors in Second Language Acquisition." *Canadian Modern Language Review* 32.3(1976):214-26.

Zampogna, Joseph, Ronald J. Gentile, Anthony Papalia, and R. Gordon Silber. "Relationship between Learning Styles and Learning Environments in Selected Secondary Modern Language Classes." *Modern Language Journal* 60.8(1976):443-47.

A Discourse Analysis of Interactions of Spanish-English Bilingual Children

Carol A. Klee

Spanish-dominant bilingual children face two major difficulties when they enter school for the first time: first, like all children, they must learn to recognize and use the rules and language patterns appropriate for the classroom speech environment; and, second, they must acquire fluency and learn to interact in the classroom in English, the weaker of their two languages. Some children are able to surmount these two hurdles more readily than others, and as a result, are more likely to succeed in accomplishing academic goals.

Research (Mehan; MacLure and French; Morine-Dershimer and Tenenberg; Willes; Wilkinson and Calculator; Wells, *Language at Home and at School*) indicates that successful participation in classroom learning necessitates the acquisition of a set of discourse rules required for that communication setting (e.g., how to successfully engage the teacher and others to acquire the necessary linguistic input for learning; when and under what conditions a turn can be successfully negotiated; how to deal successfully with a specified topic). Students differ in their communicative competence, particularly in the special aspects associated with classroom activities. Some students do not immediately recognize the special characteristics of classroom interactions and may be unable to participate effectively in classroom learning experiences. Inadequate learning of the rules of classroom discourse, then, can affect their academic performance and their overall adjustment to school as well as result in lower teacher expectations.

Clearly, the acquisition of communicative competence both in and outside the classroom becomes more complex when two languages are involved. Many children from non-English backgrounds enter school with a limited knowledge of English and must learn not only new rules for interaction in the classroom but also new rules in a new language. Their task may be further complicated by the fact that the communication patterns of students and teachers from different cultural backgrounds are not always alike (Philips; Gumperz; Guthrie and Hall), and such differences often result in mutual misunderstandings that can have unfavorable academic consequences for the children involved.

Carol A. Klee is Assistant Professor of Spanish at the University of Minnesota.

142

Studies of Spanish-English bilingual classrooms have focused, for the most part, on the teachers' functional use of the two languages during classroom interaction (Shultz; Phillips; Bruck and Shultz; Legarreta; Sapiens). The findings suggest that not one but many social variables (e.g., activity, addressee, classroom, teacher's language proficiency) must be considered in the examination of bilingual children's language-use patterns.

Other research has examined the abilities of bilingual children to use a variety of styles within a single language, as well as to choose appropriately between their two languages on different occasions (Genishi; Zentella; McClure). In general, these studies indicate that children have communicative abilities they reveal in different situations. Although studies of children's language patterns in the school setting are intrinsically interesting in that children's academic success depends, in large part, on their ability to learn the rules for successful classroom interaction, they cannot provide a complete picture of children's linguistic abilities. Reflecting on educational research in general, Bronfenbrenner urges researchers to look at a variety of settings (e.g., homes, day-care centers, schools, etc.) and to focus on the relationships among the settings since, as he points out, what happens to children in one setting inevitably affects what happens in others. In order to fully understand the communicative demands of the classroom and have a more balanced view of bilingual children's communicative abilities, it is essential to analyze speech patterns in a variety of settings.

Thus, this study was designed to yield a comprehensive description of the speech activities of a sample of bilingual children and a comparison between the language interactions and language usage within the home and school settings. The specific purposes of the study were (1) to identify the types of speech activities that bilingual students encounter in the classroom, on the playground, and at home through the early years of schooling; (2) to analyze and describe the structure and function of the oral language interactions contained in those speech activities; (3) to compare the nature of those interactions across the three communication environments; and (4) to examine the differential nature of the interactions involving high-achieving vs. low-achieving students, boys vs. girls, and students at different grade levels.

Audiotaped speech samples of four bilingual students were obtained over three years of schooling (the first through the third grades) in each of the three communication environments—the classroom, the playground and the home—on a rotating monthly schedule in conjunction with the Bilingual Reading Project of the Southwest Educational Development Laboratory. The four children were selected from four student groupings that formed part of the first cohort of students included in the Bilingual Reading Project: one high-reading achieving boy, one high-reading achieving girl, one low-reading achieving boy, and one low-reading achieving girl. These children live in or near a small town in the southern central section of Texas close to the Mexican border; the county in which they live is 97%

143

Hispanic. Their school district is characterized as a largely rural region populated by families of low socioeconomic backgrounds, with substantial numbers of Spanish-dominant children. All four children have participated in bilingual classrooms since they entered school.

The taped language samples for each child are ten to thirty minutes in length. In the classroom, standard cassette tape recorders and lapel, or lavalier, microphones were used. On the playground and in the home, the taped samples were obtained by placing an activated microcassette tape recorder in the pocket of a specially designed belt and sash worn by the student. A very small microphone extended from the tape recorder up under the sash and through a button hole at shoulder height. Thus, the microphone was ideally placed to pick up the child's speech as well as that of others nearby.

The children were taped from two to six times per year, and most were taped at least once per year in each communication environment. In the subsample of target children for the present study, the two boys were not taped in the home environment during the first year.

The audiotaped speech samples were coded using a scheme designed by Gorden Wells (*The Language Experience of Five-Year-Old Children at Home and at School*) of the University of Bristol. Minor modifications were made by this researcher to accommodate the language use of bilingual children in the three environments. In Wells' system, the unit of analysis is the utterance, which is defined as one independent unit of verbal communication, together with any other units dependent on it. Typically, a single utterance constitutes a conversational move. Moves are defined as the smallest constituents of conversational interaction and fit into a hierarchical structure consisting of *sequence*, stretches of talk having unitary topic and purpose; *exchange*, the minimal unit of conversational interaction involving initiating responding, and *move*.

In analyzing the data, an examination was first made of the types of speech activities present within each of the three communication environments. Findings reveal that, as early as the age of six, the four children engaged in a wide range of speech activities varying according to the communication environment, partly as a function of what typically goes on within a particular environment, but also partly as a function of who the available participants were within a given interactional period. 86% of the classroom interactions recorded involved instruction. However, it should be clear that other speech activities such as classroom management (1%), conversation, (1%), and play (12%) also occurred within this environment. On the playground 86% of the sequences involved play, 9% play management, and 5% conversation.

Within the home, the most common types of speech activities were play (61%) and conversation (29%). However, management of general activities (2%), engagement in adult activities (4%), instruction (1%), and play management (4%) also occurred. These speech activities, reflecting the interactions that took place from the time school ended until approximately 5:00 p.m., depended primarily on who was present to interact with the child. If only siblings or neighborhood children were available, the speech activities approximated those encountered on the playground. If an adult was present, more conversation and speech activities other than play or play management occurred. The home environment enclosed the widest variety of participants, thus it evidenced the widest variety of speech activities.

The Classroom Environment

Not surprisingly, instruction in the classroom was the most structured of the speech activities. During instructional sequences the teacher directed the interactions, initiating all sequences and almost all exchanges. Most of the exchanges during these interactions were for the purpose of display and conformed to the three-part, initiate-response-follow up structure. Students were limited to filling the middle slot, usually with a one-or two-word reply. They were sometimes reminded by their teachers that these interactions followed special discourse requirements, unlike those of other communication environments. In the first grade, for example, they were told to verbalize their answers to questions even if the response required was a simple "yes" or "no":

Teacher:	¿Qué están haciendo estos niños en el dibujo?
	[What are these children in the picture doing?]
Elena:	Están bañando.
	[They're swimming.]
Teacher:	Okay.
	¿Crees que are they having fun or not?
	[Do you think that...]
	¿Qué parece?
	[What does it look like?]
	Are they having fun?
	Se parece que sí, ¿verdad?
	[It looks like they are, doesn't it?]
	Yes or no?
Elena:	Yes
Teacher:	Yes, okay.

145

Indeed, more exchanges were completed verbally during instruction than during any other kind of speech activity.

In the third grade the teacher of three of the target children insisted that the children produce not only the correct responses to her display questions, but also formulate complete sentences:

Teacher:	Where is Hawaii located? What part or what ocean? Marta.
Marta:	Pacific Ocean.
Teacher:	Can you answer me in a complete sentence, Marta?

Marta:	The Pacific Ocean.
Teacher:	The Pacific Ocean.
	Is that a complete sentence?
	Meme, can you answer me in a complete sentence?
Meme:	In the Pacific Ocean.
Teacher:	How about Maria?
Maria:	In the Pacific Ocean.
Observer:	But what in the Pacific Ocean?
Teacher:	Let's all together answer me in a complete sentence.
	Hawaii . . .
Children:	Hawaii (in unison)
Teacher:	is
Children:	is
Teacher:	located
Children:	located
Teacher:	in the
Children:	Pacific Ocean.

The next time the teacher requested a complete answer to her question Meme knew exactly how to respond:

Teacher:	Where do you usually see these grass huts also?
Meme:	Mexico.
Teacher:	Can you answer me in a complete sentence?
Meme:	They also live in grass huts in Mexico.
Teacher:	Very good.

The children soon learned that the form of their answers was as important as the content.

However, it should be noted as an exception to the concentration on form as well as content that, during these instructional sequences, teachers did not correct the children's grammatical errors but responded to the truth value of the factual information. During Marta's first-grade interactions the following exchanges occurred:

Teacher:	Tell me what you see in that picture.
Marta:	The mother is giving to eat the little baby.
Teacher:	What do you think she's giving him to eat?
Marta:	Soup.
Teacher:	Okay.
	And what is the other girl doing?
Marta:	She's the big sister and he's putting in the bottle some milk to the baby.
Teacher:	That's right.

The same policy is evident in the third-grade instructional sequences although here the correct response is modeled:

Observer:	What do you put in the tray?
Arturo:	Water.
Observer:	Tell me in a complete sentence.

Arturo:	They place in the tray water.
Observer:	They place water in the tray.
	All right.

Classroom discourse is different from other types of discourse in a number of other ways. As noted by French and MacLure, both teachers and students employ interactive strategies to facilitate question-answer exchanges and arrive at "right answers." For example, during instructional interactions with the low-achieving students, the teachers tended to use a higher percentage of reformulated nuclear exchanges to help students get the correct answer:

Teacher:	¿Qué son estas cosas? [What are these things?]
Elena:	Niños. [Children]
Teacher:	¿Y quień [And who?]
	(silence)
	(Reformulated Nuclear Exchange) ¿Están con la mamá o no? [Are they with their mother or not?]
Elena:	Yes.
Teacher:	Yes, they are.

Students, particularly in a group, use the guessing strategy described by MacLure and French to answer the teacher's questions. They identify some item in the teacher's question as a superordinate term for a class of items, and then select items according to their membership in that class. For example, during a lesson on the three states of matter, the following question-answer sequences occurred among Arturo, his teacher, and two other classmates:

Teacher:	Oxygen is an example of a gaseous matter on this page. What else could we find there that could be an example?
Carlos:	Bridge.
Teacher:	The bridge, Carlos, is solid. And everything that is living is through what matter?
Carlos:	Solid.
Teacher:	Solid.
	Is that solid fence living?
Carlos:	No.
Teacher:	It is non-living.
	Are those trees living?
Carlos:	Yes.
Teacher:	They are absorbing food, water, and air. And another very important energy. What is it?
Arturo:	Liquid.
Teacher:	Liquid? We already said water.
	What is the most important thing that has to be provided for plants to survive?
Alicia:	Sun.
Teacher:	The sun. Very good, Alicia.

147

The high-achieving children seemed to catch on to the special requirements of classroom discourse much faster than the low-achieving children. Differences between the two groups were most salient during first-grade instructional interactions. The high-achieving children required fewer reformulated nuclear exchanges to answer questions; they completed a higher percentage of exchanges verbally and left fewer exchanges incomplete; they contributed a higher percentage of the total utterances to the interactions; they spoke more English; and their utterances reflected greater syntactic complexity with greater frequency in the classroom than in other environments. This was not true of the low-achieving children whose utterances tended to reflect greater syntactic complexity during play or conversational sequences. Thus, the high-achieving children were perhaps more able to favorably influence teacher appraisal and expectations than those in the low-achieving group.

One low-achieving child in particular, Elena, seemed to have little idea in the first grade of how to interact with her teacher. She had little understanding of the special rules of classroom discourse. For example, in the following exchange, the teacher asked her to describe a picture and apparently expected to elaborate on her response:

Teacher:	¿Hay mucha gente o no?
	[Are there a lot of people or not?]
Elena:	Yes
Teacher:	Yes, what?
Elena:	Yes, ma'am

Although Elena seemed unaware of what was expected of her during classroom instructional sequences, her teacher made few attempts to explain directly what was expected. Rather, Elena was left to intuit what her teacher wanted.

By the third grade, differences between the two groups, while still apparent, had decreased in degree, due perhaps to two reasons: the low-achieving children were more aware of the conventions of classroom discourse than before, and the children were interacting in a group with other children who assumed some of the interactional responsibility for them.

The Home Environment

Conversational interactions between children and adults at home were less structured than instructional sequences in the classroom. The adults still tended to dominate the interactions; however, the target children were not as limited as in the classroom, initiating a much higher percentage of the total utterances. Fewer exchanges were completed verbally than in the classroom, and more were completed nonverbally, completed implicitly, or left incomplete.

According to Wells and Montgomery, the quality of adult interactions with the child in the home significantly influences the child's success at school. Children whose parents extend their topics and help them develop their ideas tend to do better in school than children whose parents have more authoritarian communicative style and who insist on their own point of view. The data from these four children do not either confirm or refute Wells' views. Although from Marta's first-grade data it would appear that her father listened to her and developed her topics, only eleven utterances occurred in conversational interaction between her and her father. In the third grade language samples, she did not interact with either parent. Meme's and Arturo's third-grade home language samples contained many conversational sequences between the boys and their parents or grandparents. In both cases the boys' topics were developed to a great degree, although Meme was a high-achieving one. Elena, the child who had the least success in school, also experienced the least cooperation during conversation at home. Her mother developed her topics only 8% of the time, and Elena frequently sighed in frustration at the lack of response to her initiations.

Elena:	Mañana . . . [Tomorrow]
Mother:	(to son) Cierra la boca.
	[Close your mouth]
Elena:	. . .vamos a tener el, la, el (inaudible). . .
	[. . .we're going to have the, the, the
	(inaudible). . .]
Martin:	Luis, ¿vamos?
	[Luis, are we going?]
Luis:	Sí, vamos.
	[Yeah, let's go.]
José:	(inaudible) los huevos.
	[(inaudible) the eggs.]
Elena:	. . .y a nosotros nos dejaron muchos huevos allí.
	Los vamos a traer para acá el dia de la Pascua.
	[. . .and they left us a lot of eggs there. We're
	going to bring them here for Easter Day.]
Luis:	Hijo, se apagó.
	[Shoot, it turned off.]

Compared to the other target children, Elena had considerable difficulty in expressing herself during conversational sequences at home because of the unresponsiveness of her mother and brothers.

Play Environments

During play interactions at home and at school, the children had the fewest restrictions linguistically and were frequently the most dominant participants in initiating both sequences and exchanges. Few exchanges during these sequences were completed verbally, although the percentage of verbally completed exchanges in both environments increased between the first and third grades. Because the children interacted with larger groups of children on the playground than at home, they contributed a smaller percentage of the total utterances in the former environment. On the playground, because of the number of children engaging in play, there was also a higher percentage of text-contingent exchanges than during play at home and a greater percentage of incomplete exchanges.

The syntactic complexity of the children's utterances during play tended to be greater than during the other speech activities. Even Elena, who had great difficulty in interacting in instructional sequences in the classroom, produced complex sentences during play. It should be noted that play with peers provided the children with opportunities to practice the initiation and directing role in interactions, a role which they did not assume frequently when interacting with adults. As a result, the syntactic complexity of their utterances tended to be greater, and their verbal repertoire was also greatly increased compared to the other environments.

As the children matured, the type of play in which they engaged changed considerably. In the third grade they engaged in more conversational interaction with their peers; they completed more exchanges verbally, they shared turn-taking more equitably and, thus, contributed a lower percentage of the total utterances than in the first grade. Their play began to resemble adult conversational interaction to a greater degree acquiring more of the intricacies of conversational structure.

Language Choice

Language choice during a given speech activity in a given communication environment varied across children and across years. In the instructional interactions of the first-grade classroom, both English and Spanish were used by the children and their teachers. However, the Spanish used varied from 14% of the utterances during the high-achieving boy's interactions to 55% during Elena's, in spite of the fact that all the children were judged to be Spanish dominant bilinguals with relatively the same degree of proficiency in English at the time they entered school. By third grade only English was used during classroom instructional sequences (as this was a transitional bilingual program), except in one child's case where Spanish was used 2% of the time by the children, primarily for parenthetical comments.

During first-grade play sequences at school, the use of Spanish also varied across children: from 94% of the utterances during Meme's interactions to 62% during Elena's. In the third grade the target boys interacted primarily in Spanish during play sequences while the target girls spoke primarily English.

Language preference also varied across children in the communication environment of the home. Spanish was the language of choice in all the children's home interactions except for the high-achieving girl's third-grade play sequences. In the home interactions which occurred in the third grade, more English was used than in the first grade in all contexts.

Thus, English as the primary language of the classroom begins to pervade the other communication environments, particularly by the third grade, especially when the topics of conversation deal with school-related activities or songs and games learned in the classroom. In almost all speech activities across all environments, there is a substantial decrease in the Spanish spoken and a corresponding increase in the English spoken between grades one and three.

Even at home by third grade, the high-achieving girl, Marta, found it difficult to conduct certain speech activities in Spanish. Here she attempts to relate the story of "The Three Little Pigs" to her younger playmate:

Marta: ¿Te digo una story? (inaudible) . . . muy larga.
[Shall I tell you a story? (inaudible). . . real long.]

Bueno. Son los "Three Little Pigs," okay?
[Okay. They're the "Three Little Pigs," okay?]

Three Little. . . but in Spanish, español.

Tres marranitos. . . uno le compró ladrillos a un señor. Otro le compró pipotes y otro le compró paja.
[Three little pigs. . . one bought bricks from a man. Another bought sticks and another bought straw.]

Y luego había un lobo. Y luego el lobo era muy bravo.
[And then there was a wolf. And then the wolf was very mean.]

Y luego el lobo dijo: "Open this door or I'll blow your house down."
[And then the wolf said: . . .]

No, no, dijo: "Abre esta puerta o si no te voy a tumbar la casa."
[No, no, he said: "Open this door or if not I'm going to knock down your house."]

And he wufted and he. . . y echó aire. . .

No, te lo voy a decir en Spanish, ah, en English, mejor.
[No, I'm going to tell it to you in Spanish, ah, in English, better.]

151

Marta then begins again and relates the entire story fluently in English.

Marta's storytelling experience contrasts greatly with Elena's in the third grade. Elena is asked to retell a story that has just been read to her by her teacher in English. Elena has great difficulty relating the story in English and constantly falters for lack of vocabulary. Of the four children, she is the one whose acquisition of English is extremely limited and who in addition does not learn to read in either language.

It is difficult to determine causes for such disparate linguistic behavior. Although the results of this study are not conclusive or subject to generality due to the limited size of the sample, it is apparent that, among the subjects studied, the high-achieving students played a more active role in discourse than the low-achieving students, contributing a higher percentage of total utterances across all environments and initiating a higher percentage of exchanges and sequences in all environments except the classroom. Thus, the high-achieving children were more likely to obtain the linguistic input required for continuing and rapid linguistic development. As mentioned earlier, the high-achievers' behavior differed most from the low-achievers' in the classroom environment. Since this was the main environment in which the children heard English, the ability to obtain linguistic input becomes extremely important.

For teachers, the results of this study have a number of practical implications for classroom instruction. First, since some children are slower than others to intuit the conventions of classroom discourse, it may be helpful if classroom teachers explain those conventions explicitly during the children's first months at school. This is most important in cases like Elena's where the child has limited or unsatisfactory interaction with adults in the home. It is also especially important in bilingual and/or immersion programs in which the children's main, if not only, exposure to the target language is during classroom interaction. If children are unaware of the conventions of classroom interaction, they will be less able to take advantage of the language input and, as a result, may fall behind from the start.

Second, teachers should be aware that a child's lack of performance during classroom instructional interactions is not necessarily indicative of the child's true verbal abilities. Elena, for example, was able to interact quite well with her peers. Her verbal ability, particularly in Spanish, was far greater than what was apparent during classroom interactions.

Third, teachrs need to provide opportunities for students to use more complex sentences and to develop their thoughts more completely. In the interactions we've seen, particulary those in the third grade classroom, the children were limited to answering the teacher's information questions. Almost all instructional questions required a simple one-word answer, although the teacher requested that the students answer in complete sentences. A more effective way to encourage students to answer in complete sentences is to ask them questions which require reasoning (e.g., Why do so many people visit the Hawaiian Islands every year?) rather than questions which can be answered with one or two words. Students need to practice the full range of language functions (e.g., narration, description) in both their native and target languages. We should beware of limiting them to answering simple questions.

A tremendous number of unknowns still exist in second language acquisition research. Further studies are needed to determine more completely the causes of individual differences in communicative competence particularly within the classroom environment. As we have seen, this is especially important for children whose main linguistic input in the second language occurs during classroom interactions. With this knowledge, teachers can begin to modify their instructional practices to meet the needs of low-achieving students, both monolingual and bilingual, and to help these students reach their full potential.

References

Bronfenbrenner, Urie. "The Experimental Ecology of Education." *Teachers College Record* 78 (1976): 157-204.

Bruck, Margaret, and Jeffery Shultz. "An Ethnographic Analysis of the Language Use Patterns of Bilingually Schooled Children." *Working Papers on Bilingualism* 13 (1977): 59-91. ERIC ED 140 664.

French, Peter, and Margaret MacLure. "Getting the Right Answer and Getting the Answer Right." *Research in Education* 22 (1979): 1-23.

Genishi, Celia. "Language Use in a Kindergarten Program for Maintenance of Bilingualism." *Bilingual Education*. Ed. Hernán Lafontaine, Barry Persky, and Leonard H. Golubchick. Wayne, N.J.: Avery, 1978. 185-190.

Gumperz, John. "Conversational Inference and Classroom Learning." *Ethnography and Language in Educational Settings*. Ed. Judith L. Green and Cynthia Wallat. Norwood, N.J.: Ablex, 1981. 3-24.

Guthrie, Larry F., and William S. Hall. "Continuity/Discontinuity in the Function and Use of Language." *Review of Research in Education*. Ed. Edmund W. Gordon. Washington, D.C.: American Educational Research Association, 1983. 55-77.

Legarreta, Dorothy. "Language Choice in Bilingual Classrooms." *TESOL Quarterly* 11.1 (1977): 9-16.

MacLure, Margaret, and Peter French. "A Comparison of Talk at Home and at School." *Learning through Interaction*. Ed. C. Gordon Wells. Cambridge: Cambridge University Press, 1981. 205-239.

McClure, Erica. "Formal and Functional Aspects of the Codeswitched Discourse of Bilingual Children." *Latino Language and Communicative Behavior*. Ed. Richard P. Durán. Norwood, N.J.: Ablex, 1981. 69-94.

Mehan, Hugh. *Learning Lessons*. Cambridge: Harvard University Press, 1979.

Morine-Dershimer, Greta, and M. Tenenberg. *Participant Perspectives of Classroom Discourse* (Final Report, Executive Summary, NIE 6-78-0161). Washington, D.C.: National Institute of Education, 1981. ERIC ED 210 107.

Philips, Susan U. "Participant Structures and Communicative Competence: Warm Springs Children in Community and Classroom." *Functions of Language in the Classroom*. Ed. Courtney Cazden, Vera John, and Dell Hymes. New York: Teachers College Press, 1972. 370-394.

Phillips, Jean M. "Code-switching in Bilingual Classrooms." Masters Thesis. California State University, Northridge, 1975.

Sapiens, Alexander. "The Use of Spanish and English in a High School Bilingual Civics Class." *Spanish in the United States: Sociolinguistic Aspects*. Ed. Jon Amastae and Lucía Elías-Olivares. Cambridge: Cambridge University Press, 1982. 386-412.

Shultz, Jeffrey. "Language Use in Bilingual Classrooms." TESOL Convention. Los Angeles, March 1975.

Wells, C. Gordon. *Language at Home and at School.* (Monograph). Bristol, England: University of Bristol, School of Education, Centre for the Study of Language and Communication, 1983.

_____. *The Language Experience of Five-Year-Old Children at Home and at School* (Coding manual). Bristol, England: University of Bristol, 1981.

_____, and Martin Montgomery. "Adult-Child Discourse at Home and at School." *Adult-Child Conversation.* Ed. Peter French and Margaret MacLure. London: Croom Helm, 1981. 210-243.

Wilkinson, Louise C., and Steven Calculator. "Effective Speakers: Students' Use of Language to Request and Obtain Information and Action in the Classroom." *Communicating in the Classroom.* Ed. Louise C. Wilkinson. New York: Academic Press, 1982. 85-99.

Willes, Mary. "Learning to Take Part in Classroom Interaction." *Adult-Child Conversation.* Ed. Peter French and Margaret MacLure. London: Croom Helm, 1981. 73-95.

Zentella, Ana C. "Code Switching and Interactions among Puerto Rican Children." *Sociolinguistic Working Paper No. 50.* Austin, Tex.: Southwest Educational Development Laboratory, 1979.

Age of Second Language Acquisition and Hemispheric Asymmetry

Stuart J. Anderson,
Rory P. Plunkett,
and E. John Hammond

On the face of it, the human body appears perfectly symmetrical. On closer examination, however, we find that there are many major physical differences between the two sides of the body. Here we look at the differences between the two sides of the brain, particularly the functional differences related to language. The question posed is "In carrying out a particular function, what is the relative degree of competence, dominance, or participation of the two sides of the brain?" A function that is conducted asymmetrically in the brain's hemispheres is called "lateralised."

As neuroscientists, we study the brain processes involved in acquiring and using a second language. Our findings, we hope, have something to offer the language teacher. Although our results are inconclusive, we hope they will provoke the reader to think of designing teaching programs that exploit the basic asymmetric functioning of the brain.

155

Morphological Asymmetries of the Human Brain

Without going into detail, we shall offer a brief review of the physical asymmetries of the brain. Many are visible to the naked eye. We find that the right hemisphere has more tissure and is heavier. Its frontal region is wider and extends further forward than the left. The left occipital pole is wider and protrudes more to the posterior, and the anteroparietal and posterooccipital regions are generally larger on the left.

Regions more specifically involved with language processing are also asymmetrical. Brocca's area, which has to do with language output, is larger and has greater folding on the left. The Sylvian fissure is generally longer on the left before it bends upward while the Sylvian point is generally higher on the right. These characteristics reflect the size of that portion of Wernicke's region known as the temporal planum, which has to do with the brain's phonological system. In

Stuart J. Anderson, Rory P. Plunkett, and E. John Hammond are members of the Department of Psychology of the University of Natal. The authors acknowledge the financial support of the Human Sciences Research Council in conducting their research. Opinions and conclusions expressed are the authors' and do not necessarily reflect those of the Human Sciences Research Council.

65%-90% of the cases, the planum is larger on the left (see Kolb and Wishaw; Bradshaw and Nettleson). No one has yet demonstrated that asymmetry of size is related to asymmetry of function.

It is tempting to view the findings, especially those relating to language, as more than just coincidence. But how do we explain that other primates also show these anatomical asymmetries? Perhaps these asymmetries of the language areas support cognitive processes necessary for language functioning. Two examples are the temporal sequencing of movements and an advanced ability to discriminate rapidly changing frequencies (Bradshaw and Nettleson).

Studies of Functional Asymmetry of the Brain

The functional asymmetries of the brain have been studied using a number of techniques. Clinical and invasive studies have included (a) individuals having brain damage, including commissurotomy and hemispherectomy, (b) anesthetic injected into the major blood flow to either side of the brain, and (c) unilateral electroconvulsive shock, in cases of psychiatric disorders. Experimental non-invasive techniques will be considered in greater detail, since they seem to be the most common techniques employed on normal populations and are also used in our research.

The dichotic listening technique (Kimura, "Cerebral Dominance") exploits the major input of the left ear to the right hemisphere and the right ear's major input to the left hemisphere. Thus, if information arriving at a given ear is relevant to the processing capacities of the corresponding hemisphere, then it should be perceived better. Indeed, it is found that the right ear, which feeds into the left hemisphere, is generally more efficient at perceiving verbal stimuli.

The visual-half-field technique (McKeever and Huling) used in our experiment relies on the projection of the two visual fields (not the two eyes) to the opposite hemispheres. Thus, if the individual fixes on a particular point in space, things appearing to the right of it (right visual field) project to the left hemisphere while things to the left (left visual field) project to the right hemisphere. If the stimulus is projected fast enough so the individual cannot move his eyes, then the stimulus will arrive in just one (i.e., the opposite) side of the brain.

The electrical-recording technique, also used in this experiment, relies on the brain's creation of electrical fields that can be detected and recorded by sensitive equipment attached to the scalp. The technique we used is called the *average evoked potential* technique. Since there is a relatively invariant response by the brain to a given stimulus under a given set of conditions, a stimulus can be presented and the brain's response recorded through electrodes placed on the scalp. The problem with this technique is that the ongoing background electrical activity of the brain (noise) swamps the evoked response (signal). In other words, there is a low signal-to-noise ratio. If we average many stimulations, however, the effect of random background noise is cancelled, allowing the evoked potential to emerge more strongly. From the size of the signal at different points, we can determine the locus of different brain functions.

Language Asymmetries

Although the cerebral hemispheres are functionally asymmetrical in a number of ways, we will address only the linguistic and paralinguistic differences. The overwhelming evidence supports lateralisation of language in the left hemisphere, at least in most adults. Just a few years ago it was thought that the right hemisphere is devoid of linguistic ability, but we now know that this view has to be modified.

The effects of brain damage and electrical stimulation of the brain have served to identify the language areas. Penfield and Roberts showed that stimulation within these areas produces temporary disruption of speech, while damage in this area may produce permanent impairment of language functions (Luria, *Higher Cortical Functions* and *The Working Brain*). The critical area is confined primarily to the lateral surfaces of the left hemisphere and includes the auditory receptive areas and adjacent zones as well as the inferior Rolandic and pre-Rolandic areas, which control the articulatory organs. Within these areas, phonological, syntactic, and lexical functions can be found (Marin et al.); the left hemisphere is almost entirely dominant for these functions.

Indications are that right-hemispheric language functions lag significantly behind those of the left hemisphere. Oral language is entirely absent. However, Zaidel has shown that the right hemisphere may function syntactically in 4 to 6 year olds. Further, lexical abilities are present so that on a picture vocabulary test, left-hemispherectomy patients are able to function at the level of an 8 to 16 year old. A dichotic-listening paradigm showed that the right hemisphere is less able to identify abstract nouns than the left hemisphere (McFarland et al.). Commissurotomised patients show an ability to comprehend words presented to the right hemisphere as long as they are concrete nouns, adjectives, and descriptive phrases. However, they are poor at comprehending verbs and abstract nouns (Marin et al.). It would appear that the nature of right-hemispheric language is limited to a rather impoverished lexicon.

It is apparent that the left hemisphere is dominant for the core language functions, such as phonology, syntax, and semantics. Paralinguistic functions, e.g., intonation, emotional tone, context, inference, and connotation, seem to be located in the right hemisphere. Patients with right-hemispheric lesions are impaired in producing and perceiving the correct emotional tone of linguistic utterances, react inappropriately to humorous material, interpret metaphors incorrectly, have difficulty solving anagrams and recognizing subtleties, and have a poor appreciation of antonyms, actor-object relations, and connotations of pictures (Moscovitch). Patients with damage to the right hemisphere seem to have no difficulty comprehending individual sentences, but they do have difficulty relating a sentence to a larger context, understanding its emotional connotations, and drawing the proper inferences from it. Without the right hemisphere, communication in its broadest sense may be impoverished.

Music, Emotions, and Abstractions

There is strong evidence to suggest that speech intonation and musical abilities are largely supported by the right hemisphere. Even though left-hemispheric damage may cause severe disruption of speech, intonation and singing may remain relatively intact. Conversely, right-hemispheric damage has been shown to cause a lack of speech intonation, and some patients even lose the ability to laugh and cry (Borod et al.). Likewise, right-temporal lobectomy impairs musical discrimination (Milner), and injections of anesthetic into the blood supply of the right hemisphere depresses singing but not speech (Bogen and Gorden). The dichotic listening technique has revealed a left-ear advantage in discriminating emotional tone in natural speech (Haggard and Parkinson) and in the identification of melody (Kimura, "Right-Left Differences").

The right hemisphere's ability in musical processing and intonation has been exploited in speech therapy with those having aphasia from left-hemispheric damage. Melodic intonation therapy accentuates the modulation of phrases and sentences, or patients may be taught phrases in song. The song is then gradually deemphasised (Helm-Estabrooks).

We have already seen that the right hemisphere appears to be concerned with judging the emotional tone of speech. Damage to the right parietal region may impair the identification and production of both negative and positive emotions, even though they are conveyed verbally (Heilman, Scholes, and Watson). There is also evidence that emotional expressions are better experienced by the right hemisphere when they are presented in the split-field mode (Ley and Bryden). An interesting finding is that the left side of the face is often most expressive of emotion (Moscovitch and Olds).

Much of language is figurative. Winner and Gardner found that individuals with right-brain damage tend to perceive things more literally than control subjects. Similarly, right-brain-damaged individuals have difficulty appreciating humour, often missing the point of cartoons or jokes (Gardner et al.). The argument is that they do not integrate or perceive details in context and so miss the punch line.

There is strong evidence to suggest that the right hemisphere specialises in visual imagery (Humphrey and Zangwill; Penfield and Perot; Robbins and McAdam; Ley; and Bryden and Ley). Visual imagery may be strongly related to some language functions, as concrete words are more easily recognised when presented to the right hemisphere. There may be quicker access to the right-hemispheric lexicon since no phonological encoding takes place (Bradshaw). Imagery offers a mnemonic device to help verbal recall (see

Fitch-West). Concrete pictures are highly efficient at arousing both the visual and the verbal codes—indeed, concrete pictures have been used for the treatment of aphasics—and it does not take much imagination to realize that concrete pictures and encouragement to form images can help second language acquisition.

The point to remember is that while the left hemisphere is clearly concerned with core linguistic functions, the right hemisphere, with its paralinguistic functions, probably makes a real contribution to linguistic performance.

A Reexamination of the Nature of Hemispheric Differences

We have noted that brain functions tend to be asymmetrically distributed between the two hemispheres. However, there has been much discussion about fundamental functions that might distinguish the two hemispheres. It is popular, for example, to talk of the hemispheres' different cognitive styles, usually expressed in dichotomies such as verbal/non-verbal, diffuse/focal, serial/parallel, and analytic/holistic. These dichotomies probably miss the point. It is not so much a question of which hemisphere does the processing as the kind of processing done by each. Thus, verbal information may be processed by both the left and right hemispheres. The left hemisphere analyses the meaning of words and sentences while the right hemisphere concerns itself with the meaning of words and sentences in context.

A good example to demonstrate this point is facial recognition. Because the best strategy is to perceive the face as a whole, this function is supposed to be located in the right hemisphere. The dominance of left or right hemisphere in perceiving faces depends on the recognition strategies used. Ross and Turkenitz (see Segalowitz) presented faces for identification in the left and right visual fields. Some individuals were better in the left visual field, some were better in the right. In follow-up experiments, it was found that those who were better in the right visual field (left hemisphere) were disrupted by obscuring details on the face, such as moustache, eyebrows, and noses. Those who were better in the left visual field (right hemisphere) were disrupted by global changes made to the faces, such as inverting the face. It appears that the left hemisphere is sensitive to details or specialises in analysing a stimulus configuration, while the right hemisphere is sensitive to the overall pattern or specialises in holistic processing.

Whatever the validity of the descriptive terms used to differentiate hemispheric functioning, there is general support for the conclusion that the two hemispheres proceed in different ways. In any situation, both hemispheres are usually operative and contribute to the task. Under certain circumstances a given strategy may be most appropriate, and one or the other hemisphere will dominate in pursuing this strategy.

With this background information, we are in a position to com-

159

ment on the theory and research in the neuropsychology of bilingualism.

Theory and Research in the Neuropsychology of Bilingualism

A large part of the neuropsychological research into bilingualism has been concerned with the cerebral organisation or representation of two or more languages in the brain. The question frequently asked about polyglots is whether two or more languages occupy, or are mediated by, the same or different parts of the brain. Scovel, for example, maintains that we learn a second language in a manner anatomically different from that in which we learn our first language. He points out that in first language learning, associations are made primarily between object and name whereas, in second language learning, the key process is to translate from one language to the other without reference to the actual world of objects. Lambert and Fillenbaum distinguish between compound and coordinate bilinguals. In a *compound bilingual*, the two languages are so well integrated as to be neuropsychologically indistinguishable. In a *coordinate bilingual*, the two languages are maintained as distinct entities using two separate brain systems. There is some controversy about which type actually occurs, or whether they both do. There are both clinical and experimental approaches to be considered in addressing this problem.

Clinical Evidence

160

The clinical approach has largely looked at polyglot aphasics. Differential impairment or recovery would suggest that the two languages are dependent on different brain structures. Equivalent impairment or recovery would be evidence for identical brain systems. There is evidence that language dissociation does occur among bilingual aphasics. Albert and Obler estimate the incidence of these differential aphasic patterns at 58%; Paradis estimates a 45% occurrence. Galloway, writing in *Language Learning*, and Vaid and Genesee, writing in the *Canadian Journal of Psychology*, point out that these projections are probably inflated because it is the unusual and interesting cases that get reported. Studies on unselected cases produce more modest figures. Charlton reports two out of nine cases, and Nair and Virmani report two in thirty-three cases.

More specific hypotheses about the organisation of bilinguals' brains have been suggested by Paradis, by Obler et al., and by Sussman et al. These researchers predict greater right lateralisation of language or less-complete left lateralisation. Stated differently, they propose that at least one language is represented bilaterally. If language in bilinguals is less left-lateralised than in monolinguals, one would expect to find a higher frequency of language impairment in bilinguals with damage to the right side of the brain. Indeed, polyglot aphasics have a higher incidence of right-hemispheric damage than monoglots. Taking a retrospective look at 102 polyglot aphasics, Galloway found 15% had right-side lesions, whereas only 2% of monolingual controls manifested right-side lesions. Vaid and Genesee are not convinced, claiming that differential organisation of language among polyglots is probably not the rule but is dependent on a number of factors, such as language-specific effects, acquisitional factors, and affective factors.

Experimental Evidence

We now turn to the experimental evidence for greater right-hemispheric involvement in second language processing. Once again the picture is not a simple one; conclusions have to be qualified by a number of variables and their interactions. We have already noted the theories on distinctive hemisperic functioning. We concluded that the hemispheres are distinct, not because of the type of stimuli they process (e.g., verbal or nonverbal) but because of the way, (e.g., holistic or analytic) in which information is processed. Thus the same information can be processed by both hemispheres in different ways.

Language cannot be seen as a discrete process in the left hemisphere alone. Rather, language consists of many interrelated cognitive processes, some performed by the left and some by the right hemisphere. We should not be so concerned whether the languages of a bilingual are processed by different hemispheres. We should ask instead which hemisphere would be brought into operation according to the demands placed on the individual. The important factors that determine hemispheric involvement have been well and comprehensively discussed by Galloway, by Obler, and by Vaid and Genesee and include (a) language-specific factors, (b) acquisition factors, (c) cognitive-strategy effects, (d) proficiency factors, and (e) sociolinguistic factors. In this study we are interested in some of the factors that affect the acquisition of a second language. We shall consider age of acquisition, stage of acquisition (or proficiency), manner of acquisition, language-specific characteristics, attitude, and sex.

161

Age of Acquisition

During the early stages of development, the brain is "plastic" enough to recover a function after damage has caused its loss. The younger the child, the greater the recovery after damage to the left hemisphere. After puberty there is little recovery, and there may be reduced plasticity from as young as five years.

If two languages are acquired simultaneously in infancy, both probably follow the same course that a single language would at that age, i.e., bilateral representation followed by progressive lateralisation to the left hemisphere. A second language acquired after the loss of cerebral plasticity will be subject to different cerebral organisation. Both Galloway ("Convolutions of a Second Language") and Vaid and Genesee, ("Neuropsychological Approaches to Bilingualism") suggest that second language acquisition involves different processing strategies at different stages of development. Early in life, left-hemisperic strategies tend to predominate. Later, however, with reduced plasticity and the development of paralinguistic skills, there is a bias toward right-hemispheric strategies, as confirmed by a study by Genesee et al. using evoked-potential measures. Subjects responded to taped stimuli by pressing a button. In this study, the balanced bilinguals were divided into three groups on the basis of age of second language acquisition. When those who had acquired the second language during adolescence listened to either language, they showed an earlier N100 peak in the right hemisphere than in the left hemisphere. Those who had learned the second language in infancy or childhood showed a faster N100 peak in the left hemisphere in either language condition. This difference implied that the adolescent learners employed right-hemisphere strategies when they processed language in this identification task. Though Obler suggests that a simple proficiency difference among the groups (adolescent learners being less proficient) could have accounted for the findings, Vaid and Lambert replicated Genesee's findings, showing more right-hemispheric involvement the later the second language was acquired. It should be noted, however, that there is also evidence against differential involvement of the two hemispheres as a function of age of acquisition (see Vaid and Genesee).

Stage of Acquisition

Early during second language acquisition, the cognitive strategy is probably right-hemisphere related but later gives way to left-dominant strategy. The speech production of beginning second language learners, adults as well as children, consists of highly contextualised, formulaic utterances. The right hemisphere is quite capable of overlearned verbal responses, such as days of the week and swearing (we know this from aphasics with left-hemispheric damage). If second language learning, whether early or late, is conducted in a formal setting with the emphasis on rote learning, the right hemisphere is likely to be involved.

Speech comprehension relies on prosodic rather than phonetic features: pragmatic rather than syntactic information and content rather than function words (see Vaid and Genesee). Further, early learners are known to understand by recognizing a few words and guessing the rest. This ability to discern meaning from both linguistic and non-linguistic context is within the capabilities of the right hemisphere.

Gaziel et al. tested right-handed Israeli school children from the seventh, ninth, and eleventh grades. Hebrew was their native tongue, and English was begun in the fifth grade. English and Hebrew words were shown in the left or right visual fields. Most subjects revealed a right-visual-field effect in Hebrew while in English the left visual field emerged, most evident in the seventh grade subjects and diminishing in the higher grades. Vaid and Genesee comment on four studies that suggest that right-hemispheric involvement may persist even in the final stages of second language acquisition (Genesee et al.; Gordon; Vaid and Lambert). Gordon, Kershner and Jeng, Hardyck, and Tzeng and Wang, however, find that not all the evidence supports the proficiency or stage-of-acquisition hypothesis.

Probably one of the major points to be made is that after plasticity is lost, the general tendency to use the right hemisphere (evident early in second language acquisition) may persist since there may be an inability to transfer to a left-hemispheric strategy.

Manner of Acquisition

When discussing hemispheric domination, formal and informal language learning must be distinguished. The formal mode emphasises the structure of language and its rules. Such a method usually involves rule specification and drilling. In informal learning, the individual communicates naturally and is more concerned with content than form. When the formal mode of instruction is used, there is continual monitoring or evaluation of the process according to learned rules. This analytic process is more left-hemisphere related. Informal learning involves contextual information, intonation, facial expression, and so forth. This holistic process is right-hemisphere related.

When Kotik (see Segalowitz) compared Russian-Estonian bilinguals on a dichotic task in both languages, he observed that the Estonians showed a larger left-hemispheric advantage than the Russians. The two groups learned the second language differently: the Russians learned Estonian in everyday circumstances; the Estonians learned Russian only in school. Using a dichotic listening procedure, Gordon showed that Hebrew speakers who learned English as a foreign language in Israel did not show reduced language laterality. Hebrew speakers who had spent many years abroad in English-speaking countries showed lower laterality scores. There are of course other factors which affect the lateralisation of languages, but these will not be considered in detail.

Language-Specific Characteristics

Structures inherent in the languages of the bilingual may be conducive to right-hemispheric involvement. Reading scan, which varies among languages, is an important factor in speed of information processing fed to the right- or left-visual field. For example, for left-to-right scanning, information on the right will be perceived faster and hence is confounded with laterality factors. For right-to-left scanning, as in Yiddish or Hebrew, information in the left-visual field will be perceived faster. It is found, however, that reading scan alone cannot account for laterality differences (see Obler, 55).

Rogers et al. suggest that the Hopi language is closely associated with the perceptual world whereas English is not. As Hopi elicits appositional thought whereas English elicits propositional thought, Hopi

163

should be more related to right-hemispheric functioning and English to the left hemisphere. Monitoring the EEG of Hopi-English bilinguals listening to taped folk tales in Hopi and English revealed greater right-hemispheric suppression of alpha activity for Hopi than for English.

Vowel characteristics of the language also affect hemispheric involvement. In Japanese and in Polynesian languages, vowel sounds can be legal words and would therefore be processed in the left hemisphere. Since vowel sounds tend to comprise only part of most words in European languages, they may be processed by the right hemisphere (see Tsunoda, in Vaid and Genesee). Note, however, if the vowel sounds are reduced in length so that they are equal to those normally found in speech, then a left-hemispheric dominance resumes, probably because the brain now interprets them as part of the language system (Darwin).

Attitude

Polyglot aphasics' differential recovery of languages may be the result of associated positive and negative affect associated with the languages. Research with neurologically intact individuals has demonstrated the importance of affective variables, in particular, positive attitudes towards second language learning. Vaid and Genesee have reviewed research on attitude, so we shall not do so here.

Sex

Although Gordon ("Cerebral Organization in Bilinguals") and Vaid and Lambert ("Differential Cerebral Involvement") have emphasised its importance, the determinant of sex has received little attention in the neuropsychology of bilingualism. There is evidence for differences in morphology of brain structure between the sexes (Witelson and Pallie). Wada, Clarke, and Hamm indicated that the planum temporalum is larger on the right in the female than in the male, suggesting less asymmetry in the female. This assertion accords with the functional findings that females are less lateralised than males (Hughes; Tucker), suggesting bilateral representation of most functions in the female's brain. Among bilinguals, females appeared to rely less than males on the left hemisphere in analysing the meaning of French and English words (Gordon; Vaid and Lambert). It is possible, therefore, that females may show enhanced right-hemispheric involvement in the acquisition and use of their second language.

Recapitulation

The material we have reviewed so far clearly demonstrates that the left hemisphere is specialised in linguistic functions while the right hemisphere is more concerned with the so-called paralinguistic functions. Individuals acquiring a second language may find that they must revert to these non-lingual skills in order to discern what is being said to them or what they read. In other words, they may rely on the non-linguistic context, especially if the language is acquired in an informal setting. Such skills use linguistic context, intonation, facial expression, and the integration of these elements. Right-hemispheric involvement may therefore be a component in second language acquisition. Since females show less hemispheric lateralisation than males, perhaps this sex difference may be enhanced in learning another language. As proficiency increases, however, the individual relies more on linguistic skills than on paralinguistic elements.

We have also noted that some individuals may never lose the tendency to rely on the right hemisphere when using a second language. These individuals have probably acquired their second language after puberty. Since this timing coincides with the loss of cerebral plasticity, perhaps the reason for persistence of right-hemispheric involvement is that the brain has difficulty incorporating the language-specific characteristics of the second language into the existing language system. On the other hand, perhaps once such right hemispheric skills are acquired and used, it may simply be a case of not being able to kick the habit.

How Neuropsychology Can Contribute to Second Language Teaching

Especially in the early stages of second language acquisition, the right hemisphere is responsible for many of the paralinguistic functions that may make sense of a segment of speech or text. How would one go about "heightening" right-hemispheric involvement in second language acquisition? Perhaps one could incorporate in one's teaching the type of stimulation known to affect the right hemisphere. In a treatment paradigm for aphasics Fitch-West suggests:

> The answer. . .is to use naturalistic, conversational settings that are highly redundant and have rich contexts so that the patient is able to extract as much as possible from the non-linguistic context itself. . . . The patient can call upon holistic processing strategies which will help him gain an intuitive grasp of what is happening. As. . .[It is the right] . . .hemisphere that can recognize melodic contours, facial expressions, emotions and the like, it would be helpful to be extraordinarily expressive vocally and facially in this naturalistic setting. (217)

An Experiment concerning Hemispheric Processing of Words from Different Languages

Our experiment was designed mainly to look at the effects of age of acquisition and of sex on the differential involvement of the two hemispheres in second language acquisition. We wanted to rectify the failure of Genesee et al. to account for the variable of sex. To do this we included sex as a relevant independent variable in our study. In addition, we felt we should take the opportunity to investigate the spatial and temporal order of language processing in bilinguals. As mentioned earlier, evoked potentials tell us something about the

165

temporal order of information processing and its location in the nervous system. In other words, a stimulus evokes a series of voltage "bumps" that represent the temporal order of processing. Further, the shape and size of these bumps may vary with respect to location in the nervous system (see figure 2).

The languages we used for our study were English and Afrikaans, both official languages in South Africa and compulsory subjects in the school curriculum. Of interest to us is the fact that some words look the same in the two languages but differ in meaning (e.g., "loop" in Afrikaans means "walk"). The only way that such words can signify meaning is if the subject knows which language is being used. Since some evoked potentials are sensitive to the physical structure of the stimulus, we felt that by using such ambiguous words the differences that would arise in the evoked potentials would be due only to their "accessed" meanings.

If a particular hemisphere is alerted or "primed" by telling the subject which language is being used, we might expect the right hemisphere to show greater response to the second language while the opposite should be true for the first language. Since early processing of information in the nervous system is probably of simple physical features such as shape or size of the stimulus (Hillyard and Woods; John) we might expect little difference between the languages using ambiguous stimuli. On the other hand, since the appropriate hemisphere is primed, it is possible that even at the earliest levels of processing we may find language differences.

Our subjects were 18 young adult bilinguals (somewhat more fluent in English than Afrikaans). On the basis of their age at the time of second language acquisition, they were divided into three groups of six: (a) "infant bilinguals" who acquired both languages at the same time in infancy, (b) "childhood bilinguals" who acquired Afrikaans between the ages of 6 and 12, and (c) "adolescent bilinguals" who acquired Afrikaans after the age of 12.

Stimuli were presented on a visual display unit (VDU). The evoked potentials were recorded on a Medelec ER94 averager interfaced to a BBC microcomputer. The microcomputer controlled the sequence of trials, generated and displayed the words, and stored the evoked-potential traces. The arrangement is depicted in Figure 1.

Stimulus material consisted of eight common English four-letter words and their Afrikaans translations. These were unambiguous across languages: no Afrikaans or English word was also a word in the other language. A further eight were ambiguous across languages: they could have been English or Afrikaans (though they would have different meanings in each language). See Table 1.

The procedure involved placing four active electrodes on the scalp in standardized positions (01, 02, P3, P4). Two electrodes were placed on each hemisphere, one at the lower end and one at the higher end of the assumed information processing system. Recordings were taken from all four electrodes simultaneously under four different experimental conditions. In this way, sixteen separate, averaged traces were obtained and stored on a floppy disc for later manipulation and analysis.

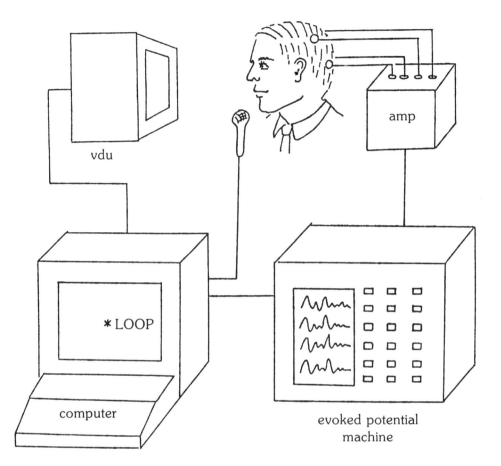

Figure 1. The experimental setup. The computer displayed a word on the VDU and triggered the averager. The subject pronounced the word, activating the next presentation.

Table 1. Stimulus Words Used in the Experiment

Unambiguous Words		Ambiguous Words*
English	Afrikaans	
take	neem	gang
read	lees	kind
show	toon	stem
side	kant	slim
city	stad	bang
turn	keer	held
wood	hout	loop
cold	koud	skip

*Ambiguous words are those that can be read, albeit with different pronunciation and meaning, in both languages.

The subject sat 50cm from the VDU, fixing on a point in the middle of the screen. Words were flashed in random order for 200 milliseconds (msec) to the left or to the right of this point. For each block of word presentations, the subject was told whether the stimulus was to be English or Afrikaans but not whether it was ambiguous. The subject responded by saying the word as it was presented. A voice-activated switch then initiated the cycle for the next word. Each block thus used words in one of the two languages. Eight of the words were unambiguous and eight were ambiguous. Each word was presented three times in each hemifield. These combinations were presented in random order and yielded 96 presentations per block.

One of the less central findings of our study suggests that there is a marked difference in the proficiency of brains relative to sex. Figure 2 clearly demonstrates that females not only respond more intensely to verbal stimuli but also process verbal stimuli much faster than males.

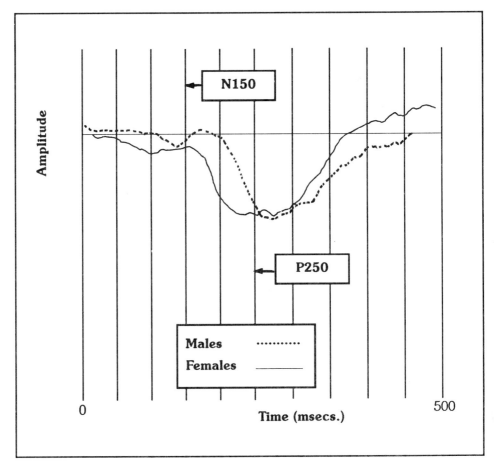

Figure 2. Average evoked potentials for male and female participants. The amplitude is in arbitrary units, with a peak-to-trough displacement of about 100 microvolts. The female trace shows evidence of more rapid response to stimulation of the order of 25-30 msec.

In Figure 3 responses in the brain's parietal locations are shown for ambiguous and unambiguous stimuli; each of these categories is further divided into relatively early and relatively late evoked potential components. Figure 2 demonstrates amplitude measurements in arbitrary units over a range of 100 microvolts. Negative deflections in amplitude (N) are conventionally displayed upward from 0; positive deflections (P) appear below the zero point. The numbers 0 - 500 refer to milliseconds. The early component is defined as a response from N150 to P250, and the late component was taken from P250 to the highest subsequent negative point. Figure 2 shows a strong P250 component for both men and women.

The *early components* of the evoked potential involve the processing of the superficial features of the stimulus (Hillyard and Woods). It may be that ambiguous words that do not differ superficially may be treated no differently in English and Afrikaans. On the other hand, since these words were presented in the context of a particular language and the subject was told what language to expect, the appropriate side of the brain may have been primed to respond to a given language.

Figure 3(a) shows that there is no substantial relationship between age of acquisition and responsiveness of the right hemisphere to cues in Afrikaans. Our hypothesis was therefore not supported. It is apparent, however, that there are definite group differences. Indeed, a three-way analysis of variance (ANOVA) showed that these differences were statistically significant on the left ($p = 0.02$) and on the right ($p = 0.045$). Such differences between the groups in either hemisphere irrespective of language are not easily explained. We may speculate that the tendency for Group 3 (the adolescent learners) to show greater responsiveness to both languages may have something to do with lower proficiency in the second language.

According to Hillyard and Woods, the *late components* involve the processing of deeper features of the stimulus, such as meaning. Figure 3(b) demonstrates a significant lateralised effect in relation to age of acquisition. The right hemisphere clearly showed more intense processing of English words in the adolescent learners but more intense processing of Afrikaans in the infant learners. A three-way ANOVA showed that this interaction between language and group was significant ($p = 0.044$). This finding contradicts the predicted outcome. There were no significant intergroup differences similar to those found for early-component responses.

The presentation of unambiguous words differed from that of the ambiguous words not only because the subject was primed about which language to expect but also because there were clear surface cues characteristic of the given language.

With respect to early components, Figure 3(c) shows no clear relationship between age of second language acquisition and the tendency to use the right hemisphere for second language processing. However, once again there are definite group differences. The adolescent learners (group 3) show greater responsiveness to both languages in both sides of the brain. Indeed, a three-way ANOVA

Figure 3. Amplitude measures of EPs in response to words in the two languages. Panels (a) through (d) show group by hemisphere differences. (a) and (b) show results for ambiguous words; (c) and (d) for unambiguous words. (a) and (c) are early component (i.e., N150)

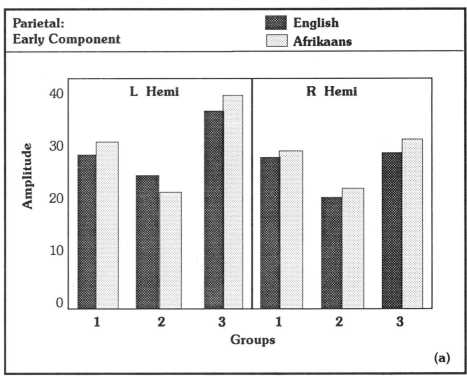

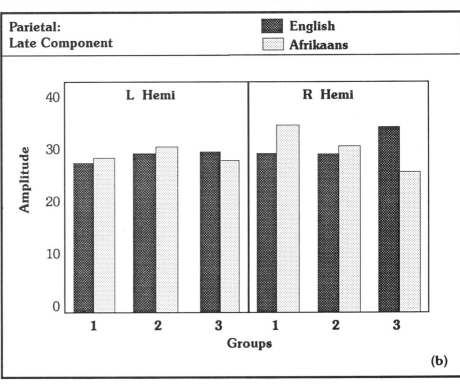

amplitudes; (b) and (d) are late component (i.e., P250) amplitudes. Panel (e) shows sex by hemisphere differences for unambiguous words, late component.

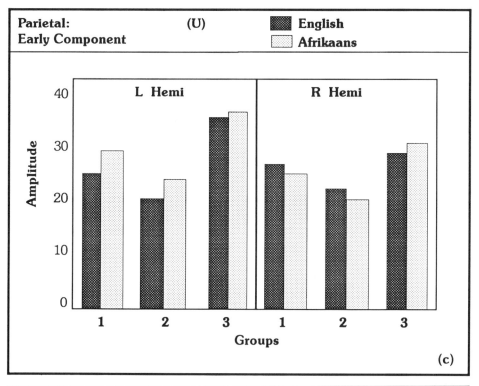

(c)

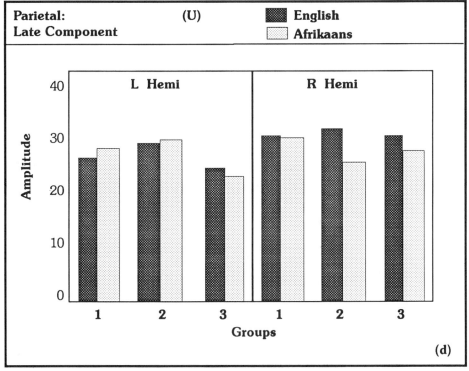

(d)

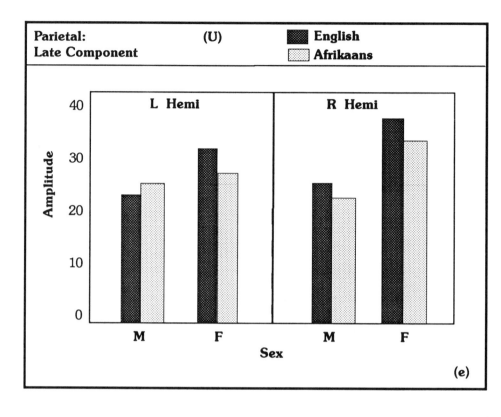

revealed a significant group effect on the left (p = 0.058) and on the right (p = 0.035). This occurrence in both hemispheres suggests that the adolescent learners are generally more responsive. Once again this could be due to a proficiency factor.

Looking at the late components in Figure 3(d), we find no significant relationship between age of acquisition, language, and intensity of processing. Neither were there any significant group effects. However from Figure 3(e) we see that females demonstrate a greater right-hemisphere responsiveness in both languages (p = 0.035). This did not prove true for the left hemisphere. This finding is consistent with the prevailing view of reduced laterality in females; the present study shows that this trend extends to English and Afrikaans language processing. In other words, females are more proficient than males in right-hemispheric linguistic ability and perhaps employ a processing strategy mediated by the right hemisphere. The female preference for processing meaning in the right hemisphere led Vaid and Lambert to conclude that there is an "intriguing possibility that the meaning is processed more efficiently in the right hemisphere for this group" (104).

Our conclusions must be tentative. Nevertheless, we have found supporting evidence for greater right-hemispheric involvement in second language processing. There are indications, however, that the adolescent learners allocated more processing resources to both languages, possibly because they were less proficient and put more effort into the task as a whole. Further, there is a sex differential in bilingual language processing; females make greater use of a right-hemisphere-based processing strategy.

We anticipate two major criticisms of our experiment. First, our groups were not balanced. The adolescent group had used the second language for less time than the others and had probably attained less proficiency. This led to a bias in the effort put into processing language in general. The evoked potentials we have considered vary in relation to the magnitude of resources allocated to the stimulus. Relatively unfamiliar stimuli may require greater resources than familiar ones. It is our contention that the adolescent learners were less proficient at Afrikaans than the other groups and therefore required greater neural resources for processing language in general. Second, the experimental conditions were so artificial that the usual paralinguistic functions were probably not invoked as they might have been in a more naturalistic setting. Thus, the visual presentation within an obvious linguistic and paralinguistic context may have failed to bring the right-hemispheric functions into operation. A design which purposely included a number of paralinguistic cues might have provided better support for our hypothesis. Spoken stimuli with language-characteristic prosodic cues, placed in a natural linguistic context such as a sentence, may be the sort of experimental setting that would lead to the predicted results.

References

Albert, Martin L., and Loraine K. Obler. *The Bilingual Brain: Neuropsychological and Neurolinguistic Aspects of Bilingualism.* New York: Academic Press, 1978.

Bogen, Joseph, and Harold Gordon. "Musical Tests for Functional Localization with Intracarotid Amobarbital." *Nature* 230 (1971):524-25.

Borod, Joan C., Elissa Koff, and Herbert S. Caron. "Right Hemispheric Specialization for the Expression and Appreciation of Emotion: A Focus on the Face." *Cognitive Processing in the Right Hemisphere.* Ed. Ellen Perecman. New York: Academic Press, 1983. 83-110.

Bradshaw, John L. "Right-Hemisphere Language: Familial and Nonfamilial Sinistrals, Cognitive Deficits and Writing Hand Position in Sinistrals and Concrete-Abstract, Imageable-Non-Imageable Dimensions in Word Recognition. A Review of Interrelated Issues." *Brain and Language* 10(1980):172-88.

_____, and Norman C. Nettleton. *Human Cerebral Asymmetry.* Englewood Cliffs, N.J.: Prentice-Hall, 1983.

Bryden, M.P., and Robert G. Ley. "Right Hemispheric Involvement in Imagery and Affect." *Cognitive Processing in the Right Hemisphere.* Ed. Ellen Perecman. New York: Academic Press, 1983. 111-23.

Charlton, M.H. "Aphasia in Bilingual and Polyglot Patients: A Neurological and Psychological Study." *Journal of Speech and Hearing Disorders* 29 (1964):307-11.

Darwin, C. "Ear Differences and Hemispheric Specialization." *Hemispheric Specialization and Interaction.* Ed. Brenda Milner. Cambridge, Mass.: MIT Press, 1975. 57-64.

Fitch-West, Joyce. "Heightening Visual Imagery: A New Approach to Aphasia Therapy." *Cognitive Processing in the Right Hemisphere.* Ed. Ellen Perecman. New York: Academic Press, 1983. 215-28.

Galloway, Linda M. "The Convolutions of a Second Language: A Theoretical Article with a Critical Review and Some New Hypotheses towards a Neuropsychological Model of Bilingualism and Second Language Performance." *Language Learning* 31 (1982):439-64.

Gardner, Howard, Paul K. Ling, Laurie Flamm, and Jen Silverman. "Comprehension and Appreciation of Humorous Material following Brain Damage." *Brain* 98 (1975):399-412.

Gaziel, T., Loraine K. Obler, Shlomo Bentin, and Martin L. Albert. "The Dynamics of Lateralization in Second Language Learning." Paper presented at the Boston Univ. Conference on Language Development, 1977.

Genesee, F[red], J[osianne] Hamers, W[allace E.] Lambert, L. Manonen, M[ichael] Seitz, and R[ichard] Starck. "Language Processing in Bilinguals." *Brain and Language* 5(1978):1-12.

Geschwind, Norman. "Asymmetries in the Brain: New Developments." *Orton Society Bulletin* 29(1979):67-73.

_____, and Walter Levitsky. "Human Brain: Left-Right Asymmetries in Temporal Speech Region." *Science* 161(1968):186-87.

Gordon, Harold W. "Cerebral Organization in Bilinguals." *Brain and Language* 9(1980):255-68.

Haggard, Mark P., and Alan M. Parkinson. "Stimulus and Task Factors as Determinants of Ear Advantages." *Quarterly Journal of Experimental Psychology* 23(1971):168-77.

Hardyk, Curtis, Ovid J.-L. Tzeng, and William S.-Y. Wang. "Cerebral Lateralization of Function and Bilingual Decision Processes: Is Thinking Lateralized?" *Brain and Language* 5(1978):56-71.

Heilman, Kenneth M., R. Scholes, and Robert T. Watson. "Auditory Affective Agnosia." *Journal of Neurology, Neurosurgery and Psychiatry* 38(1975):69-72.

Helm-Estabrooks, Nancy. "Exploiting the Right Hemisphere for Language Rehabilitation: Melodic Intonation Therapy." *Cognitive Processing in the Right Hemisphere*. Ed. Ellen Perecman. New York: Academic Press, 1983. 229-40.

Hillyard, Steven A., and David L. Woods. "Electrophysiological Analysis of Human Brain Function." *Handbook of Behavioural Neurobiology*. Vol. 2, Neuropsychology. Ed. Michael S. Gazzaniga. New York: Plenum Press, 1979. 345-78.

Humphrey, M. E., and Oliver L. Zangwill. "Cessation of Dreaming after Brain Injury." *Journal of Neurology, Neurosurgery and Psychiatry* 14(1951):322-25.

Hughes, Mirinda. "Sex Differences in Brain Development: Process and Effects." *Brain and Behavioural Development*. Eds. John W. T. Dickerson and Harry McGurk. Glasgow: Surrey Univ. Press, 1982. 233-61.

John, E[rwin] Roy. *Neurometrics: Clinical Applications of Quantitative Electrophysiology*. Vol. 2, Functional Neuroscience. Hillsdale, N.J.: Erlbaum; New York: Wiley (Halsted), 1977.

Kershner, John, and Amy Gwan-Rong Jeng. "Dual Functional Hemispheric Asymmetry in Visual Perception: Effects of Ocular Dominance and Postexposural Processes." *Neuropsychologia* 10(1972):437-45.

Kimura, Doreen. "Cerebral Dominance and the Perception of Verbal Stimuli." *Canadian Journal of Psychology* 15(1961):166-75.

_____. "Left-Right Differences in the Perception of Melodies." *Quarterly Journal of Experimental Psychology* 16(1964):355-58.

Kolb, Bryan, and Ian Q. Wishaw. *Fundamentals of Human Neuropsychology*. San Francisco: W.H. Freeman and Co., 1980.

Lambert, Wallace, and S. Fillenbaum. "A Pilot Study of Aphasia among Bilinguals." *Canadian Journal of Psychology* 13(1959):28-34.

Ley, Robert G. "Cerebral Laterality and Imagery." *Imagery: Current Theory, Research, and Application*. Ed. Anees A. Sheikh. New York: Wiley, 1983. 252-87.

_____, and M.P. Bryden. "Hemispheric Differences in Processing Emotions and Faces." *Brain and Language* 7(1979):127-38.

Luria, Aleksandr R. *Higher Cortical Functions in Man*. New York: Basic Books, 1966.

_____. *The Working Brain*. Harmondsworth: Penguin, 1973.

Marin, Oscar S. M., Myrna F. Schwartz, and Eleanor M. Saffran. "Origins and Distribution of Language." *Handbook of Behavioural Neurobiology*. Vol. 2, Neuropsychology. Ed. Michael S. Gazzaniga. New York: Plenum Press, 1979. 179-213.

McFarland, K. M., L. McFarland, J. D. Bain, and R. Ashton. "Ear Differences of Abstract and Concrete Word Recognition." *Neuropsychologia* 16(1978):555-61.

McKeever, Walter, and Maurice Huling. "Lateral Dominance in Tachistoscopic Word Recognition: Performance Obtained with Simultaneous Bilateral Input." *Neuropsychologia* 9(1971):15-20.

Milner, Brenda. "Laterality Effects in Audition." *Interhemispheric Relations and Cerebral Dominance*. Ed. Vernon B. Mountcastle. Baltimore: Johns Hopkins Univ. Press, 1962. 177-95.

Moscovitch, M[orris]. "The Linguistic and Emotional Functions of the Normal Right Hemisphere." *Cognitive Processing in the Right Hemisphere*. Ed. Ellen Perecman. New York: Academic Press, 1983. 57-82.

_____, and Janet Olds. "Asymmetries in Spontaneous Facial Expressions and Their Possible Relation to Hemispheric Specialization." *Neuropsychologia* 20(1982):71-81.

Nair, K. R., and V. Virmani. "Speech and Language Disturbance in Hemiplegias." *Indian Journal of Medical Research* 61(1973):1395-1403.

Nottebohm, Fernando. "Origins and Mechanisms in the Establishment of Cerebral Dominance." *Handbook of Behavioural Neurobiology*. Vol. 2, Neuropsychology. Ed. Michael S. Gazzaniga. New York: Plenum Press, 1979. 295-344.

Obler, Loraine K. "Right Hemisphere Participation in Second Language Acquisition." *Individual Differences and Universals in Language Learning Aptitudes*. Ed. Karl C. Diller. Rowley, Mass.: Newbury House, 1981. 53-64.

_____, Robert J. Zatorre, Linda Galloway, and Jyotsna Vaid. "Cerebral Lateralization in Bilinguals: Methodological Issues." *Brain and Language* 15(1982):40-54.

Paradis, Michael. "Bilingualism and Aphasia." *Studies in Neurolinguistics*. Vol. 3. Ed. Haiganoosh Whitaker and Harry A. Whitaker. New York: Academic Press, 1977. 65-121.

Penfield, Wilder, and Phanor Perot. "The Brain's Record of Auditory and Visual Experience: A Final Summary and Discussion." *Brain 86(1963): 595-696*.

Penfield, Wilder, and Lamar Roberts. *Speech and Brain Mechanisms*. Princeton, N.J.: Princeton Univ. Press, 1959.

Robbins, Kenneth I., and Dale W. McAdam. "Interhemispheric Alpha Asymmetry and Imagery Mode." *Brain and Language* 1(1974):189-93.

Rogers, Linda, Warren Ten Houten, Charles D. Kaplan, and Martin Gardiner. "Hemispheric Specialization of Language: An EEG-Study of

Bilingual Hopi Indian Children." *International Journal of Neuroscience* 8(1977):1-6.

Scovel, Tom. "Foreign Accents, Language Acquisition and Cerebral Dominance." *Language Learning* 19(1969):245-53.

Segalowitz, Sidney J. *Two Sides of the Brain.* Englewood Cliffs, N.J.: Prentice-Hall, 1983.

Sussman, Harvey M., Philip S. Franklin, and Terry Simon. "Bilingual Speech: Bilateral Control?" *Brain and Language* 15(1982):125-42.

Tucker, Don M. "Sex Differences in Hemispheric Specialization for Synthetic Visuospatial Functions." *Neuropsychologia* 14(1976):447-54.

Vaid, Jyotsna, and Fred Genesee. "Neuropsychological Approches to Bilingualism: A Critical Review." *Canadian Journal of Psychology* 34(1980):417-45.

Vaid, Jyotsna, and Wallace E. Lambert. "Differential Cerebral Involvement in the Cognitive Functioning of Bilinguals." *Brain and Language* 8(1979):92-110.

Wada, Juhn A., Robert Clarke, and Anne Hamm. "Cerebral Hemispheric Asymmetry in Humans." *Archives of Neurology* 32(1975):239-46.

Winner, Ellen, and Howard Gardner. "The Comprehension of Metaphor in Brain Damaged Patients." *Brain* 100(1977):717-29.

Witelson, Sandra F., and Wazir Pallie. "Left Hamisphere Specialization for Language in the Newborn." *Brain* 96(1973):641-46.

Zaidel, Eran. "Auditory Language Comprehension in the Right Hemisphere following Cerebral Commissurotomy and Hemispherectomy: A Comparison with Child Language and Aphasia." *Language Acquisition and Language Breakdown: Parallels and Divergencies.* Eds. Alfonso Caramazza and Edgar B. Zurif. Baltimore: Johns Hopkins Univ. Press, 1978. 229-75.

Classroom Management: Maintaining a Viable Learning Environment

Donald R. Jacoby

Classroom management is very aptly defined by Daniel L. Duke in *Classroom Management: The Seventy-eighth Yearbook of the National Society for the Study of Education*: "Classroom management constitutes the provisions and procedures necessary to establish and maintain an environment in which instruction and learning can occur" (xii). The foreign language teacher in an intensive elementary foreign language program may wish to append to this otherwise accurate and all-encompassing definition "in a classroom full of lively, enthusiastic children, where instruction occurs in a new language." It is precisely here that managing a classroom in such programs distinguishes itself from classroom management in general and requires specific management techniques. For our purposes classroom management might be further defined as "constituting the provisions and procedures necessary to provide an environment where instruction occurs in the target language in an atmosphere where the young child feels adequately secure and comfortable enough to communicate in the target language."

This paper will enumerate the salient characteristics of the elementary school language learner and discuss their relevance to our particular task. In conjunction with this description, I shall propose specific classroom techniques that have proven particulary effective in an elementary school intensive language program. Finally, I shall examine the significance of the relationship between the adult teacher and the child, focusing on the relevance of this relationship to successful language teaching and learning.

Those programs offering intensive foreign language instruction at an early age, with continuity and articulation in later stages, appear to be most successful, i.e., the public school magnet programs in Cincinnati and Milwaukee as well as the French-English immersion programs in Canada. Most language educators would agree that the optimum age for beginning foreign language instruction is best stated by the well-worn adage "the sooner, the better." Of course, our reasons for supporting this statement may differ. Some might cite the child's innate ability to grasp foreign language, while others might attribute the success of such programs to the length of exposure to the

177

Donald R. Jacoby teaches second grade in the Fairview German Bilingual School, Cincinnati, Ohio.

foreign language where mastery is the result of constant exposure and practice over an extended period of time. Still others, including Ronald Macaulay, point out that the primary grade pupil is a likely candidate for foreign language instruction since the child is at a stage in linguistic development where communicative skills are being honed, thereby creating a desire to communicate. The foreign language teacher therefore exploits this natural desire as he directs his pupils' quest for mastery of the target language (29).

Given the optimum candidate for foreign language mastery, the task of the primary school foreign language instructor should be far less demanding and complex than that of our colleagues on the secondary and college level. However, this is not necessarily true. Anyone who has faced a classroom full of squirming, fidgeting yet eager first or second graders would support this statement.

It is the special task of the elementary school language teacher to harness the energy of his charges and channel it into effective foreign language acquisition. This goal needs to be accomplished in an environment where the exclusive use of the target language is a prerequisite for optimum second language learning. To accomplish this end, the instructor must employ specific techniques that capitalize on those characteristics of the child that facilitate teaching while controlling those that could impede the learning/acquisition process. The former include:

- natural curiosity
- lack of inhibitions
- appreciation of humor
- freedom from prejudices against other cultures and other languages
- willingness to experiment
- playfulness
- willingness to accept an adult as a model
- innate desire to please
- natural desire to communicate with others

At the other end of the spectrum are those attributes that could, if allowed to do so, impede the language learning process. These characteristics include:

- a relatively short attention span
- need for freedom of movement
- susceptibility to distraction from various sources
- undeveloped listening skills
- propensity for spontaneous, irrelevant outbursts
- ignorance of the rules of proper classroom behavior

In light of these categories, then, I propose teaching techniques that promote the establishment and maintenance of a viable learning environment in the elementary language classroom, by utilizing the natural tendencies of the primary pupil conducive to language learning and modifying those tendencies that negatively affect the teaching/learning process.

Returning to the original definition of classroom management, we note the important role of the word "provision" or "providing." This provision becomes the focal point of the following discussion concerning practical measures that ensure the proper environment in the classroom. The basic strategy is to establish a well-organized, structured classroom environment from the outset. On the first day of instruction, ground rules need to be stated, guidelines provided and daily routines established as a prerequisite for proper learning conditions. At this point, too, the concept of communicating in the target language should be introduced.

Here the teacher needs to rely upon the child's natural curiosity and desire to please. An attractive flag of the country in question can encourage cooperation. When the flag is standing in the classroom, the target language is spoken. Most children are interested in the attractive, strange flag, and are at the same time eager to find out about the country and the culture that it represents. It is usually accepted willingly as the official signal for speaking the target language.

Raising the flag is synonymous with transforming the American classroom into a cultural island where specific ground rules apply and a foreign langauge is spoken. Students begin to associate the teacher with the flag and the culture it represents. A routine should be established that allows individual children to raise and lower the flag at the appropriate times each day. Gradually, the children accept the significance of the flag and its importance in the daily routine and vehemently oppose the slightest deviation from the established routine. Children who either deliberately or inadvertently disregard the raised flag by speaking English are frequently subjected to a firm reprimand from their peers.

The development of good listening skills is an important ingredient in any teaching approach; however, it is especially critical in the foreign language classroom. Simply stated, listening is the prerequisite to speaking. It is in the development of listening skills that the foreign language instructor in the primary grades encounters significant obstacles, produced in part by the natural tendencies of the young child.

To ensure that the classroom is a place where children have the opportunity to hear what others say and to create an atmosphere conducive to productive, give-and-take conversation, an important ground rule needs to be established: a raised hand signifies the need or desire to speak. No one speaks without having first given the correct signal. Initially, this rule should be strictly enforced with gradual relaxation as the school year progresses so as not to stifle spontaneity.

Combat inattentiveness by involving as many children as possible in classroom activities and language drills. Elicit responses randomly so that children gradually learn the advantage of being alert. Move to a child who is obviously inattentive and touch her head or playfully pull an ear or a nose. Make some gesture that indicates to her that you are aware of her inattentiveness. Actions often speak louder than words, and a verbal reprimand may not be necessary.

Capitalize on the child's playfulness by conducting specific listening drills that are entertaining as well as instructional. Conduct a sound-discrimination drill where a sequence of correct sounds or words is followed by one that is incorrect. Recognition of the incorrect form is acknowledged by a clap or a hissing sound from the pupil or pupils.

Example: Teacher - "Kopf, Kopf, Kopf, Kopf"
Class - (silence)

Example: Teacher - "Kopf, Kopf, Kopf, Koff"
Class - "Pssst!" (or clap)

A simple ball game can further the development of listening skills while providing necessary physical activity for the youngsters. The teacher throws the ball to individual children who must count in sequence. They must be attentive in order to know the correct number in sequence. Any child failing to produce the correct response is eliminated from the game. The old standby "Simon Says!" lends itself well to the language classroom, fulfills basically the same purpose, and is very popular with the children.

Take whatever measures necessary to eliminate distractions. To eliminate outside noises, keep doors and windows closed, weather permitting. Ask colleagues in a diplomatic manner to refrain from interrupting language sessions. This same request should be made of office personnel.

Assist the pupils in developing a good listening posture: feet on the floor and hands resting on the desks. This guideline must be established so that children know what a good listening posture is. Obviously, we do not expect young children to sit at rigid attention for long periods of time. Therefore, the instructor needs to be flexible in the use of his ground rule but also must curtail flagrant violations at once so that a good listening atmosphere is maintained. When the teacher commands, "jetzt hört bitte gut zu!" [now listen carefully], it is reasonable to expect the children to assume a good listening posture.

The successful management of a classroom full of six- and seven-year-olds requires active and alert teachers prepared with a repertoire of activities enabling them to adjust to any given situation. A change-of-pace activity may be needed at a moment's notice when the instructor feels that a change in tempo is necessary to stimulate a lethargic group or awaken a drowsy, inattentive class on a warm spring afternoon. This repertoire should include various activities requiring some movement: calesthenics, counting/clapping exercises, songs with gestures, rapid-fire exchange drills, etc.

As mentioned previously, handling discipline problems while maintaining exclusive use of the target language requires some specific measures. Without disturbing the momentum of the class, the teacher needs to take immediate action to squelch any form of disruption. A fidgeting child is best controlled by swift action. The teacher moves briskly to the offender, places a hand on the child and demonstrates physically what is expected. Sometimes a hand placed on the head or on the hands is all that is needed to correct the child. Many times, just moving to the source of disruption is enough to restore order. At any rate, speed is of utmost importance. This may mean moving very rapidly from one end of the classroom to another and back again. Much energy is needed in extinguishing the sparks of disruption before they become a blaze that engulfs the entire class.

The need for quick, decisive action goes hand in hand with the need for brevity. The message needs to be succinct and easily understood. To accomplish this, the teacher should possess a certain number of phrases in the target language. They should implicitly state the teacher's expectations. Words and phrases such as "good, not good, stand up, sit down, quiet please," coupled with appropriate gestures readily convey the message while eliminating the need for lengthy explanations or reprimands.

Often a stern look of disapproval will suffice in calling a child back to order. A finger held up in warning accompanied by a brief verbal warning: "Vorsicht" [careful] serves the same purpose. A child who is unable to sit quietly can be asked to stand for a few minutes as a reminder of what is expected.

When all else fails and a child remains disruptive, inattentive, or uncooperative, the instructor removes the student from the classroom and communicates privately in the child's native language. This serves a dual purpose: the instructor is able to remove the source of the disturbance, yet need not compromise the principle of exclusive use of the target language in the classroom.

Conducting a language session of forty-five or fifty minutes in the target language is no easy task. The teacher is called upon to channel the energies of twenty-five to thirty active youngsters into structured activities that further the development of linguistic skills and meet the goals of the curriculum. Experience has proven that a lively approach with a variety of activities is needed to achieve this. Especially in the early stages of instruction, fifteen to twenty minutes is the maximum time to be spent on any one activity and even that should be one that the majority of the children enjoy. Except for writing and reading exercises introduced at later levels of instruction, brevity should be the keyword when introducing and reinforcing grammatical concepts, new vocabulary, and syntactic elements. Any scenario or drill that lasts longer than fifteen minutes runs the risk of being ineffective. Rather, one should concentrate on clear, concise conversational patterns in which pupils interact with one another as well as with the instructor.

When conducting language activities, the teacher should make an attempt to include as many children as possible. Begin an exercise with the ablest children serving as examples and then gradually allow others to participate. With encouragement, even the most reluctant child will usually welcome the opportunity to participate in a given activity. On the other hand, if a child is struggling, defensive, and intimidated, the teacher should not press the issue. It is far better to receive no response than to coerce an unwilling child into responding. This technique does not mean ignoring the child. It simply suggests waiting for an appropriate opportunity to allow the child to respond correctly. Elicit the correct reply from a confident student,

181

then allow the more reluctant child to repeat the correct response. Avoid intimidation whenever possible.

Adjusting to a child's sense of humor may require some effort on the part of the teacher. Children often find humor in situations that seem totally devoid of such to the adult. The teacher needs to accept children's humor, allowing them to laugh when it seems sincere. Laugh with them if possible. Rather than stifle the outburst which is usually contagious, patiently allow it to run its course and reestablish order by indicating that it is now time to settle down and return to the business at hand. Give a visual signal, turn the lights off, ring a bell, clap your hands, count to ten in the target language. Do whatever is necessary to regain the pupils' attention.

Because of the child's inherent playfulness, the use of puppets as an instructional prop can serve many useful purposes:

- Capturing the children's attention by appealing to their sense of humor and need for play, thereby serving as superb models for introducing scenarios and grammatical concepts.
- Serving as an acceptable extension of the instructor as controlling agents engaging in playful, humorous admonition.
- Helping the teacher overcome inhibitions when communicating with children on a child's level; sometimes outrageous, yet humorous statements emanate readily from the puppet's mouth, enlivening potentially monotonous exchanges.

The teacher can appeal even further to the child's sense of humor by including humorous items among classroom realia: one-legged dolls, trucks driven by dogs and cats (à la Richard Scarry).

Sometimes teachers might find themselves objects of the child's humor. While the older child will practice a certain amount of discretion when confronted by a potentially humorous situation, the younger child might react with child-like spontaneity to the teacher's disheveled hair, muddy shoes, stains on shirt, chalk on clothing, missing buttons, etc. In these instances the ability to laugh at oneself can be an invaluable asset for the teacher.

Once an atmosphere of discipline and control has been established, teachers can gradually relax their authority, step aside, and allow children to take over their role in the prescribed classroom scenarios. At this point creativity and spontaneity often develop while the teacher plays a secondary, supporting role removed from the scene of the action.

One of the keys to a successful foreign language program in the elementary school lies in focusing upon the world of children and addressing their needs, desires, and concerns. The foreign language teacher must be committed to identifying those characteristics that make the young child a willing and usually successful learner. Yet this journey into the world of the child is replete with a multitude of deterrents, for in no other phase of the education process is the age gap between teacher and pupil as great.

Not only is the adult teacher a great deal older than his pupil, but his physical superiority is also quite evident and potentially intimidating. If this physical superiority is misused by the adult, the goal of establishing a relationship based on mutual trust and respect may never be attained. In overcoming the age barrier, the adult teacher needs to step into the world of the child, to interact with pupils, and to become acutely aware of their specific likes and dislikes, their fears and frustrations. It is important to gain the child's trust, to demonstrate that you the adult, despite your intimidating physical superiority, care for each child, respect each's feelings, acknowledge each's problems and concerns.

That trust is enhanced by interacting with students outside the classroom. There might be an opportunity to observe them at play during the school day. Give them words of encouragement or consolation as they participate in games on the playground. Show your interest in their activities. Join in a game if invited, even if only for a short period of time. Show the child that you care by being a good listener. What may seem an extremely mundane or irrelevant matter to the adult may be of utmost importance to the child. Children are extremely sensitive to rejection, so if time prohibits you from listening at a given moment, tell the child when you will be available. Be sure to follow through with your intentions. Children take promises seriously and are affronted by a broken promise.

Extend your contact time with the pupils by accompanying classes on field trips or other school functions. Offer to step in for the classroom teacher if the need arises. Step into the everyday environment of your pupils. See how they function outside your classroom, how they interact with other adults and with their peers. Participate in class activities: holiday festivities, parties, sharing time, etc. Attend class plays and similar performances. Eat lunch with the children if the opportunity presents itself. Above all, let them see you as a person with many of the same needs and concerns.

While I advocate the development of mutual trust and respect, I am in no way suggesting unbridled permissiveness on the part of the teacher. On the contrary, from the outset, the teacher needs to establish authority. Certain decisions will, by necessity, be made by the teacher. The message should be made clear: we will work well together, we will enjoy each other, but I have certain expectations concerning behavior in my classroom and these expectations shall be met. Interact with the children, joke and laugh with them, share their thoughts and concerns as much as possible, allow them to express themselves freely, but set limits and above all never relinquish your authority.

In this presentation I have drawn upon my seven years' experience as a second-grade German instructor in the Cincinnati German Bilingual School. I have provided insights into the personality of the elementary school language learner and suggested practical methods for establishing and maintaining a lively, effective, child-oriented elementary school language classroom. My purpose has been to provide an impetus for the evaluation of one's own managerial skills in the classroom. By borrowing once again from Ronald Macaulay, I reiterate the thrust of this paper:

183

...since none of us adults knows much about how the child develops his or her linguistic competence, we can only try to provide an environment that best allows that development to take place. In the final analysis this probably means creating a situation in which the child can be his or her natural self: happy, curious, and talkative. At least we know in which direction we ought to move. (6)

Keeping this in mind, we press onward with the firm commitment to assist young children in their attempts to acquire a second language.

References

Duke, Daniel L., ed. *Classroom Management. The Seventy-eighth Yearbook of the National Society for the Study of Education, Part II.* Chicago: NSSE, 1979.

Macaulay, Ronald. *Generally Speaking: How Children Learn Language.* Rowley, Massachusetts: Newbury House, 1980.

Schuh, Hermann. *Komm Bitte! Ein Deutschkurs für Kinder.* München: Max Hueber Verlag, 1983.

"Syllabus: Level II" Fairview German Bilingual School. Cincinnati, Ohio, 1974. (unpublished)

Laying the Foundation: German in the First Grade

Marianne Ryan

As a six-year veteran of laying the foundation for German language skills with six- and seven-year-olds, I would like to record observations on the introductory phase of a program that has been functioning effectively for a decade. Since materials acquisition in this field presents a special problem, I would also like to share, in a brief annotated bibliography, what published teaching aids I have found to be specifically useful with school beginners.

Established in 1974 to promote voluntary racial integration in the large urban public school system of Cincinnati, Ohio, the German-English Bilingual Alternative School (GEBAS) set out to lure students from the entire school district to two centrally located, racially isolated neighborhood schools with declining enrollments by means of a unique offering: high-quality, intensive foreign language instruction beginning in the first grade.

All classes from kindergarten through grade five are now consolidated at Fairview School on Stratford Street in Clifton Heights, near the University of Cincinnati campus. Urban decay and regeneration are juxtaposed in the lower-middle-class area as they are within the school. Kindergarten and first grade classes occupy a "new" building, erected in 1957, bright, airy and clean but sterile and undistinguished, while the upper grades are housed in a separate building erected in 1888, a huge, ominous, turreted Cincinnati Gothic monstrosity, no doubt worthy of historical preservation. The small, bleak, black-topped playground, dwarfed by two huge television broadcasting towers, has recently been enhanced with sturdy climbing equipment, a gift of our superbly energetic parent organization. Fair is the view of the distant silvery bend of the Ohio River, shabby the immediate environment in which a venturesome program prospers.

While academic excellence has been a primary goal of GEBAS from the outset, selective admission by academic criteria has not been permitted. Neither language aptitude tests nor screening interviews are allowed. Aside from considerations of racial balance, students are admitted in order of application.

A few elementary statistics might sketch a profile of my present first

185

Marianne Ryan teaches first grade in the Fairview German Bilingual School, Cincinnati, Ohio.

grade class. In four first grade homerooms, 118 students commenced German in September 1984. At mid-year, the end of January 1985, 111 remain, with an average class size of 28. The sexes are equally distributed, girls having a majority of only one, and the races very nearly so: 45.9% are black, 2.7% are oriental, 51.4% are white. For 16.2% of the students, our "walkers," the neighborhood school has not closed but merely added "fringe benefits." Most students arrive by yellow bus from near and far, especially for those "fringe benefits." Among twenty-nine magnet programs available in 1984, they chose the German Bilingual Alternative. Why? In an informal letter/questionnaire which I sent to the parents of all first graders at the beginning of the school year, and to which 82.2% responded, by far the most frequently cited reason—by 57.7%—was the general academic reputation of the GEBAS program. Another 29.9% were convinced of the value of foreign language study at an early age, but only 8.3% admitted to any German being spoken in their home, while another 16.4% mentioned a German background or some other German experience. Thus, with fewer than one fourth of the students having any "German Connection," ours is not a bilingual maintenance program responding to the needs of a minority culture. Among the first graders, 15.5% have siblings or relatives already in the program, and for 12.4% it was the proximity of the school that mattered most. (Since several reasons were given by many, these percentages total more than 100.)

The first grade student body reflects our modern fractured society: fewer than one half of the children (47.7%) live in a "traditional" family with both their parents. (Another 2.7% have step-parents.) Considerable financial distress is evidenced by the fact that 45.9% receive free and 54% reduced-fee lunch at school, totalling 51.3% on nutrition assistance. The occupational status of parents varies greatly: from construction worker to construction company owner, from university professor to pre-school teacher, from sales clerk to sales manager, from police sergeant to social worker, from housewife to computer programmer, from mechanic to engineer, from attorney to activity therapist, from the self-employed to the unemployed, from investment counselor to clergyman to funeral director. Since students' cumulative records are frequently imprecise, incomplete and out-of-date, a socio-economic classification was not attempted. Suffice it to say that the range is great.

In academic achievement, as measured by the Metropolitan Reading Readiness Test (administered to kindergartners in the spring of each year), the range is equally great. In a normally distributed population 23% would fall into the *below* average range (stanines 1–3), 54% into the *average* range (stanines 4–6), and 23% into the *above* average range. Thus 79.3% of our present first graders stand at or above average in achievement, only slightly better than the national average of 77%. The first grade student body is not elitist, despite a greater than normal share of the ablest students; 17.1% are expected to be retained, while 10.8% are presently repeating. I perceive a high correlation between general academic achievement and first grade German language proficiency. While even the best first graders are slow in acquiring vocabulary and syntax, those experiencing difficulty in most aspects of school work are rarely outstanding students of German. In this diversity lies the challenge!

While funding for the German bilingual program has never been luxurious, it has been consistent, even in times of extreme fiscal emergency. Super-numerary language specialists represent the costliest recurrent budget item. The initially very generous appointment of two full-time coordinators made it possible to overcome two obstacles to long-term success: a scarcity of teachers with ideal formal qualifications and a dearth of published language material in German suitable for young children. In 1974 Margith Stern and Larry Stevenson were real innovators, though nowadays their bilingual concept seems conservative, little more than an expansion of earlier FLES programs. However, their model of fractional immersion, fully integrated into the schedule and curriculum and carefully programmed for continuity and articulation, is seen by the GEBAS community as the key to balanced success for our type of student.

In first grade an average of 50 minutes per day is allocated to German instruction. The entire class has 30 minutes of German in the afternoon, and on alternating mornings about half the class is "immersed" for another 40 minutes, the others remaining to be instructed in English. Morning groups are selected by the homeroom teacher to coincide with reading or mathematics groupings. In first grade both homogeneous and heterogeneous morning combinations result. All are exposed to essentially the same, entirely oral curriculum. Comprehension and speaking skills are fostered in first grade. Reading and writing are deliberately not taught until second grade. Four first grade classes fill the teaching schedule of one itinerant language specialist with a fixed abode: a separate, full-sized classroom that can be arranged to suit distinct pedagogical and aesthetic needs. Our younger students migrate, not the teacher, as in earlier years of the program.

All German specialists appointed to our program combine high academic qualifications (M.A. minimum) with genuine bilingual proficiency. None, however, has elementary certification. To remedy the lack of age-appropriate experience and materials, the original coordinators began the time-consuming but ultimately rewarding tradition of writing, for each grade level, a voluminous lesson-plan syllabus (of some 200 pages each) containing precise directives for daily instructional activities. Given the liberty to adjust, abridge, extend, or supplement the curriculum, teachers appreciate the syllabus for the consistency, and assurance it provides—and the labor it saves.

The curriculum developed by Stern and Stevenson, the thrust of which has not been changed in recent revisions, is an eclectic one. Linguistically, methodologically, and philosophically, it is most heavily indebted to Hermann Schuh's *Komm bitte!* project, the *Grundkurs* of which forms the structural framework of our foundation year. Originally developed for the instruction of the children of foreign workers in German-speaking countries, the audio-lingual course is equally suitable for teaching German as a second language to elementary school children in foreign countries. It assumes no prior knowledge of German; neither does our first grade curriculum. Approximately one third of the first graders are new to the school, the remainder repeating the year or graduating from our kindergarten, where German instruction is limited to one hour per week. The learning of colors, numbers, songs, and games breaks the ground, but the foundation for coherent discourse is not laid until first grade.

Komm bitte! implicitly embraces—but with moderation—many second language teaching techniques being advocated at present; its action-centered fun-and-games approach is nonthreatening and communicative, its psychology is appealing to seven-year-olds, its limited scope is manageable within the time frame for most of our students. Its carefully structured progression guides the teacher in "direct method" presentations that do not overwhelm and discourage school beginners.

The linguistic material presented in the 24 units of the *Grundkurs* is summarized in large type on five small pages of the "Einführung" (pp. 7-11). It provides the core for daily lessons of about 25 minutes' duration, each over an entire school year. Its judicious selectivity strives to afford maximum opportunity for correct but genuine communications. Authentic quality matters to Schuh, not inaccurate quantity. This linguistic material is presented in cohesive models: phrases and short sentences that form building blocks for dialogues gradually increasing in length and complexity. Puppets frequently aid in conveying these dialogues in dramatic, supposedly self-explanatory situations. These are then imitated by the children, first chorally, then individually, acted out, re-combined in new situations with subtly different connotations. Eventually, with prompting, long exchanges can take place. It is expected that, in the course of the year, students progress from vague global to an ever more precise understanding of the selected structures.

In an action-centered approach, as the title would imply, the principal emphasis is on verbs and their varying forms. Of the approximately 190 words prescribed by Schuh in the *Grundkurs* only 13 are nouns: *Auto* [car], *Ball* [ball], *Puppe* [doll], *Tasche* [bag], *Buch* [book], *Wagen* [car], *Fenster* [window], *Tür* [door], *Schrank* [closet], *Rad* [bicycle], *Roller* [scooter], *Eis* [ice cream], and *Pflaster* [band-aid]. The three toys *Ball, Auto,* and *Puppe* assume generic status in an attempt—largely futile—to impress German gender classification on the non-analytic minds of seven-year-olds. Against the advice of Schuh and in conformity with tradition, our own syllabus greatly extends the range of nouns to be learned. Care is taken, however, to embed these nouns into the syntactical framework provided by Schuh. Some 140 supplementary nouns cover conventional topics in elementary courses: clothing (17), parts of the body (24), days of the week (7), weather (3), animals (24), family (7), birthday celebrations (4), foods (32), house, rooms, and furniture (15), and money and shopping (5).

Schuh introduces only eight adjectives: *fertig* [finished], *schön* [beautiful], *gross* [large], *klein* [small], *krank* [sick], *schnell* [fast], and *langsam* [slow]. We add many words of praise and criticism (for global comprehension only!), as well as *alt* [old], *neu* [new], *jung* [young], *lang* [long], *kurz* [short], *dick* [fat], *dünn* [thin], *laut* [loud], and *leise* [soft, low].

More than half the entire vocabulary introduced in the *Grundkurs* consists of verbs and their varying forms (86). Age-appropriate action words, they are internalized naturally and spontaneously through total physical involvement. In order of appearance these are *kommen* [come], *dürfen* [be allowed], *machen* [make, do], *sein* [be], *zeigen* [show], *haben* [have], *spielen* [play], *holen* [fetch], *helfen* [help], *können* [be able], *gehen* [go], *sagen* [say], *wissen* [know], *warten* [wait], *fahren* [drive, ride], *fragen* [ask], *gehören* [belong], *verlieren* [lose], *weinen* [cry], *suchen* [look for], *finden* [find], *läuten* [ring], *klopfen* [knock], *klatschen* [clap], *flüstern* [whisper], *rufen* [call], *husten* [cough], *schlafen* [sleep], *bluten* [bleed], *fangen* [catch], *hinfallen* [fall down], *weh tun* [hurt], and *sehen* [see]. Of course, these are not fully conjugated from the very first encounter. Instead, various inflections and word order patterns are very gradually introduced, with the present tense prevailing until Unit 20, close to the end of the academic year. The present perfect tense of strong and weak verbs may be comprehended but is certainly not mastered by the end of first grade. Imperative and interrogative forms are amply practiced, as are the first and second person singular indicative, while the third person singular and plural forms appear quite late (Units 17 and 19). The polite form is deferred until second grade. The verb *kommen* is used generically: its usage pattern illuminates Schuh's methodology. "Komm!" [come!] is the core of Unit 1, "Komm bitte, 'rein!" [Please come in!] of Unit 2, "Komm bitte nicht!" [Please don't come!] of Unit 3, "Komm bitte mit!" [Please come along!] of Unit 4. "Darf ich kommen?" [May I come?] is featured in Unit 6, "Soll ich kommen?" [Shall I come?] in Unit 9, "Dann Kommst du!" [Then it is your turn] in Unit 12, "Ich weiss, wer kommen soll" [I know who shall come] in Unit 13, "er/sie kommt" [he/she is coming] in Unit 17, "wir kommen alle" [we are all coming] in Unit 19, "er/sie ist gekommen" [he/she has come] in Unit 20, "wir sind alle gekommen" [we have all come] in Unit 22. Entrance and opening routines, drills, games, and dialogues afford regular opportunities for verb practice. Schuh's verbal largesse for active usage is only slightly extended in our syllabus with verbs relating to supplementary topics like weather, clothing, foods, and shopping. Passive comprehension ranges widely, fostered by giving instructions for all activities in German and by the learning of rhymes and songs.

Crucial to authentic communication, according to Schuh ("Einführung" 27), is the intuitive application of invariables (including adverbs, prepositions, conjunctions, interrogatives, and exclamations), which receive commensurate emphasis amongst his structures (56 of 190). Especially appealing to children are the snappy repartees of casual conversations and the many, almost untranslatable exclamations—*ach so* [oh], *ach ja* [oh yes], *o ja* [oh yes],

189

na endlich [at last], *mal* [for a bit], *denn* [then], *na so etwas!* [well now], *schade!* [a pity], *Entschuldigung!* [Sorry!], *Vorsicht!* [look out!], *bestimmt* [certainly] *natürlich* [of course], *ein bisschen* [a little] ...which are skillfully woven into the very earliest exchanges, and mimicked with delight.

Remarkably effective in this context are the *Tonband-Bildszenen* of Units 12, 15, 18, and 21. On tape, familiar linguistic material is fused into extensive conversations, with sequential, colored, cartoon-style illustrations depicting the progression of action. The tape-picture scenes deal with recurrent problems of social interaction among youngsters: taking turns, resolving disagreements (painfully with aggression or sensibly with compromise), helping and sharing, concern and cooperation. Children are attentive, they imitate with alacrity the distinctive voices and expressive intonations of the young speakers, they applaud spontaneously and evaluate episodes critically. The introductory scene (12 a) is never surpassed in popularity. Most students are satiated, however, well before they can recall the dialogues for smooth re-enactment without prompting.

Prompting, indeed, seems to be the despairing instructor's main function for some six months of the first year, while students appear to be repeating the dialogue lines quite mechanically, when suddenly the ablest and most out-going begin to use acquired patterns independently, playfully, even wittily—but not always accurately! "Ich sehe die Unterhose. Die ist weiss und grau und bedeckt" [I can see the underpants. They are white and grey and covered.] "Frau Ryan, du bist böse. Du bist draußen!" [Mrs. Ryan, you are naughty. You are outside.] "Er habe die Haare ein bißchen weg." [His hair is a little gone.] "Ich habe zwei Brüder. Meine Brüder haben Schokoladeneier. Kleine. Ich nicht!" [I have two brothers. My brothers have chocolate eggs. Little ones. I don't!]. Simple sentences — like snowdrops, harbingers of spring.

Just as weeds will grow among flowers, Hermann Schuh's *Komm bitte!* has its trouble spots. It seems excessively restrictive to defer the use of the indefinite article until Unit 16 and third person singular verb forms until Unit 18. It is unlikely that one can encourage children to play "catch" in the classroom (Units 2 and 17) so as to learn verb forms *affektgeladen* [emphatically] and yet have a controlled environment where grammatical insights are commonplace. It is unfortunate that the *Geräuschreihe* [sound series] of Unit 18 with verbs like *klopfen* [knock] and *klatschen* [clap], *husten* [cough], *weinen* [cry], and *lachen* [laugh] has to be taught just when spring fever is peaking. It appears impossible to play games with twenty-eight volatile school beginners without often being authoritarian. Yet judiciously applied, Schuh's "leisure-pleasure" principle taps the eagerness of first graders to communicate without inhibition, without resentment at corrections, with excellent pronunciation and intonation, within the limited realm of their concerns.

Schuh's skeletal "200 Wörter und was man damit machen kann" [200 Words and what one can do with them] is easily doubled in our syllabus, and so are the troubles of vocabulary learning. In an oral course, all review must take place in the classroom, and it should be brief, frequent, varied, and fun. Visuals are mounted in gender groups (masculine on the left, neuter in the center, feminine on the right) on the *Bildtafel* [picture board] and drilled in varied ways: by pointing and individual or choral repetition with changing speeds, intonations, and rhythms. Hints on novel procedures are sprinkled thoughout the syllabus, and more are always wanted. Realia—culturally authentic or unusual ones are sought, while fashionable American ones are avoided to limit the impulsive injection of English—are manipulated in a multitude of guessing games. A *Nikolaussack* [Santa's sack] made of burlap has turned out to be an ideal container for such vocabulary reinforcement games. Vocabulary illustrations are colored at the teacher's direction, personal *Bildtafeln* [picture boards] are pasted up, paper dolls are cut out and dressed by boys and girls alike (with outlines for such activities conveniently supplied in the syllabus, bingo games, (mostly teacher-made) are played, counting and finger rhymes and songs are learned. Near the end of the year, students can and do appreciate familiar stories like "Goldhaar und die drei Bären" [Goldilocks and the Three Bears], "Hänsel und Gretel" and "Rotkäppchen" [Little Red Riding Hood] entirely in German.

Although less than twenty percent of the school day is devoted to second language instruction, a solid foundation for comprehension and communication skills in German is laid in the first grade. In a multi-ethnic setting, where a student can playfully say to the teacher "Du bist meine Mutti" [You are my mom] to be corrected swiftly but without rancor "Nein, sie weiss, du schwarz" [No, she (is) white, you (are) black], students begin to appreciate cultural diversity before stereotypes are firmly rooted. By tasting German foods—sweet *Gummibärchen* [gummy bears] and *Nutella,* not Sauerkraut—by seeing German homes on slides, by lighting real candles on an advent wreath or pine branch, children are enticed to look a little beyond the hills of Cincinnati. Armed with several hundred German words firmly fitted into Hermann Schuh's "structures," they might already not be totally lost by the real Rhine.

Annotated Bibliography

Textbooks.

Göbel, Heinz, Traudel Müller and Martha Schneider. *Du und Ich: Unterrichtspraktisches Handbuch für Deutsch als Zweitsprache im Kindergarten.* (Item 49990); *Medienvorlagen.* (Item 49991); *Liederheft.* (Item 49992). Berlin: Langenscheidt, 1983. Available from Langenscheidt Publishers, Inc., 46-35 54th Road, Maspeth, NY 11378. A treasure-trove of creative ideas, songs, games and media that can be integrated with *Komm bitte!*

Schuh, Hermann. *Komm bitte!* Ismaning bei München: Max Hueber Verlag, 1972. 3rd ed. 1979. (U.S.A.: Midwest European Publications, Inc., 915 Foster Street, Evanston, IL 60201). Basic text for the first grade syllabus of the Fairview German Bilingual School in Cincinnati, Ohio.

Visual Aids.

American Guidance Service. *Peabody Language Development Kits. Stimulus Cards for Level #1.* Minnesota: AGS, 1965. Large, clear illustrations, though many are outdated.

Bruna, Dick. *Animal Frieze.* London: Methuen Children's Books Ltd., 1975.

_____. *1 2 3 Frieze.* London: Methuen Children's Books, Ltd., 1974. (Methuen Children's Books Ltd., 11 Fetter Lane, London EC4P 4EE) Colorful, excellent for long-term display.

Family Face Puppets (White-No. 1185; Black-No. 1186) Animal Face Puppets (No. 1189), *Instructo* Corporation, Paoli, Pennsylvania 19301.

Pienkowski, Jan. *Colours Frieze; Homes Frieze* (Gallery Five F/65 1977); *Weather Frieze;* William Heinemann Ltd., (10 Upper Grosvenor St., London WIX 9PA.) These friezes, when trimmed of their English captions, make useful and well-liked displays for regular practice.

Reidel, Marlene. *Eine Weltkarte für Kinder: Großposter* (108/80 cm. Item 758); *Kinderreime: Großposter (*98/114 cm. Item 694); Sellier Verlag GmbH, Erfurter Str. 4, D-8057 Eching bei München. Many beautifully illustrated posters, friezes and books for young children are available from the same publisher.

Song Books and Records.

Haffner, Gerhard, ed. *Unsere schönsten Volkslieder.* Mit Noten zum Singen und Spielen am Klavier. München: Delphin, 1979.

_____. *Grosses Buch der Weihnachtslieder.* Mit Noten zum Singen und Spielen am Klavier. München: Delphin, 1979.

Kreusch-Jacob, Dorothee. *Ravensburger Liederspielbuch für Kinder.* Ravensburg: Otto Maier Verlag, 1978. Over 70 songs and verses with practical and creative suggestions for activities to accompany traditional and modern songs and games.

Grüger, Heribert and Johannes. *Die Lieder der Liederfibel: Die schönsten Kinderlieder zum Mitsingen.* Kindermusikstudio Saarbrücken. Leitung: Christa Frischkorn. Schwann: Hören und Lernen H + L 103 Düsseldorf: Schwann, 1977.

_____. *Weihnachts Liederfibel* mit Schallplatte. Düsseldorf: Schwann, 1976.

Sing mit — Spiel mit: 22 fröhliche Kinderlieder zum Mitsingen. Schwann Hören & Lernen H + L 102 Düsseldorf: Schwann, 1976. Records and *Bildernotenbücher* produced by the Pädogogischer Verlag Schwann-Bagel GmbH, Düsseldorf, are appropriate for classroom teaching because of their simplicity, clarity, pitch, and speed. Texts of songs are not provided. Ample material for early elementary grades, despite some duplication.

Games.

Baird, Mary. *International Bingo.* New York: Gessler, 1982. Illustrations only have been used to make composite Bingo games. *Number Bingo.* Trend Enterprises, Inc. T-102.

Liebowitz, Dorothy Gabel. *Basic Vocabulary Builder:* 32 Duplicating Masters, each containing 16 illustrations of basic vocabulary words grouped by subject. National Textbook Company, 4255 W. Touhy Ave., Lincolnwood, IL 60646-1975. Selected illustrations are repeatedly used in the curriculum for discrimination testing, for composing Bingo games and for making gender-grouped *Bildtafeln.*

Elstner, Frank. *Spiel mit: Das große Spiele-Buch des Deutschen Sport-*

bundes für Sport, Spiel und Spass. Dortmund: BAKA-Druck, 1979. Indoor and outdoor games for all age groups.

Glonnegger, Erwin. *Spiele - Spiele - Spiele.* Ravensburg: Otto Maier Verlag, 1965. Pocket book edition 1977. Instructions for traditional children's games, including "Faules Ei" which is manageable with an entire class on the playground.

Neue Kinderspiele: 260mal Spiel und Spass für 4- bis 12jährige. Erlenbach + München: Pamir Verlag, 1979. Well-organized, clear instructions for many games; suitable for first graders.

Slides.

Inter Nationes. Kultureller Tonbanddienst. D-5300 Bonn-Bad Godesberg, Kennedyallee 91 - 103. Excellent sets of slides and other cultural material may be obtained free of charge by schools, not individual teachers, from *Inter Nationes.* Cultural material suitable for first graders may be culled from the following sets: *Was möchten Sie wissen?* (70 slides); *Das Land, in dem wir leben.* (180 slides); *Themen aus dem Alltag.* (100 slides); *Wer kommt mit? Eine Reise durch die Bundesrepublik Deutschland.* (110 slides).

Filmstrips.

Die drei Bären (Goldilocks and the Three Bears), Item 7120 or 7121, Gessler Publishing Co., Inc., 900 Broadway, New York, NY 10003-1291. *Hänsel und Gretel,* Item S-5010; *Rotkäppchen* (Little Red Riding Hood), Item S-5020; Catalogue of German Materials, Goldsmith's Music Shop, Inc., 301 East Shore Rd., Great Neck, NY 11023.

193

Fairy Tales in the ESL Classroom

April Haulman

Teachers of English as a second language (or any second or foreign language, for that matter) wishing to diversify their instructional approach should consider that fairy tales offer a richness of experience in the target language and culture. There are several lines of reasoning that demonstrate the appropriateness of fairy tales in the second language classroom. (For my purposes in this paper, "fairy tale" will refer to a rather broad category of folklore, legends, fables, and other forms of children's stories incorporating elements of magic and/or fantasy.)

First of all, when introduced and optimally utilized, fairy tales provide a glimpse of the target language group's values, lifestyles, customs, and historical traditions. Children can examine how a given group has dressed, how and what they ate, and what they held dear in their day-to-day lives. Since fairy tales, for the most part, evolved as a way of instructing and inculcating the young in the ways and mores of a people, they offer an understanding of the target group's perception of their environment and their relationship to it. Moreover, fairy tales provide the opportunity for children to explore folk wisdom and assist in clarification and evolution of their own value systems.

Second, children's stories offer a variety of language contexts appropriate for expanding and refining vocabulary, and for developing a larger repertoire of linguistic structures. The storytelling genre, by its very nature, provides ample opportunity to demonstrate role-specific language in many different settings and circumstances. The fairy tale often incorporates both narrative and conversational interactional styles. Although the specific language of certain stories may seem outdated (e.g., "porridge" in *The Three Bears*), or too unusual for everyday usage (e.g., "Fe, fi, fo, fum, I smell the blood of an Englishman" in *Jack and the Beanstalk* or "not by the hair of my chinny, chin, chin" in *The Three Little Pigs*), it can still portray many sociological aspects of the language. A popular discourse-structuring device for children's stories is the sequential build-up of the plot, which provides frequent repetition and predictability and thus enhances comprehension. Consider, for example, *The Three*

April Haulman is Director of Bilingual Education at Oklahoma's Central State University.

Bears', "Someone's been eating my porridge," or *The Gingerbread Man's* "Run, run as fast as you can," or *The Little Red Hen's* "Who will help me plant this wheat?" and the never-forgotten response "Not I." These examples also highlight the usefulness of fairy tales for focusing on specific linguistic structures or functions, (e.g., tenses as in "...been eating..." or questions with "who") and for introducing idiomatic expression in context-embedded situations (e.g., "...and broke it all to pieces" or "...and ate it all up").

The final argument for studying fairy tales in the foreign/second language classroom is supported by current research in the field of second language acquisition. In *Principles and Practice in Second Language Acquisition* (New York: Pergamon Press, 1982) Stephen Krashen states there are two necessary conditions for second language acquisition to occur naturally in the classroom setting: (1) comprehensible input in the target language; and (2) lowered affective filter of the second/foreign language learner (33). By incorporating variations of child-oriented themes and/or fantasy, fairy tales can pique and maintain a young person's interest, thus affectively engaging the child in the story's content. While focusing on the action, the characters, and the plot, in combination with some repetitive and predictable language and situations, the fairy tale, when creatively introduced, can provide the necessary "comprehensible input" and lower the "affective filter" at the same time. Thus, fairy tales offer a varied medium for cultural, cognitive linguistic, and affective stimulation in a second language classroom.

Suggested steps for the use of fairy tales in the ESL classroom may be outlined as follows.

1. *Introduction.* The vocabulary should be introduced and any unusual concepts embedded in the story explained or demonstrated. Depending on the level of linguistic ability of the students, motivating statements about the story or the story's lesson (if it has one), would be an appropriate introductory activity.

2. *Story Presentation.* After the introduction, the story is presented using whatever props and dramatic techniques are necessary to make the content enjoyable, e.g., flannel board, puppets, picture-telling, or even, in some instances, films or filmstrips.

3. *Language Activities.* Next, activities designed to practice, review, or extend the vocabulary or structures in the story should be presented. Pattern drills, games, songs, worksheets, puzzles, or any activities that provide variations and practive with language are appropriate.

4. *Reinforcement or Follow-up Activities.* After manipulating the language of the story, children should be given an opportunity to review and summarize the story content or to reinforce the story's values or implications. (e.g., Little Red Riding Hood should not have spoken to a stranger when she was alone in the woods.)

5. *Springboard Activities.* As a last step, use the language, themes, or topics of the fairy tale as a springboard to other content area activities. While these activities may only be tangentially related to the fairy tale, they can demonstrate to the ESL student the usefulness

195

and transferability of language to other important subject matter. For language minority students in particular, it is essential to make the connection between language study and academic areas such as math, science, social studies, or cultural studies. Springboard activities could include field trips, guest speakers, science projects, or math problems. The focus will depend on the creativity of the teacher and the interests of the students.

Suggestions for using some old favorites in the ESL classroom follow. All but the first, i.e., *Jack and the Beanstalk*, were suggested in brainstorming sessions at Central State University by graduate students in the program of teaching English as a second language.

Suggestions for ESL Instruction using Fairy Tales

Jack and the Beanstalk

1. Introduction
   a. Vocabulary presented using pictures and explanations:
      poor, food, cow, beans, beanstalk, giant, wife, gold, harp
   b. Motivation: Have you ever done something your mother told you not to do?
2. Story
      Read story from picture book with large, colorful pictures using full voice characterizations.
3. Language Activities
   a. Have students sequence picture cards of the cow, beanstalk, and giant, and write or explain the part of each in the story.
   b. Make a character pyramid.

(person)	Jack
(adjective)	young poor
(verbs)	sells climbs runs

   c. Practice command forms. Students write out simple commands and take turns playing parts.
      - Mother's orders to Jack. (e.g., "Take the cow to town")
      - Giant's orders to his wife.
   d. Pattern/drills to practice comparative adjective, e.g., "The beanstalk grew taller and taller."
   e. Prepare an interview with Jack's mother for her side of the story or with the giant for his.
   f. Make a board game with a beanstalk. Each leaf has a vocabulary word from the story on it. As students try to reach the treasure up in the sky, they must spin and move "up the beanstalk." When they land on a leaf, they must use the word in a sentence to stay there.

4. Reinforcement and Follow-up Activities
   a. Students draw pictures depicting the sequence of events.
   b. Students dictate the story to the teacher, or retell it in their own words into a tape recorder.
   c. Students talk about the meaning or moral of the story.
5. Springboard Activities
   a. Discussion of vocabulary relating to family relationships, e.g., mother, son, husband, wife.
   b. Activity relating to the five senses: I see..., I smell (as in "I smell an Englishman")..., I hear..., I taste..., I touch (or feel)....
   c. Planting of beans, watching and recording their growth.

The Little Red Hen

1. Introduction
   a. Vocabulary: names of farm animals and farm-related vocabulary.
   b. Motivation: What do you do to help around your home?
2. Story Presentation
   Use flannel board or puppets to tell the story using animal sounds.
3. Language Activities
   a. Tell what sounds the animals make, e.g., "The hen says cluck, cluck."
   b. Dramatize the story.
   c. Retell the story using different animals.
   d. Practice drills using interrogative forms.
   e. Sing "The Little Red Hen" song.
4. Reinforcement
   a. Make a picture collage of animals on the farm.
   b. Play a game in which children act out jobs—helping others.
5. Springboard Activities
   a. Make bread, take a field trip to a bakery.
   b. Teach about farms and their products.
   c. Visit a farm and record the event on language experience charts.

The Three Little Pigs

1. Introduction
   a. Vocabulary: straw, stick, brick, pig, wolf, chimney.
   b. Motivation: (1) If you were building a house, what would you use? (2) Do you ever want to play instead of doing what you know you need to do?
2. Story Presentation
   Students listen to dramatic interpretation on tape and follow along in picture book.
3. Language Activities
   a. Sequence pigs in their respective houses.
   b. Practice ordinal numbers.

197

  c. Practice drills with comparatives and superlatives: "the strong, stronger, strongest house."

  d. Discuss other words for house, e.g., home, pad, place.

  e. If you were the man selling the straw (bricks, sticks), how would you convince the pig to buy your product?

  f. Discuss pigs' feelings at different points in the story.

4. Reinforcement and Follow-up

  a. Dramatize the story with props.

  b. Draw a picture of your favorite character or scene in the story.

  c. Discuss moral: "If you threaten someone, you may be your own victim," or "Why do people work? What would happen if they didn't?"

5. Springboard Activity

  a. Discuss materials used to build houses.

  b. Study kinds of houses around the world.

Cinderella

1. Introduction:

  a. Vocabulary Categories:

  (1) household work: sweep, wash, dust, scrub, cook, stir, mend, sew, comb hair

  (2) family: stepmother, sisters, father, daughter, stepchild, godmother

  (3) emotions: sad, cry, mean, brag, arrogant

  (4) clothes: shoes (slippers), gown, rags, apron, skirt, jewelry

  b. Motivation: Have you ever felt as if you had to work harder than everyone else?

2. Story Presentation
Students watch a filmstrip of the story and then a puppet reenactment.

3. Language Activities

  a. Arrange sentence strips in sequence.

  b. Identify commands of stepsisters, stepmother and fairy godmother and act them out.

  c. Discuss a picture of Cinderella's family and discuss the children's families.

  d. Talk about Cinderella's feelings at different points in the story.

  e. If you had a fairy godmother, what would be your wish?.

4. Reinforcement
Students tape story for younger students and learn songs from *Cinderella* movie.

5. Springboard Activities

  a. Discuss textures and appearance of types of cloth (shiny, smooth, rough, etc.).

  b. Discuss feelings about not receiving invitations to parties.

  c. Discuss parties, e.g., dancing, music, games, types of parties, and different clothing worn.

Short Stories in the Elementary Classroom: "El camello que se perdió"

Cida S. Chase

Although there are significant differences between the two concepts, the terms foreign language and second language are usually employed interchangeably. According to William Littlewood's distinction, foreign language implies that the learner has to travel to another land in order to use the language in a truly realistic framework or that the learner can use it as a means of communication with foreigners. On the other hand, a second language can be used to communicate inside the learner's country, perhaps in his own community. In this context, Spanish is a second language in the United States where many communities have a Hispanic population and the students are able to use the language learned in the classroom to communicate with over twenty million American citizens.

Among the "non-linguistic factors which many people believe (from observation, statistical evidence, or both) to influence success in second language learning," one can point out two of great importance to all learners, especially children: motivation and opportunity for learning (Littlewood 53). The teacher can strengthen the children's motivation by using interesting, attractive materials that demonstrate cultural and aesthetic values and that are appropriate to their grade level. The teacher can also promote motivation for learning the second language by fostering a healthy attitude toward the second language community. Hence one can see the importance of selecting materials that lead to a positive cultural analysis and enlighten the learners about cultural and historical events involving the second language community.

The Hispanic literature of the American Southwest constitutes a valuable source of materials for the Spanish elementary classroom. It contains numerous tales, myths, legends, and fables in which a child's dream world and day-to-day reality are skillfully combined as in all great works of children's literature. One charming tale that belongs to this body of literature is "El camello que se perdió" ("The Lost Camel"), included in José Griego y Maestas and Rudolfo A. Anaya, *Cuentos: Tales from the Hispanic Southwest*, a bilingual col-

Cida S. Chase is Associate Professor of Spanish at Oklahoma State University.

lection of short stories with a wide range of tales appropriate for different age groups.

"El camello que se perdió" concerns a group of merchants traveling to another country to sell their products. When it became dark and they were ready to make camp, they realized there was a camel missing. They met a man and asked him if he had seen it. He answered that he had not seen it but that he could offer them information on the missing camel. He told them that the camel was carrying a load of wheat on its left side, and on the right side it was carrying jars of honey. In addition, the man told them that the camel was blind in one eye and that it had a tooth missing.

Extremely surprised and somewhat suspicious, the merchants demanded to know how this person knew so much about their camel. He answered patiently:

> "I know he was carrying wheat on his left side because grains had fallen along the left side of the path. The bag was probably cut by some branches. Ants were gathering the grains on the left side of the trail. I know he was carrying jars of honey because on the right side of the path flies were swarming where the honey had dripped." (85)

The merchants continued to question him:

> "Fine, but how do you know he is blind in one eye?"
> "Because I noticed he had been grazing only on the right side of the path," the man answered.
> "And how do you know he has a tooth missing?"
> "Because where he had chewed the grass he left a clump in the middle of the bite." (85)

After his explanation, the man told the merchants where to look for the camel. The merchants found the camel and handsomely rewarded this honest man who had such refined powers of observation.

This story is suitable for fourth or fifth grade students of Spanish as a second language, provided they have had previous training in the language. At these levels the learners' listening skills are usually sufficiently developed to appreciate it. The story provides some enlightening background on the Hispanic presence throughout the American Southwest. A historical introduction relating when and how the Spanish first came to the United States and what legends and traditions they brought with them facilitates a cultural analysis. The teacher can even expand and include information about the Moors in Spain and the Spanish knowledge of *A Thousand and One Nights*. Some of these tales came with the Spanish to the American Southwest, where they blended with indigenous tales and traditions and remain today as part of the rich Hispanic folklore of the United States.

In addition, the students can be informed that in the old Southwest, stories like "El camello que se perdió" had several purposes. They taught Hispanic children about animals around the world but above all they domonstrated to children the value of environmental awareness. Many Hispanic children were sheepherders and had to observe their animals' behavior and detect special markings on their animals. Also, early recognition of wild animals' tracks or the presence of hostile Indians in the area were critical factors for the survival of these youngsters in the hills. Such valuable background can be provided in either English or Spanish depending on the linguistic ability of the students.

"El camello que se perdió" is truly a short story, for the Spanish version is no longer than one page. It is narrated almost entirely in concrete terms. With a knowledge of the twenty-five nouns that constitute the heart of the story, the children can comprehend the story in Spanish. Children are more successful in second language when exposed to simple, concrete speech they can relate to their experience (Littlewood 60). The number of concrete terms suggests narration using visual stimuli without resorting to the use of English. Pictures, mounted on construction paper, can be prepared depicting the camel, the merchants, the man, the countryside, the swarming flies, the ants carrying grains of wheat, the grass, and all the other nouns that make up the story.

To encourage comprehension of verbs, actions and mime can accompany the pictures. The merchants who "viajaban a otro país a vender sus productos" [were traveling to another country to sell their products] can be acted out by the teacher while holding the appropriate illustration. Although the story makes use of a wide range of verb tenses and is an excellent example of the use of the preterite and imperfect tenses, it can be dramatically narrated to children using mainly the present tense.

The adjectives and participles number only thirteen, and they can be dramatized and illustrated without using English. The use of "derecho" [right] and "izquierdo" [left] provides the opportunity to practice directions and positions in Spanish. These terms can be used later in a follow-up activity combined with the presentation or review of the parts of the body, e.g., "el ojo derecho" [the right eye], "el ojo izquierdo" [the left eye], "la mano derecha" [the right hand], "la mano izquierda" [the left hand].

After the students have had a rewarding listening experience with "El camello que se perdió," they can engage in play activities, graded in difficulty, designed to elicit Spanish words and sentences. The teacher must be sure that the young learners will experience success and satisfaction in these activities. Therefore, the initial exercises should be group activities.

A very useful game to provide vocabulary review is "¿Qué es esto?" Knowledge of definite and indefinite articles, singular and plural, are required for this activity. In order to avoid student errors in gender, the instructor should review these items before playing the game. In this game the teacher holds the pictures up one at a time and asks the students: "¿Qué es esto?" [What is this?]. Choral responses of the students are "Es un hombre" [It is a man], "Es el campo" [It is the countryside], "Es una hormiguita" [It is a little ant].

201

The game can continue until all the nouns of the story are reviewed or until interest in the activity wanes.

A "Sí o no" game, in which the students are provided with two alternatives, can follow. In this activity the children repeat together the correct alternative while reviewing the sequence of events in the story. They are presented with questions such as "¿Los mercaderes perdieron un camello o no perdieron un camello?" [Did the merchants lose a camel or did they not lose a camel?]; "¿Los mercaderes encontraron un hombre o no encontraron un hombre?" [Did the merchants meet a man or did they not meet a man?]; "¿El hombre les dijo que había visto el camello o que no había visto el camello?" [Did the man tell them that he had seen the camel or that he had not seen the camel?]; "¿Llevaba carga el camello o no lievaba carga?" [Was the camel carrying a load or not carrying a load]; "¿El camello es tuerto o no es tuerto?" [Is the camel blind in one eye or is it not blind in one eye?]. If the teacher has chosen to narrate the story in the present tense, all these questions must be posed in the present tense. In addition, the use of visual aids is valuable in this activity.

A game of "Verdad o mentira" can be played with the teacher making a series of statements and the students answering, "Es verdad" [It is true] or "Es mentira" [It is not true]. If the teacher says, "Las hormiguitas estaban recogiendo los granos de trigo" [The little ants were gathering the grains of wheat], the students react by saying, "Es verdad," but if the teacher says, "Al camello no le falta un diente" [The camel is not missing a tooth], the students respond, "Es mentira."

The verbs learned in the story can be reviewed with "Un juego de acertijos" [charades] in which the teacher performs actions like *agarrar* [to grasp], *buscar* [to look for], *caminar* [to walk], *derramar* [to spill], *indicar* [to indicate], *recoger* [to gather], *robar* [to steal], *tirar* [to throw], and many other verbs that can be demonstrated through mime.

After carrying out several class activities, the students will be ready to perform in small groups and individually. A small-group activity that children will enjoy is the game "¿Qué tengo?" [What do I have?]. The teacher divides the class into groups of four or five children, distributes the pictures and requests that the students not reveal the picture they have. The children take turns asking "¿Qué tengo?" and select members of their group to guess what pictures they have. The students selected pose questions such as "¿Tienes el hombre?" [Do you have the man?] or "¿Tienes la carga?" [Do you have the load?]. The groups can later exchange pictures and continue the game as long as interest is sustained. These activities are important because they offer the students the opportunity to participate in the review of the story and because the learners practice the newly acquired vocabulary. The activities can be distributed over several class periods, and the teacher can use them with discretion.

A short story like "El camello que se perdió" is worthwhile material in the elementary Spanish classroom. It offers the opportunity to learn by providing entertaining listening activity which can be successfully accompanied by non-linguistic resources such as mime, gestures, and other visual stimuli. In effect, listening is a critical element for language acquisition in young children as well as in adults. A great deal of listening must take place in order to stimulate speech production, and "listening comprehension may map the blueprint for speaking" (Wolfe and Jones).

"El camello que se perdió" provides the opportunity to develop awareness of a large minority group in the United States. Through its use in the classroom, the teacher can project a positive image of the Hispanic community, furthering the motivation of the young learners who may want to continue learning and enjoying Spanish in the classroom.

References

Griego y Maestas, José, and Rudolfo A. Anaya. *Cuentos: Tales from the Hispanic Southwest*. Santa Fe: Museum of New Mexico Press, 1980.

Littlewood, William. *Foreign and Second Language Learning*. London: Cambridge Univ. Press, 1984.

Wolfe, David E., and Gwendolyn Jones. "Integrating Total Physical Response Strategy in a Level I Spanish Class." *Foreign Language Annals* 15.4 (1982):273-80.

Teaching Methodology:
A Child-Centered Approach

Marcia H. Rosenbusch

Interest in second language acquisition seems to be strongest in this country in areas where second languages are more commonly spoken: in large cities, around international ports and border states, and in communities where large groups of immigrants settled and maintained their first language. But in the central part of the United States, interest in second language acquisition has not been strong.

The Iowa Governor's Task Force Report on Foreign Language Studies and International Education (1983) describes Iowans as responsible, hard-working, and inclined to accept what they believe to be the "practicalities of life." According to the report, the typical attitude toward second language education of Iowans can be illustrated by the following statements: "No one ever uses a 'foreign' language." "Learning a foreign language is a waste of time and money." "Travel is expensive and difficult, given our location" (11).

Yet not all Iowans would agree with these statements. Parents of grade school children are demonstrating a desire to provide second language classes for their children in spite of the school's reluctance to add new programs. In the last year, at least four central Iowa communities have begun extracurricular programs of foreign language in the elementary school (FLES).

Another good sign is that the Iowa Humanities Board, in conjunction with the National Endowment for the Humanities, has provided funding to launch an Iowa FLES Newsletter, available on request to all Iowans interested or involved in FLES programs. The first issue was published in April, 1985.

How did this interest in FLES develop where support for foreign language programs has not been strong in the past? Although it is impossible to identify all the reasons, three factors surely have had an impact:

1. The report of the President's Commission on Foreign Language and International Studies (1979) stimulated thinking about second languages and incited the governor of Iowa to name a commission to study the situation of second language education in the state and to make recommendations based on its findings.

2. The Iowa Governor's Task Force Report on Foreign Language

Marcia H. Rosenbusch teaches in the Department of Foreign Languages and Literature at Iowa State University.

Studies and International Education (1983) made several recommendations, one of which was to "promote a comprehensive foreign language and international studies program for Iowa." The report stated that this "program should extend from kindergarten through college and beyond, in a coordinated effort to reach all Iowans" (19).

3. Media information about ongoing model FLES programs has also had an impact. The FLES program in Ames, Iowa, was featured in the Iowa Public Television program *Take One* (1983). After this presentation we received numerous requests for information and visits by persons interested in beginning similar programs in their own communities.

The Ames FLES program was started in 1976 by several parents who were interested in providing a second language experience for their grade-school children. They hired a person fluent in Spanish who was also trained in elementary education and arranged for the Spanish classes to be held at their neighborhood school in the morning before the regular school day. Within two years, parent volunteers had organized the Ames Foreign Language Association, which sponsored extracurricular classes in French, German, and Spanish in all eight elementary schools. In just two years, 466 children were enrolled in these classes. Currently, parents pay $50 -$60 for 36 hours of class during the school year. The classes meet twice a week for 45 minutes over a period of 24 weeks.

At first, the tutors planned their own lessons, but it soon became evident that the program would be stronger and more respected in the community if curriculum guidelines were developed to unify the goals and methodology of the program. I volunteered as curriculum coordinator and, together with another tutor, began the task of defining the curriculum.

The first step was the review of available curriculum guides to see how others had approached the problem. We found that most second language educators had adopted an audiolingual instructional approach (as advocated by Donoghue in 1968) in which conversational skills are taught first, and reading and writing are delayed. Grammar is taught inductively, vocabulary is learned in meaningful context, and translation is avoided.

Even though we accepted this basic approach, the suggested methodology and classroom activities in the curriculum guides we reviewed seemed tremendously boring to children. We couldn't imagine children getting excited about learning to say in a second language: "Good morning. How are you? I am fine. What is your name? My name is Mary." The stilted question-and-answer approach used in most guides reminded us of the books about Dick and Jane that so many of us had used in learning to read. Those books transmitted such a limited version of life that many children could not relate to them. Most real children don't speak or act like Dick and Jane, nor do they speak English as they were being taught to talk in the second language!

We suspected that part of the problem for educators developing programs for elementary-school children was that they were writing a curriculum based on their training and experience teaching junior and senior high school. We decided to approach curriculum development from the other direction: we sought to gain a better understanding of the elementary-school child's interests and needs by examining the stages of development through which these children had just passed, and which continued to affect their ways of thinking and acting.

Need for Real Objects

Consider the infant who has just learned to grasp objects. The first thing that happens to any such object is that it finds its way to the child's mouth, where the infant explores the taste and texture of the object. During the next few years, the innate curiosity of children will lead them to grasp and explore as many objects of their immediate world as they possibly can. They will discover differences and similarities in textures, tastes, smells, sounds, and color. This period of exploration is of fundamental importance to the child's growth, providing the basis for all later intellectual understanding.

Through the preschool years, children learn that they cannot always satisfy their curiosity first-hand. There are times and situations in which they must be satisfied by "just looking," not by touching and manipulating objects. By the time children are in the elementary school, they can usually judge fairly well when it is acceptable to touch a new object and when it is not. But during the elementary-school years, children still are very curious and still derive tremendous pleasure from touching and exploring objects. It makes good sense to utilize this attraction children have for objects in the second language classroom.

It is true that elementary-school children are well acquainted with the look, smell, feel, and taste of an apple and that they can be taught the word for "apple" in the second language without using a real apple. But how much more memorable and pleasurable for them if you teach the word "apple" by having them first close their eyes, then repeat the word "la manzana" as you hold the apple close to them so that they can smell it and guess what "la manzana" means. Next have them open their eyes to see the apples as they hear and repeat "la manzana." Finally, cut the apple into slices and let the children, in the second language, ask for it to be passed to them so that they can savor the flavor and texture of the apple as they learn the word for it: Pásame la manzana, por favor. (Pass me the apple, please.)

There are other advantages to using real objects in teaching vocabulary besides stimulating the children's interest and motivation in learning. Real objects eliminate the need for translation. Children will avoid developing the cumbersome habit of translating into English each word they learn in the second language. They will be accustomed to seeing the object and knowing that it is "la manzana" from direct experience with the object, just as they learned the names for objects in their first language.

Real objects also provide variety in the classroom. Using several objects to represent each vocabulary item will make the frequent review, an essential part of teaching a second language to children, more interesting and enjoyable. How might the word "apple" be reviewed?

(1) plastic apple,
(2) cardboard cutout,
(3) flash card drawing, or
(4) flannel cutout.

Not every representation of the subject is acceptable, however. There are three questions to keep in mind as you evaluate an object for use in the classroom:

1. *Is it attractive?* You want the object to motivate the children to participate in the activities. If it is unattractive to them, it will not. Objects that are too familiar to them—a regular ball point pen, for example—aren't especially attractive, whereas a giant ball point pen would be. Unusual size can make an ordinary object appealing. Be sure that the object is not more distractive than attractive. Wind-up toys that click and clatter are not good choices, no matter how interesting they may be to the children!

2. *Is it sturdy?* A papier-mâché cow would be attractive to the children but it would be easily broken; a cow made of durable plastic would be a much better object to use in the classroom. A colorful cutout of a butterfly from a magazine would also be attractive, but it would be almost as delicate as a real butterfly. Laminating it would make it sturdy enough for the children to use. All materials should be sturdy enough for the children to handle without fear of breaking them.

3. *Is it a clear symbol?* It is important that the object be easily identifiable. If an object is to represent the concept "lion," it must look enough like a lion not to be confused with a cat or tiger. All teaching materials should clearly symbolize the concept being taught.

Real objects are especially important for the younger elementary-school child and for beginning students in the language, but even the older elementary-school children, who have moved on to conversation without objects present, still enjoy reviewing vocabulary with these objects.

Need for Physical Activity

Let's consider now another important characteristic of the elementary-school child by looking first at the toddler, the young child who has just learned to walk. What an exciting stage this is for children because it expands their world so much. Now they can

207

move about and put themselves into contact with so much more of their surroundings. And "move about" is something that they do a lot of! Toddlers have an amazing level of physical activity. To understand clearly how different they are from adults, just try imitating every move that a toddler makes. Before long you will be exhausted, but the toddler will still be full of energy. Their bodies seem to be compelled to keep in constant motion.

Some of this tremendous need for physical movement is still evident in elementary-school children. These children are not physically able to sit quietly for long periods of time as adults do. Instead of concentrating only on intellectual and verbal activity in the second language classroom, it is wise to incorporate physical activity as an integral part of the classroom activities!

How can this be done? With action verbs! When children have learned several nouns such as "cow," "flower," "dog," and "banana," teach them to use these words together with an action verb command, for example: "Touch the cow, please." "Throw me the flower, please." "Pass me the dog, please." "Draw the banana, please."

With these commands children have a legitimate reason for being physically active in the classroom. They love this possibility and remain interested longer and more intensely in the learning activities than if they were participating in traditional, physically passive activities such as: "What is this?" "It is a dog." "What color is this?" "It is red."

In addition to allowing direct physical involvement in the classroom, there are other reasons for using commands in the foreign language classroom:

1. When children ask to have an object passed to them and they receive it, they have a chance to explore that object first-hand, and we know that they love this.

2. Within the limits that the teacher imposes on an activity, the children decide what they want done to which object and by whom. They create their own sentences, simulating the model to express what they have decided: "John, throw me the dog, please." The fact that children have this decision-making possibility allows them to actively participate, intellectually as well as physically. How much more enjoyable this is than activities based on mere repetition and rote memory!

3. One of the most important reasons for using commands is that commands allow children to communicate meaningfully in the second language. Instead of answering questions or describing or defining objects, they are communicating their wants to their companions. As their companions respond physically to their commands, they experience concretely the success of their communication. They get results from what they have learned to say; they know that this second language "really works!"

4. There are also advantages for the teacher in using active commands. The teacher can evaluate easily whether a child

understands the meaning of a command or remembers what object a particular word represents. If the child who is asked to pass the dog, throws it, the child has not learned to differentiate between these two commands. The child who passes the cat instead of the dog has not yet clarified the meanings of these two words.

5. Another advantage for the teacher is that commands provide variety in the classroom activities. The various objects that represent a particular word can be used together with the basic commands: touch, throw, pass, put on, and remove. By combining these five commands with five representations of a vocabulary item—the real object, a toy model, a flash card, a paper cutout, or a flannel cutout—you can review the word "apple" in twenty-five consecutive class periods without repeating the same activity once. The children enjoy the variety and so will you.

Need for Creative Expression

Let us consider another important characteristic of children, one which has been virtually ignored in all the second language teaching programs we reviewed — children's innate creative abilities. If you have had the opportunity to be around preschool children, you know that at this age children are particularly imaginative, spontaneous, and expressive. They love to create the most unusual situations and scenes in their everyday play or conversation. Every parent or preschool teacher can recall many examples of their refreshing outlook. Which of us would think of answering the question, "Why aren't you eating that last meatball on your plate?" with, "I can't eat it, it's taking a sunbath!"

But as delightful as their ideas may be, a degree of conformity is necessary in learning the basic skills taught in the elementary school. The children will soon have to make an "A" look like an "A" instead of laying it on its side because "It's sleeping." Too often, in the name of order, discipline, and the importance of learning the basics, our school systems squelch children's creativity.

It is not impossible to have our cake and eat it too! Children are much more likely to learn enthusiastically when their creative nature is respected. As teachers of second languages, we need to recognize methods that allow children to express their thoughts and that incorporate their ideas into our teaching. We will find that our students become more dedicated to learning a second language when they know that their teacher appreciates their input.

One way we demonstrate a respect for children's thinking, creative nature is in allowing children to use commands. This structure permits children to decide and express what they want done to objects instead of asking them to participate in repetition of material which has little interest or meaning for them. Traditionally, only very advanced students are encouraged to use the language they have been studying in communication with others. But by then, we have lost

209

many of the less persistent students. Using the commands as a first step in the language, even beginning students can experience the joy of meaningful communication in the second language.

There are many other opportunities for encouraging children's creative nature in regular classroom activities. The same activity can stimulate or discourage self-expression, depending on the way the teacher organizes it. For example, when the children are using the felt cutouts of the face parts, the teacher will ask them to place the parts in their normal positions while the children are still affirming that "la nariz" means "the nose." But when the children know the face parts well and these materials are being used in review, why not let the children place them in as crazy a position as possible? Children find it satisfying and funny to place the mouth on the forehead and the ear on the chin, and why not? The review activity is more interesting to them, and they appreciate the fact that the teacher enjoys their imaginative ideas, too.

This same principle can be applied when using the command "Draw." Why not allow a child responding to the command "Draw the eye" to draw a giant bloodshot eye? It may not appeal to our esthetic taste, but if the child has learned to respond correctly to the command "Draw" and this kind of eye does not interfere with learning, why not? The important quesiton that determines what we will and will not allow in our classrooms is, will it interfere with learning the language? It makes good sense to incorporate the children's ideas for activities, or variations of activities, as long as those suggestions do not impede learning and stay within the basic guidelines of respect for persons and things.

210

Combining objectives in novel ways makes learning more interesting to the children. Instead of always using the command "Touch the house" in the logical manner of touching the house with the hand, the children have suggested touching the house with other body parts. It is certainly more interesting to watch John touch the house with his nose or ear than with his hand! And it necessitates the learning of another pattern in the second language. Now that basic command "Touch the house" is expanded with a new phrase, "Touch the house with your ear."

Another activity that the children have enjoyed is placing the family members, cat, and dog in the toy house. The children describe what they are doing as they place the object in the house, e.g., "I put the mother in the kitchen." After repeating this activity several times, the children suggested placing the farm animals in the house: "I put the cow in the living room."

Songs and games also stimulate children's creative suggestions. Many songs and games offered in second language teaching materials are dull and lifeless. For example the song "One, Two, Three Little Indians" is often suggested for use in second language classes because the tune is already familiar, because it uses numbers, and because its repetitiveness makes it easy to learn the new words of the second language. But it is also quite boring. What suggestions have the children made? Substitute cats, dogs, or even noses for the ndians! It is also possible to use the numbers 11-20 or 21-30 instead of 1-10.

A commonly used song by Spanish teachers of children is one about "Los Pollitos" (The Chicks). In it the chicks say "pío, pío, pío" when they are cold and hungry:

Los pollitos dicen
Pío, pío, pío
Cuando tienen hambre
Cuando tienen frío

This song lends itself very naturally to the substitution of other animals instead of chicks. Soon the children will sing about the dog who said "guau, guau, guau" when it was hungry and cold. It doesn't take the children long to suggest that they could pretend to be those animals they sing about. Sometimes the whole group imitates the animal and, at other times, only one child or several children do.

Another way to make a familiar song or poem with a strong rhythm more enjoyable for children is to encourage them to accompany the rhythm physically. We have a favorite Spanish poem about a kitten that runs away down San José Street, and who will be given coffee and French bread when it returns:

Mi gatito se me fue
Por la calle San José.
Cuando vuelva le daré
Una taza de café
Con pan francés.

After the children learned the poem well, I suggested that they keep the rhythm individually by clapping their hands. Seated in a circle, they would clap first their own hands, then they would clap with their neighbors. The children then planned as partners how they would keep the rhythm. They enjoy inventing new ways and love to share their invention with the group. Another variation on this activity is to ask the children to keep the rhythm with their heads, feet, or eyes. In keeping time with their eyes, some children blinked, others switched their gaze from side to side, and still others crossed and uncrossed their eyes!

Some songs lend themselves to dramatization. Remember that child's play is frequently dramatic play; they are experts at dramatization. A Spanish song the children have enjoyed enacting describes a big bear and a little bear who go to the woods together, the big bear in front, and the little bear behind. The little bear says the nonsense words "pa-pa, pa-pa, pa-pa" and the big bear responds, "pa-pa, pa-pa, pa-pa." The little bear is tired and can't walk any more, so what does the big bear do? He spanks him, "chas, chas, chas."

Because of the spanking, I hesitated to use this song. But it didn't seem to worry the students; in fact they thought it would be fun to dramatize! Since only two children could be bears, the others simulated the woods, placing themselves in positions as bushes, rocks, and broken or fallen trees.

El oso y el osito
Al bosque juntos van.
El oso va delante
Y el osito va detrás.

El osito le dice
"Pa-pa, pa-pa, pa-pa,"
El oso le contesta.
"Pa-pa, pa-pa, pa-pa."

El osito, cansado,
El oso enojado
Le pega: chas, chas, chas.

Need for Special Activities

No matter how interesting each class period is for the children, a complete break from normal routines with the use of special activities revitalizes the teacher and the children. Although other special activities can be used, I use original plays in Spanish because of the special benefits they provide:

1. *Motivation to continue learning.* The children enjoy the preparation and presentation of the plays so much that it is the single most important reason why children return year after year to continue their study of Spanish.

2. *Outlets for creativity.* The children provide input as we choose the theme, develop the story line, and select props and costumes.

3. *Development of expressive speech.* As the children learn the lines for the play, they are encouraged to "act angry when they say angry words": scowl, stamp their feet, shake their fingers. The children begin to believe that with the second language they are learning they can express anger, joy, sorrow, and disbelief, just as they do in English. Most learners of a second language do not experience the expressive possibilities of the second language. After all, in the second language classroom, they rarely observe emotional expression.

4. *Development of self-confidence.* One mother confessed that she would not have believed that was her son performing in front of a group. Until his performance in the second language, he had refused to participate in school and church programs. His participation in the development of the play had gradually involved him so much he did not want to miss being a part of the performance!

5. *Talent development.* The plays are a good opportunity for children to explore their talents and interests. One boy who delighted us with his depictions of bungling doctor, bland father, and lovable spider went on to take part in community theater and even had a lead role.

5. *Parent involvement.* The plays encourage parent involvement in the second language program: parents help with makeup and costumes, provide props, take photographs or videotape the plays, and provide the treats afterwards. Since our program is extracurricular, the commitment of parent volunteers is essential to its vitality. The Spanish plays help convince parents of the value of the second language program.

How are the original plays developed? The first step is to review the vocabulary theme areas that the children have been learning through the year and identify those themes around which a play might be developed. For example, last year I suggested to one group animals of the forest or breakfast foods.

The second step is to have the children brainstorm ideas for a play that might utilize the newly learned vocabulary. Depending on the group, no further suggestions for themes may be necessary, but be prepared to stimulate their thinking (for example, by asking them to think of books, stories, or TV programs they have liked that might be adapted to a play). Also remind them of the basic tenet of brainstorming: no criticism of another person's idea.

The ideas suggested by the children can cover quite a range; the group that was considering forest animals and breakfast foods seemed to favor the forest animals. Their suggestions ranged from very involved and difficult plots to more manageable ones. Their suggestions were *The Dark Crystal*, a story based on *The Littles*, house-sized people who live in the walls of a house without adults' knowing about them; a big man who tries to rule the earth and is defeated by Super Rabbit; and a boy who is lost at the zoo and is helped by the animals there. The favorite idea and the one that shaped the play was an adaptation from a book. A deer was shot and its antlers taken by two hunters; all the forest animals plot to capture the hunters and thus teach them to respect the animals' desire to lead a safe life in their home, the forest. In the end, the deer gets its antlers back, and the hunters and all the forest animals become friends (See Appendix).

As a third step, develop the rough draft of the play. Make sure that the play contains natural dialogue even though the children will be using new grammatical constructions they have not yet studied. It is important to make the dialogue as realistic as possible. Be sure the plot has dramatic tension: something needs to be wrong and, in the resolution of the play, be corrected. Also consider the following factors:

The group's ability with the second language. Beginning groups have shorter lines, more repetition, the addition of songs, and a simpler plot than do more advanced groups.

The number of children in the group. If there are few children in the group, they may have several parts. If there are many children in the group, they may share lines, or a line may be broken up among several persons.

The feasibility of props and costumes. Parents shouldn't go to expense and effort to provide costumes for the children. A child can be a snake with a piece of shiny, draped fabric rather than a homemade

213

sequined costume. The important thing is to feel like a snake: with child's imagination, this is not hard to do.

When the rough draft is completed, share it with the children ar ask them to make further suggestions to "polish it." Add these fin adaptations to the play. If the play is long, ask each child to bring blank cassette tape on which you record his/her part. Leave a sile space after each line so that the child can repeat the line after yo The children use these tapes to practice at home.

Next, use class time to practice the play. Be sure to remind t children to be expressive, to speak loudly, and to keep their fac toward the audience when they are speaking. You may take all only part of the class period for practicing the play. When the play learned well and the costumes and props are ready, hold a dre rehearsal, asking parents to take photographs or videotape the pla Invite parents, friends, and teachers to a program at which ea group presents its play. The children enjoy seeing the other plays much as they enjoy performing their own.

Too often the foreign language itself is the only considerati when a curriculum is planned for an elementary-school langua program. Teachers should not lose sight of the children when pla ning a program! They need to consider the children's needs for r objects, physical activity, creative expression, and special activiti The children will enjoy the program more, the parents are more thusiastic, and so is the teacher.

References

Donoghue, M.R. *Foreign Languages and the Elementary School Ch* Dubuque, Iowa: William C. Brown, 1968.

Iowa Governor's Task Force. *Report of the Governor's Task Force Foreign Language Studies and International Education to the Honoro Terry E. Branstad, Governor, State of Iowa.* Des Moines, Iowa: Auth 1983.

Mitchell, R. (Field Production), and Halgren, M. (Narrator). *Take One.* Moines, Iowa: Iowa Public Television, February 23, 1983.

President's Commission on Foreign Language and International Stud *Strength through Wisdom: A Critique of U.S. Capability, A Report to President from the President's Commission on Foreign Language and ternational Studies. Modern Language Journal* 64.1 (1980):19-57.

Rosenbusch, M.H., and Graber, A. *Conversational Spanish for Childr A Curriculum Guide.* Ames. Iowa: Iowa State University Press, 1982

Appendix

¡Amigos Somos Ya! (We're Friends Now!)

by Marcia H. Rosenbusch, with the assistance of

Sara Britson	Elizabeth Furr
Aprille Clarke	Tina Limbird
Aaron Dietz	Mairym Pinero
Suzanne Dietz	Justin Readhead
Sarah Freed	Adrian Rosenbusch

Characters:

El pájaro (bird)	*La ardilla* (squirrel)
La serpiente (snake)	*El oso* (bear)
El conejo (rabbit)	*El ciervo* (deer)
El zorrino (skunk)	*El cazador 1* (Hunter 1)
El lobo (wolf)	*El cazador 2* (Hunter 2)
	El cazador 3 (Hunter 3)

Scene 1: *The animals are just waking up in the forest.*

El pájaro:	Pío, pío, pío. Buenos. . . [Peep, peep, peep. Good. .]
La serpiente:	. . .días-s-s-s. . . [morning. . .]
El conejo:	. . .a todos, a todos, a todos! [to everyone, to everyone, to everyone!] *Said while hopping around.*
La ardilla:	*(counting his nuts)* Buenos días, amigos![Good morning, friends!]
El oso:	*(yawning)* ¿Qué hacemos hoy? [What are we doing today?]

The deer yawns and goes back to sleep, snoring softly.

El zorrino:	¿A ver, a ver? [Let's see, let's see?]
El lobo:	¿Qué día es hoy? [What day is today?] *scratching his head.*
El pájaro:	¿Navidad? [Christmas]
La serpiente:	¿Mi cumpleaños-s-s-s-s? [My birthday?]
El conejo:	¿Vacaciones? [Vacation]
La ardilla:	¡Es lunes, amigos! [It's Monday, friends!]

A shot rings out.

El oso:	¿Qué pasa, qué pasa? [What's happening? What's happening?]
El zorrino:	¡Es un cazador! [It's a hunter!]

All animals except the deer begin to tremble with fear.

El lobo: ¡Tengo miedo! [I'm afraid!]

The deer stretches slowly and yawns.

La serpiente:	. . .notic-c-c-c-cia [bad. . .]
El conejo:	. . .malísima! [. . .news!]
El ciervo:	*(stretching)* Pero, qué es un cazador? [But, what is a hunter?]
La ardilla:	¡Un cazador. . . [A hunter. . .] *trembling*
El oso:	. . .es un hombre. . . [. . .is a man. . .]
El zorrino:	. . .que mata . . . [. . .who kills. . .]
El lobo:	. . .a los animales! [. . .animals!]
El ciervo:	¿Qué? Yo no tengo miedo! [What? I'm not afraid!]

Another shot rings out. All the animals except the deer dash off trembling to stage left. The deer stretches again, admires the reflection of its antlers in the water, and takes a drink.

   Off stage, hunters sing to the tune of "A-hunting We Will Go."

Los cazadores:

> ¡Cazando vamos ya! [A-hunting we will go!]
> ¡Cazando vamos ya! [A-hunting we will go!]
> ¡Qué felicidad [What happiness]
> Cazando vamos ya! [A-hunting we will go!]

As they come onstage, they see the deer and immediately stop singing and prepare their guns.

Cazador 1:	¡Un ciervo! [A deer!]
Cazador 2:	¡Qué grande! [How big!]
Cazador 3:	¡Qué cornamentas! [What antlers!] *Indicating the antlers by pointing to his own head.*

Cazador 1:	¡Es mío! [It's mine!] *He shoots and the deer falls.*
Cazador 2:	¡Las cornamentas. . . [The antlers. . .]
Cazador 3:	. . . son para casa! [. . .are for our house!]

They take off the antlers and all three leave singing their song again and carrying the antlers. The animals all return quickly to where the deer is lying.

El pájaro:	¡Oh no!
La serpiente:	¡Pobre c-c-c-c-ciervo! [Poor deer!]
El conejo:	¡Está muerto! [He's dead!]

They all begin to cry.

El ciervo:	Oh-o-o-o *He begins to move and look about, dazed.*
La ardilla:	¡El ciervo está bien! [The deer is OK!]
El oso:	Pero pobrecito. . .[But the poor thing. . .]
El ciervo:	*Looking at the bear in surprise.* ¿Qué pasa? [What's wrong?]
El zorrino:	Tú no tienes. . . [You don't have. . .]
El ciervo:	¿Qué pasa, qué pasa? [What's wrong, what's wrong?] *worriedly*
El lobo:	No tienes las cornamentas! [You don't have your antlers!]

The deer reaches for its antlers and when it discovers that they aren't there, begins to cry.

El pájaro:	. . .No llores. . . [Don't cry. . .]
La serpiente:	. . . nosotros-s-s-s-s. . . [. . .we. . .]
El conejo:	. . . te ayudaremos! [. . .will help you!]

They whisper together, making their plan.

Scene 2: The hunters are at their camp admiring the antlers.

Cazador 1:	¡Qué cornamentas! [What antlers!]
Cazador 2:	!Qué grandes! [How big!]
Cazador 3:	¡Qué bellas! [How beautiful!]

A moaning sound is heard. The hunters take their guns and investigate. They find the bear lying on the ground.

Cazador 1:	¡Un oso! [A bear!]
Cazador 2:	¡Qué grande! [How big!]
Cazador 3:	!Qué piel! [What fur!]

They get ready to shoot, but the other animals throw a net over them. The hunters tremble in fear while the animals all sing the following song to the tune of "A-hunting We Will Go." They dance around the captured hunters.

Animals:

¡Cazando vamos ya¡ [A-hunting we will go!]
¡Cazando vamos ya¡ [A-hunting we will go!]
¡Qué felicidad [What happiness]
Cazando vamos ya! [A-hunting we will go!]

El pájaro:	¿Dónde están. . . [Where are. . .]
La serpiente:	. . .las-s-s-s cornamentas-s-s-s. . . [. . .the deer's. . .]
El conejo:	. . .del ciervo, del ciervo, del ciervo? [antlers, antlers, antlers.] *hopping about excitely*
El cazador 1:	¡Socorro! ¡Socorro! [Help! Help!]
El cazador 2:	¡Sálvanos! ¡Sálvanos! [Save us! Save us!]
El cazador 3:	¡Ahí están! [There they are!] *pointing to the antlers by the campfire.*

La ardilla:	¡Ahí están! [There they are! There they are!]
El oso:	*putting the antlers on the happy deer* Bueno, amigo. . [Well, friend. . .]
El zorrino:	Y con los cazadores. . [And with the hunters. .]
El lobo:	¿Qué hacemos? [What shall we do?]

Cazador 1:	Perdón. . . [Forgive us. . .]
Cazador 2:	Señor ciervo. . . [Mister Deer. . .]
Cazador 3:	Perdón. . . [Forgive us. . .]
Los cazadores:	¡No cazaremos más! [We won't hunt anymore!]

The animals all whisper together. Then they let the hunters out. The hunters break their guns and throw them away.

El oso: Bueno, ¡aprendieron su lección! [Well, they learned their lesson!]

All the animals cheer. The animals and hunters hold hands and dance in a circle, singing together the following song to the same tune as before.

Amigos somos ya! [We are friends now!]
Amigos somos ya! [We are friends now!]
Qué felicidad! [What happiness!]
Amigos somos ya! [We are friends now!]

All come to the front of the stage and bow.

Bilingual Language Arts through Music

Sheryl L. Santos

Promoting the incorporation of music into the bilingual curriculum has come about as a result of experiencing, observing, and documenting the positive reactions of students and teachers to music in the classroom. As the guitar is tuned or the record player readied, an air of expectancy, unity, and excitement envelops the classroom.

As songs are introduced in the second language to speakers of other languages, it is not long before each student is involved in an authentic cultural experience. In addition, students develop such linguistic competencies as pronunciation, intonation, vocabulary, and comprehension effortlessly and naturally. For example, when a song is taught in Spanish to a linguistically mixed student body, the native Spanish speakers display delight and pride in assisting the English-only students with mastery of the melody, pronunciation and meaning. The English speakers, on the other hand, eagerly strive for perfection of the newly acquired skills in Spanish. In addition to learning a second language and becoming familiar with a new mode of cultural expression, the students perceive the positive values of bilingualism and elevate the status of the non-Anglo culture. Similarly, a song introduced to the same students in English affords the Spanish-dominant pupils an opportunity to develop linguistic competencies in the second language, to work closely with their English-speaking peers in a tutorial situation, and to acquire a feeling for the Anglo culture through personal involvement.

Music and Ethnicity

Dr. Ricardo Trimillos, ethnomusicologist at the University of Hawaii, speaks of the great potential of the interface between ethnomusicology and education in the following statement:

> One of ethnomusicology's primary purposes in education is to educate the individual *through* music as well as *to* music. For example, learning an ancient hula involves an understanding of music, dance, language, geography and social values. It presents a mode of thinking, a style of moving, and a way of hearing... The study and presentation of ethnic music in the schools points up the existence of alternative and valid

Sheryl L. Santos is Associate Professor of Bilingual Education in the Department of Elementary Education, East Texas State University.

cultural expressions, which are of critical importance to the American of an ethnic minority background. A polycultural approach to music can reinforce positively his identity as a "hyphenated American." Negative marginality thus becomes positive biculturality; it allows him to experience and explore another part of his own heritage without feeling that he is weakening or rejecting the American orientation. (32)

Culturally relevant music (i.e., traditional and folk music representative of a specific ethnic population) can be integrated into the school's curriculum in order to make the total educational program more compatible with the cultures and languages of minority children. As Cárdenas and Cárdenas indicate:

An instructional program developed for a white, Anglo-Saxon, English-speaking middle class school population cannot be and is not adequate for a non-white, non-Anglo-Saxon, non-English-speaking, or non-middle class population. To reverse the pattern of failure for non-typical children, it is necessary that the instructional program and the characteristics of the learner be compatible. (1)

Others have also recognized the need for culturally oriented curriculum materials that are useful and stimulating in both the cognitive and affective domains. Responding to this awareness, Franklin and Nicholson in their study of 157 randomly selected black students reported statistically significant differences in achievement according to (1) the type of music the students were exposed to (culturally oriented or not), (2) the attitudes of the teachers toward the culturally oriented music program, and (3) the entry attitudes of the students themselves toward music representative of their culture. They concluded that positive attitudes toward the home culture coupled with a culturally based curriculum can inspire greater pupil achievement.

In an informative publication, B. Lee Cooper, vice-president for academic affairs of Newberry College, develops two innovative instructional approaches using popular music as a resource for teaching contemporary black history: (1) the use of biographies of popular music artists and (2) the analysis of social themes through song lyrics. Cooper laments that although black music has always been at the vanguard of the community's feelings and consciousness, the lyrics of black artists have rarely been introduced into the academic setting. He believes that black musical artists' contributions to the rich oral Afro-American tradition can no longer be overlooked.

The power of music as an enculturator contributing to positive cultural identity, self-esteem and group cohesiveness is examined by Johnston in research concerning the role of Eskimo and Indian music vis-a-vis Alaskan native social adjustment. Addressing educators with his extensive, well developed rational, Johnston advocates native music in the classroom at every grade level. He believes that continued research can eventually help solve intercultural and intracultural problems in a rapidly changing, pluralistic society.

Music and the School Curriculum

The versatility of music as a vehicle for achieving educational success in academic disciplines such as reading, foreign language, mathematics, and language arts has also been documented in the literature. (Arrellano and Diaper; Donlan; Lloyd; Crow; Jolly; Cardelli). In addition, interdisciplinary uses of music are often proposed to enhance and unify the entire academic curriculum. (Mulligan; Williams)

One important curricular area, reading, has been given considerable attention by educational practitioners and researchers. In a state-of-the-art review, Sullivan found three prevalent types of publications pertaining to the teaching of reading through music: (1) testimonials concerned with motivation and the affective domain, (2) research on the relationship between reading and musical abilities, and (3) research on the effects of music instruction on acquisition of reading skills. Sullivan concludes that, despite inconclusive evidence and insufficient research investigations documenting gains in the affective domain to support using music instruction to improving language reading attainment, "it would appear that if one likes the music/reading approach, that is, using songs in teaching reading skills, it can be successfully utilized as part of the instructional program for reading" (8).

In noting the many ways that music can benefit the curriculum, music's appeal and usefulness with special populations (e.g., mentally retarded, pre-school, emotionally disturbed) should not be overlooked (Groves and Groves; Simons; Andres). In one interesting case study by Deutsch and Parks, for example, music is used as a reinforcer to increase appropriate conversational speech. The subject of their research was a moderately mentally retarded fourteen-year-old boy with severe emotional problems. Rewarding Glen with the opportunity to hear continuous music as long as he demonstrated appropriate behavior and conversational dialogue proved to be a successful motivator. After eighteen sessions, his use of "conversation-like" sentences increased significantly. The researchers suggest that music be considered a primary reinforcer with autistic and mentally ill patients.

Methodology

Prior to incorporating music into the curriculum and thus reaping the benefits of this instruction, one should strive for mastery of a comfortable method for introducing and teaching songs in a foreign language. A teacher who isn't proficient in the target language can rely on a parent volunteer, consultant, student, or recording. Once the method itself is internalized, it can be passed along to the one who will ultimately be responsible for teaching the song.

The successful teaching of a song in a language not yet mastered by the students depends on the teacher's technique, method, patience, and awareness. The awareness of students' abilities, interests, and mastery levels will enhance and facilitate the completion of the task. The time it takes to pass through the four phases of the recommended methodology will vary according to the complexity of the song, the students' experiential backgrounds, the time allotted daily to this activity, and the students' attention span. The following suggested methodology can be adapted for compatibility with the teacher's style of teaching and the pupil's style of learning.

Motivation. Before introducing the song, orient the students by briefly discussing the content, origin, central theme, historical relevance, or any other information available to you about the song. Follow the orientation by playing a recording or by singing the song to the class. As the melody becomes increasingly familiar, encourage the students to hum or sing along.

Participation. To encourage student involvement, begin by teaching the most repetitive parts of the song such as the chorus or refrain. This phase familiarizes the student with the verses and creates an early sense of accomplishment.

Analysis. Once the students are completely familiar with the tune and with the chorus or other refrains, move on to teaching the correct pronunciation and meaning of each line of the song. It is important to translate in a meaningful way, as opposed to a word-by-word literal translation. The analysis phase can be accomplished in the following manner:

1. Decide the key words in each line in advance. If the students have a personal copy of the lyrics, have them underline the key words and write the translation on the top of each one. Repeat the difficult words several times to encourage correct pronunciation.
2. Following the mastery of the key words, move on to longer phrases using a technique called "backward buildup," a standard feature of the audiolingual method. (See section on sample methodology.)
3. As each line is mastered, sing the song through from the beginning for practice and reinforcement until the stanza is completed. Teach subsequent stanzas following the satisfactory performance of each previous one.

Performance. After all phases of the lesson are completed, sing frequently. It is often fun to sing together as the day begins, while waiting in line for the lunch bell to ring, or at the end of the day. On a selected day, small groups of children may want to perform for the class, or an individual student may want to sing a solo. The main points to remember are that singing is an enjoyable class activity and that the mastery of a song serves as a catalyst for many related learning activities in other content areas.

As your class expands the repertoire, students may enjoy performing for various audiences, including other classes at your school or at a neighboring one. Parents, nursing home residents, hospitalized

221

children, or community service club members may enjoy the performance also.

Sample Methodology

An example of the recommended methodology applied to the popular Spanish folk song, *De colores* follows. Refer to the *Cancionero bilingüe*, p.17.

Motivation. De colores means "of colors." It is a Spanish folk song to which a myriad of lyrics have been added over the years. The song has become the theme song of the Cursillo movement, an experience of rededication to the Roman Catholic Church which began in Spain in 1949.

Participation. Encourage students to sing along each time the phrase "de colores" is sung. Introduce the refrain, "Y por eso los grandes amores de muchos colores me gustan a mi." This refrain is repeated several times throughout the song.

Analysis. After the teacher has chosen the key vocabulary, the following may be introduced and the students may make notations on their paper as follows:

                       countryside   spring
De colores, de colores se visten los *campos* en la *primavera.*

                       birds   from afar
De colores, de colores son los *pajaritos* que vienen *de fuera.*

                   rainbow   shine
De colores, de colores es el *arco iris* que vemos *lucir.*

For this particular song, it might also be a good idea to point out how Spanish speakers and English speakers differ in their cultural perceptions of animal sounds.

                   cockadoodledoo
Canta el gallo, canta el gallo con el *quiri, quiri, quiri, quiri, qui.*

                   cluck, cluck
La gallina, la gallina con el *cara, cara, cara, cara, ca*

To teach the pronunciation of the longer phrases such as "se visten los compos en la primavera," begin with smaller parts starting at the end of the phrase. This "backward buildup" would be introduced thus: "en la primavera" ... "los campos en la primavera" ... "se visten los campos en la primavera."

In the event of a particularly difficult phrase such as "los pajaritos que vienen de fuera," you might repeat the difficult words several times prior to attempting the entire phrase. The techniques of backward buildup can be used as an added reinforcement. "Los pa-

222

jaritos ... los pajaritos que vienen ... los pajaritos que vienen de fuera ... de fuera ... que vienen de fuera ... los pajaritos que vienen de fuera."

Performance. After teaching the song in both English and Spanish, there are several alternatives to encourage a group sing-along. One idea is to divide the class in two and have each group sing its version simultaneously in either English or Spanish. Languages can be switched after the first stanza. Another idea is to have the girls sing the first stanza in English or Spanish and then have the boys sing the second stanza in the other language. By alternating languages, students are given practice in both languages and are encouraged to develop fluency and control in each.

Language Arts Learning Activities

The introduction of the language arts activities should follow the learning of the song in the students' second language so that they will be familiar with the phonetics, syntax, and semantics of the lyrics. The suggested activities that follow are designed to achieve varied objectives in the areas of oral language development, reading, listening, and writing. If the song is in the students' native language, these activities can also be adapted to promote growth in oral language, new knowledge of grammatical relationships and patterns, spelling, cultural information, creativity, and other language arts skills.

Oral Language Development Skills

1. After teaching the students specific vocabulary, allow these to be substituted in a song in which the syntax might still be preserved although the meaning is somewhat altered. The following activity is adapted from Jacovetti.

   De la sierra morena ...

   　　mis padres y mis tíos
   　　Tomás y su hermana
   　　vienen bajando
   　　Unas orejas grandes　　　...vienen bajando

   　　una niña bonita
   　　mi amigo Miguel
   　　un buen conocido　　　...viene bajando

   Corriendo y brincando, cielito lindo, de
   　　saltando y jugando
   　　　contrabando.

   　　　Ay, ay, ay, ay, canta y no　　　...bailes
   　　　　　　　　　　　　　　　　　　grites
   　　　　　　　　　　　　　　　　　　te quejes
   　　　　　　　　　　　　　　　　　　te vayas ...

223

In English.

Down from the mountain top
       zoo
       market
       school

My dearest
   darling
   love
   sweetheart

There come those ... pretty dark eyes
                 tremendous ears
                 great big feet

A ... pair of pretty dark eyes
   bushel
   dozen

My dearest ... stealthily coming toward ... me
         sneakily   us
         rapidly   you
         slowly   him
         noisily   her

2. Instruct students to search the lyrics for a particular element. These might include such things as words of emotion or words expressing the senses. The use of dictionaries and glossaries should be encouraged to develop the students' self-help and resource skills. Once the assignment is given, the students can carry out such instructions as underlining, defining, searching for synonyms or antonyms, writing original sentences or others.

> Example: Después de estudiar la versión en español de *Cuando calienta el sol* (25) haga lo siguiente:
> 1. Subraye todos los verbos
> 2. Tradúzcalos al inglés utilizando el diccionario bilingüe
> 3. Usando la grabadora, grabe una oración original para cada verbo (en inglés o en español)

3. Ask specific questions, such as: Who is singing to whom? What is the tone or mood of the song? Why do you think this song was written? What cultural elements are in it? How does this song make you feel?

4. To encourage creative expression, have students invent a scenario for the song in question. Allow them to make up a story or invent characters about whom the song might have been written. Students may also look for pictures in magazines that seem to depict scenes from the song. These can be used to illustrate an

original story booklet about the song. When completed, all students tell their stories to the class.

5. Have students draw or paint their interpretations of a specific part in the song that has meaning for them. Display these drawings or have the students talk about what their own drawings represent.

6. Employ a guided discussion method for students who cannot yet speak English fluently. Have the students choose the correct response from the model provided to encourage their use of complete sentences and correct grammatical patterns. Example: (Refer to *Brown-Eyed Children of the Sun*)

who	*what*	*where*	*how*
You	toil	California	lined
	back	Mexico	bent
wife	eyes	Sacramento Valley	wrinkled
children	picking		smiling
	working		
	life		
	face		
	age		

Up to (where) from (where) (who) come
To the (where) to (what) in the sun
Your (what) is (how) and (how)
Your (who) and (who) are (what) everyone...
Your (what) is (how) and (how)
And your (what) is 41: Your (what)
dying time has come. Your children's (what)
are (how) their (what) is just begun...

Reading Activities

These sample activities will be based on the song, *Feelings*.

1. The cloze technique (deletion of a phoneme or word) can be employed to strengthen the phonic, syntactic, and semantic cueing systems in the following ways:
    Phonics. Delete a selected phoneme or pair of phonemes each time these appear in a word. Have the students complete each word. Variations of this activity might include deleting only beginning, ending, or medial consonants, blends, or digraphs, according to the chronology of the reading skills sequence. For example:

    ____eelings, no____ing more ____an ____eelings.
    Trying to ____orget my ____eelings of love.

    Syntax. Delete words following a key grammatical structure. For example.

    Can you find a home for these words? "than," "to," "of," "on."

    Feelings, nothing more _____feelings, trying _____

225

forget my feelings _____ love. Teardrops, rolling down _____ my face...

Additionally, words in the lyrics that are crucial to the meaning of the song may be deleted. Instruct students to replace those words with their own words, provided that they make sense syntactically, in order to create a song with a different meaning. For example,

_____, nothing more than _____, trying to _____ my _____ of _____.
_____, rolling down on my _____....

2. Sight word activities are excellent for helping young readers identify very common words in a context they can understand. In the song *Feelings*, there are many sight words that students can search for and circle in context. These include "than," "to," "my," "of," "for," "all," "it," "I," "you," "come," "in," "and," "girl," "have," "down." Similarly, sight words in Spanish are "cuomo," "mis," "de," "si," "yo," "que," "aquí."

3. Purposeful oral reading can be encouraged as questions are asked that will require students to locate specific answers in their texts and read these aloud. For example, the teacher can ask a student to locate the line in the song that tells what the singer is trying to forget. Or perhaps the student will be instructed to locate the information which states what the singer wishes for with respect to his girlfriend.

4. Reading comprehension can be encouraged by asking questions that are inferential or evaluative as opposed to literal. For example, inferential questions requiring the students to infer information about the characters in the song might include the following opening phrases: Why do you suppose...? Why is it probable or not that...? What do you believe caused...?

Writing Activities

1. Have students create a story with characters centering around the mood evoked by the song or around the song itself. For example, *Brown-eyed Children of the Sun* evokes the trials of a migrant family struggling to survive as best they can, while the popular romantic tune, *Cuando calienta el sol*, evokes a scene of young lovers at the height of their relationship.

2. Extract poetic phrases and have students explain these in their own words or by using another poetic simile. In *Brown-eyed Children of the Sun* there are such phrases as: "your dying time has come," or "your children's eyes are smiling."

3. To enhance spelling skills, have students identify misspelled words within the song text. For example, the song *Eres tú* has ten spelling errors. Instruct students to underline each misspelled word and write each word correctly on a separate page.

Como una promeza, erres tú, eres tú
como una manana de berano
Como una sonriza, eres tú, eres tú
Así, así, eres tú.
Como mi esperansa, eres tú, eres tú,
Como lubia fresca en mis manos
Como fuerte briza eres tú, eres tú
Así, así, eres tú
Eres tú como el agwa de mi fuente
Eres tú el fuego de mi ogar.

4. Have students write a summary of a song using essay form in which they tell what the song is about. For example, an essay about *Autumn Leaves* might include the following:

   Autumn Leaves is a sad song telling about a person who is remembering a lost love. The leaves are dying. This represents the death of the relationship. The singer can see many things in his mind like leaves, lips, kisses, and sunburned hands. Even though the love is ended, the singer is not angry and still misses the beloved person.

5. For students who cannot yet write creatively in English, written responses can be encouraged by providing a guided discussion model for students to follow. Refer to the English version of *Solamente una vez* for the following example.

who	*what*	*when*
You	heart	now and forever
our	start	not long ago
we	stars	while
	guitars	

   (who)   belong to my   (what)   ,   (when)
   and   (whose)   love had its   (what)   ,   (when)
   (who)   were gathering   (what)   ,   (when)
   a million   (what)   played our love song...

Listening Activities

1. Ask students to identify rhyming words. For example, in the song,
   Cielito lindo,
   bajando/contrabando
   nido/perdido
   boca/toca
   pasión/corazón
   supe/Guadalupe
   fragua/agua
   ver/volver

2. Ask students to identify beginning, medial, or ending letters of words as the teacher or a chosen student reads the text of a song. The teacher reading the lyrics in English of *De colores* will stop after each word the class is to work with and indicate one of the following: identify beginning letters; identify medial vowels; identify ending letters: e.g., *l*iving colors embrace all with *love* in the springtime.

3. Ask students to listen for intonation to determine when a question is being asked, or when a statement or negative sentence is being said.

4. Have students complete phrases, predict outcomes, or substitute synonyms or antonyms as a listening/speaking activity.

References

Arrellano, Sonya I., and Jean E. Diaper. "Relationship between Musical Aptitudes and Second Language Learning." Florida State University, 1970. ERIC ED 050 621.

Cardarelli, Aldo. "Twenty-one Ways to Use Music in Teaching the Language Arts." Evansville, 1979. ERIC ED 176 268.

Cardenas, J.A., and B. Cardenas. *The Theory of Incompatibilities.* San Antonio: Intercultural Development Research Association, 1977.

Cooper, B. Lee. "Popular Music: An Untapped Resource for Teaching Contemporary Black History." *Journal of Negro Education* 48(1979):20-36.

Crow, Warren. "Mathematics and Music." *School Science and Mathematics* 74.8(1974): 687-691.

Deutsch, Marily, and A. Lee Parks. "The Use of Contingent Music to Increase Appropriate Conversational Speech." *Mental Retardation* 16.1 (1978): 33-36.

Donaln, D. "Music and the Language Arts Curriculum." *English Journal.* 63.7 (1974): 86-88.

Franklin, Jacquelyn C., and Everett W. Nicholson. "Relationship between Teacher Viewpoints towards a Culturally Oriented Music Program and Black Pupils Achievement and Viewpoints towards the Program." *Education* 98.3 (1978): 307-10.

Groves, Saundra L., and David Groves. "Music as a Vehicle for Life Enrichment and Expanded Content for Special Audiences." *Adolescence* 15.57 (1980): 195-200.

Johnston, Thomas F. "Alaskan Native Social Adjustment and the Role of Ethnic Studies." *Journal of Ethnic Studies.* 3.4 (1976): 21-36.

Jolly, Yukiko S. "The Use of Songs in teaching Foreign Languages." *The Modern Language Journal.* 59.1 (1975): 11-14.

Lloyd, Mavis J. "Teach Music to Aid Beginning Readers." *The Reading Teacher.* 32.3 (1978): 323-27.

Mulligan, Mary Ann. *Integrating Music with Other Studies.* New York: The Center for Applied Research in Education, 1975.

Simons, Gene M. "A Rationale for Music in Early Childhood." *Education* 99.2 (1978): 141-44.

Sullivan, Emilie P. "Using Music to Teach Reading: State of the Art Review." Paper Presented at the National Reading Council Annual Meeting, San Antonio, 1979. ERIC ED 184 109.

Trimillos, Ricardo. "Ethnomusicology." *Educational Perspectives* 14.2 (1975): 31-32.

Williams, Polly F. "Musical Creativity: An Interdisciplinary Approach." *The Creative Child and Adult Quarterly* 11.3 (1977): 148-150.

Appendix. Resources for Spanish-English Bilingual Classrooms

The following selections include song books, indexes, recordings, unique curricular materials in the content areas, classroom guides, and the names and addresses of recording companies that specialize in international folk music.

Lyric Guides and Reference Books
Cancionero popular americano. Washington, D.C.: Pan American Union.

Chase, Gilbert. *A Guide to the Music of Latin America.* New York: AMS Press, 1972.

Fourteen Traditional Songs From Texas. Trans. Gustavo Duran. Washington D.C.: Pan American Union, Music Division, 1942.

Ehret, Walter. *The International Books of Christmas Carols.* Englewood Cliffs, New Jersey: Prentice-Hall, 1963.

Havlice, Patricia Pate. *Popular Song Index.* Metuchen, New Jersey: Scarecrow Press, 1975.

National Anthems of the American Republics. Washington, D.C.: Pan American Union, 1949.

Paz, Elena. *Favorite Spanish Folk Songs: Traditional Songs from Spain and Latin America.* New York: Oak Publishing Co., 1965. The songs in this book are available in recordings from Folkways Recording Co., 43 W. East Street, New York 10023. Telephone (212) 586-7260.

Prieto, Mariana. *Play it in Spanish: Spanish Games and Folk Songs to Children.* Pennsylvania: Day, 1973.

Robb, John Donald. *Hispanic Folk Songs of New Mexico.* Albuquerque: University of New Mexico Press, 1954.

_____. *Hispanic Folk Music of New Mexico and the Southwest.* Norman: University of Oklahoma Press, 1980.

Rockwell, Anne. *El Toro Pinto and Other Songs in Spanish.* New Jersey: MacMillan, 1971.

Yurchenco, Henrietta. *A Fiesta of Folk Songs from Spain and Latin America.* New Jersey: Putnam, 1967.

Curricular Resources for Classroom Use
Badias, Bertha et al. *Cantando y aprendiendo.* Bronx, New York: Curriculum Adaptation Network for Bilingual/Bicultural Education, March 1974. ED 108 499. The illustrated teacher's songbook contains 18 songs and games to be used with the SCDC (Spanish Curriculum Development Center) publications and other materials. The objectives are designed to develop children's listening and comprehension skills, music appreciation, and rhythmic expression.

Canyon Records. 4143 North 16th Street, Phoenix, Arizona 85016. International folk music for children and adults.

Forming an Estudiantina and Symbols of Music Notation. Dissemination and Assessment Center for Bilingual Education, 7703 North Lamar, Austin, Texas 78752. Bilingual teacher's guide for music instruction at all levels.

Includes words, music, and instrumentation for beginning singing groups; music and notation; vocabulary; and costume sketches.

G. Ricordi and Company: Paseo de la Reforma 481-A, Mexico 5, D.F. Mexico. Specializing in musical scores in Spanish.

Guardarrama, Eduardo. *Un sueno musical.* Fall River, Massachusetts: National Dissemination and Assessment Center for Bilingual Education, 1978. ED 177 908. Spanish children's reader for grades 1-3 in a bilingual setting. Tells us about the cultural contributions of Indians, Spaniards and blacks to Puerto Rican Music.

Jacovetti, Raymond. *Teacher's Manual for Escuchar y Cantar.* New York: Holt, Rinehart and Winston, 1965. This manual provides teachers with the lyrics and scores of 30 popular tunes in Spanish. Each song is followed by a series of suggested activities to help students with language patterns and grammatical structures. Recordings are also available.

Joan Baez Sings De Colores. Autin, Texas: DACBE. This is a 30 minute cassette tape which also includes a number of poems and vignettes written by DACBE staff. Attractive posters also available.

Neil A. Kjos Music Co., 4382 Jutland Drive, San Diego, California 92117. Specializing in recordings in Spanish.

Mills, Alvin, and Josefa P. Mills, editors and arrangers. Christmas Songs: *Canciones de Navidad.* Available from ARRC Educational Sales Co., Box 14525, Long Beach, California 90803. Bilingual Christmas songs in Spanish and English to enrich the musical experiences of beginning singers. Arranged from Spanish folklore materials.

————. *Canciones folkloricas infantiles de España.* Fourteen bilingual musical poems available on record or cassette.

Perkins, Carol. *Songs by Carol Perkins.* Caper Records, 6100 Cherrylawn Circle, Austin, Texas 78723. A series of original lyrics and recordings designed to help young children learn English or Spanish through music and kinesthetic movement.

Something Educational, Box 3476, McAllen, Texas 78501. This company carries the following musical curricular resources: *Matematicas Musical: Mexican Ethnic Music Kit; Folkways Series of Music from Latin America and Texas Mexican Border Music.*

Soy. Rosa. *Bilingual Education through Music.* Master's Thesis, Kean College, New Jersey. July 1975. ED 141 473. In addition to a very informative and thorough review of the literature, this publication provides a series of language arts readiness activities utilizing the music and the lyrics of the traditional Cuban writers such as Jose Marti.

Vela, Irma Saldivar. *Bailes a colores.* Available from American Universal Artforms Corporation, Box 4574, Austin, Texas 78765. This is a simplified color-keyed system for use in teaching the steps of 5 dances popular in the United States and Mexico. It comes with a record, step chart, cassette, workbook, mini-manual, and map of origins.

Andress, Barbara. *Music: Experiences in Early Childhood.* New York: Rinehart, and Winston, 1980.

Grammar and the Reluctant Learner: A Games Approach

Robert Williston

Grammar remains the proverbial dirty word among foreign language learners, particularly among reluctant ones. Yet grammar remains a vital ingredient in all approaches to language learning. Games, though widely used tools in language teaching, are virtually all vocabulary oriented. Required are games for reinforcing grammar. This paper presents several models teachers can use to design games that are inexpensive, highly motivational, and congruent with their program. The model for each grammatical structure maximizes time-on-task during game time as well as provides students with excitement that may override their reluctance.

Every teacher has resistant students: those who would rather be anywhere else or do anything else. Probably because they are so well-mannered, they are not hostile, just reluctant. The phenomenon is perhaps more noticeable in mandatory foreign language courses, as a result of students' conditioning at home or among peers to consider other cultures (and thus other languages) inferior to one's own. This circumstance does not mean such courses should not be compulsory but rather that teachers should consider this resistance a challenge.

"Grammar" is usually the straw that breaks the reluctant student's determination. Students often consider grammar irrelevant because the need for it is outweighed by the difficulty of learning it. For most students memorizing rules is indeed boring. Whole generations of students never learned to speak another language because of the perceived difficulty or irrelevance of grammar.

Grammar instruction is so notoriously unappealing, in fact, that many English teachers avoid it. This increases the foreign language teacher's difficulty because it is not at all unusual to find secondary students who do not know what a noun or a verb is. Moreover, students today have frequently been indoctrinated with the notion that we can all do quite well without grammar. The fact of the matter is that no speaker or writer of any language can communicate well without good grammar. Even in this day when "communicative approaches" are considered state of the art, grammar remains, next to vocabulary, the most vital component of effective communication.

Consider for a moment that an acceptable goal for some foreign

231

Robert Williston teaches French at Harkins Junior High School, Newcastle, New Brunswick, Canada.

language student may be a level of grammar equivalent to that of an illiterate native speaker. That represents a tremendous number of grammar rules in any language, as well as all the usual exceptions accompanying them. It is truly difficult to face this grammar fact without reverting to the old grammar-translation method. Whether it is referred to as "grammar" or the "order of words in a sentence," the need for drill is inevitable. The teacher's dilemma is often stated thus: "How does one drill grammar rules and still have fun?" More precisely put, "How can one drill this rule to death and have any survivors from the process?"

Recalcitrant students need motivation as do other students, of course. It is the teacher's responsibility to provide this stimulation; one must never assume any student feels the need to learn what is taught. Everyone else—teachers, parents, and society at large—may recognize the need, but students rarely do.

Language teachers require a gadget to induce even reluctant students to "jump" over the grammar hurdles. Games are, of course, an obvious gadget, but the games needed to interest students in grammar have to be special. They have to endure extended periods of use as well as ensure that students apply the grammar they have been taught in order to win the game. They must qualify as "time on task." And it helps if they are exciting. If a game fulfills these conditions, and the students play it out of class time, then it is a successful educational game.

This paper presents several game models that serve as an approach to grammar drill; they should not be considered a teaching method as such. Since all students have particular areas of weakness, concentration on specific grammar items without the stigma of a formal grammar review can be beneficial.

Hundreds of clever, effective, entertaining games have been devised to drill vocabulary. Language teachers are proficient in the art of simulations. But one gadget has been greatly underused: blank playing cards. They are identical to traditional playing cards, except that the suits and numbers are missing. They provide endless possibilities for experimentation, and even the emergence of computer games has not diminished the intrigue or rivalled the portability of a good card game.

The game models explained here are actually skeletons to which teachers may append their own vocabulary, so they may review whatever rules they choose. Though appropriate for vocabulary review, they are exceptional for grammar review. Most important, they are adaptable to any program, language, and age group.

To design a game, one should exploit the principle that "human beings do not mind paying the full price for gratification." A teacher should not depend on the hypothesis that students prefer game playing to regular classroom activities. Students, in fact, find some games boring and uninteresting. The teacher can, however, exploit a corollary of the game principle: "A student will learn grammar to play a game that satisfies a need." This is accomplished by establishing that a knowledge of grammar is the price to pay (or prerequisite) for playing and winning the game.

Students have some easily recognized needs. Though they may seem unimportant as far as language learning is concerned, they can still be exploited because students actually *feel* the need for the following:

1. *Diversion*. All students become bored with a regular routine. A good game is great for a break.
2. *Adventure*. There is a bit of the gambler or adventurer in all of us. Every game one designs should provide some element of chance. Occasionally chronic losers get a chance to win. Losing is something we must learn to face from time to time, and losing a game is much less serious than losing in real life.
3. *Discipline*. While playing games, students practice rules of interaction. They organize themselves to take turns and build sentences in the correct order. They learn that laws (or rules of the game) transcend the individual. Disorganized students tend to repond to the discipline a structured game gives them.
4. *Investigation*. Every future trial lawyer will love looking for "linguistic loopholes" to winning. Investigation and experimentation are great assets to language learners.
5. *Self-expression*. It is wonderful to watch students at play. Their self-expression in language classes is not spontaneous, but in playing games, they can respond naturally to events in the game. It is sometimes amusing to observe an arrogant student sweating a bit, but it is ever so satisfying to see a smile on the face of a student who never smiled in class before.

In summary, such games need elements of competition, frustration, anxiety, chance, and thereby the thrill of winning. The more elaborate the rules, the more often students will be willing to return to the game.

The following game models, in reality, are well structured grammar exercises. They pass as games because they encompass all the game elements; if the techniques for introducing chance, frustration, and competition are ignored, the games will revert to traditional exercises.

Old Maid Model

The simplest to use, this game model drills the relationship between two groups of items, e.g., the agreement between nouns and adjectives or between subjects and verbs. Take the Spanish verb *hablar* as an example. We can compile two lists of words, subjects and verbs, that must agree:

yo	hablo
tú	hablas
usted	habla
él	habla
ella	habla
nosotros	hablamos
vosotros	habláis
ustedes	hablan
ellos	hablan
ellas	hablan

233

An exercise can be devised by rearranging the items in each group and having the students join the words that agree. It is doubtful, though, that this exercise would work a second time, much less a twentieth time. To add excitement to this exercise, print each word on a separate blank playing card. Then add one other card, one with an uncomplimentary name on it. (*Tonto*, which means something like "stupid", is a good one for Spanish.) Thus you have created a deck of cards that has an equal number of cards in each of the two groups to be matched and the uncomplimentary name card for the odd card out.

An optimum pack size of 50 to 60 cards can aim for a match of at least 25 pronouns and 25 verbs. With the resulting pack, we can apply the following rules:

Old Maid Rules

1. All the cards are shuffled and dealt one at a time around the table until all the cards are distributed.
2. Players find all the pairs they can in their hand and discard them. (In the case of the above game, "Tonto," this means a subject and a verb which agree.)
3. The players then take turns drawing a card from the hand of the player on their left and discarding pairs whenever they can be made.
4. When a player discards his last cards, he is then safe and out of the game and does not draw any more cards from the player on his left. The rest of the players proceed until they have discarded all their cards.

Obviously, no one really wins at this game. One only hopes not to become the *Tonto*, as happens in the traditional Old Maid game.

This game usually begins quietly, and the excitement builds to the end of the game. However, the student who simply does not learn the agreement between subjects and verbs will have a much greater chance of losing, because he will not recognize pairs in his hand.

One problem that may occur in this type of game must be avoided, or a game may not end. In a French game I have called "Grosse Panique," which specializes in subject pronouns and irregular verbs, the diagram below indicates possible pairs that can be made with four cards.

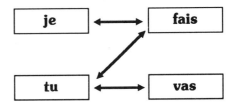

What very often happens in this combination is that someone makes a pair using *tu* and *fais*, leaving *je* and *vas*, which cannot be paired. The solution to this problem is to color code the cards. An additonal rule to the efffect that only cards of the same color may be paired prevents this impossible situation from occurring, as demonstrated in the diagram below.

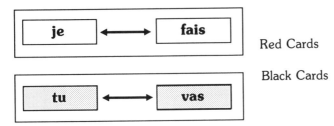

Red Cards

Black Cards

In this game model, the excitement is derived from the presence of the one card that gives the holder an uncomplimentary name. The students play to avoid it, but they go through an unending drill of matching cards correctly or the player must bear the righteous wrath of the other players.

Waterworks Model

The second model, also easy to use, provides an exercise in sentence building, with a few controls built in by the teacher. Let us assume a Spanish teacher has recently taught the differences between *el profesor* and *la secretaria*, between *un* and *unos*, between *es* and *esta*, and between expressions like *en la escuela* and *por la mañana*. These expressions can all be built into sentences in various combinations.

The first step to designing a Waterworks game is choosing "starter cards," cards (or words) with which one may start all the sentences in the game. It is appropriately frustrating if there are only a few of these cards (three to eight). Fewer than three can be too frustrating, and more than eight can become too easy or too akward.

Let us use *el*, *la*, *los*, and *las* for starter cards, as I have in designing the game "Viva." This means that all the sentences made in the game must start with one of these four words, distinguished from the other cards in the pack in some manner, as with an arrow pointing to the right. The sentence must also be punctuated with a special card. It is appropriate that the name of the game appear on that card and that the game have a "winning" name. There should be two punctuation cards in the game. So far, as in the game "Viva," we have the following cards:

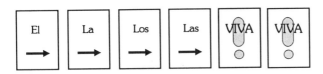

235

The next step is to make sure that there is at least one card (preferably two or three) to follow each word in the sentence. To do this, the teacher should plan in flow-chart manner the vocabulary for the game. Such a chart would resemble the following one for "Viva." Each block represents a card in the pack. The arrows indicate the possible routes through the pack of cards, building sentences that begin with the word *El.*

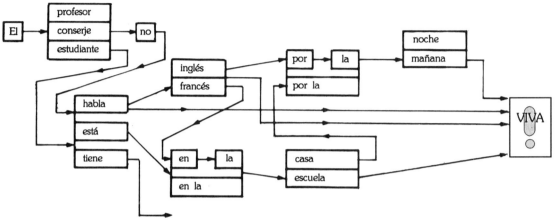

As one can see from this chart, it is possible with 21 cards to make many different sentences. Since one may end the sentence with a punctuation card at any logical time in the sentence-building process, the possibilities are for sentences from three words in length ("El profesor habla!") to eleven words. ("El profesor no habla inglés en la casa por la noche!")

Following the same procedure for *La, Los,* and *Las* does not mean one will end up with 80 cards to complete the pack. Adding the cards *La* and *secretaria* to the above group almost doubles the number of possible sentences, as one can say *La estudiante* or *La secretaria* and complete the sentence with any of the previously used combinations of cards.

Assuming then that approximately 50 cards have been developed, the rules of the game are as follows:

Waterworks-Model Rules

1. The cards are shuffled and each player is dealt four cards. The remaining cards become the draw pile.
2. Each player follows in sequence the steps listed below for his turn:
   (a) He checks to see if he can play a card. If he cannot, he proceeds as in step (b). If he can, he proceeds as in step (c).
   (b) He places any one of his cards face up on the discard pile and draws another card from the draw pile to replace it. If he can then play, he proceeds as in step (c). If he cannot, his turn is over.
   (c) He plays an appropriate card, gets points for it (see Rule 6),

236

and draws another card to replace it. This step is repeated until the player is unable to play another card.
3. All players contribute to one sentence, even though they score points individually.
4. The first card played in the game must be a starter card. It is the first word of the sentence. Each card played thereafter must be a logical continuation of the cards played before it, conforming to grammar rules and common sense.
5. There is no required number of cards for any sentence. The punctuation card may be played in turn if the cards previously played make a complete and sensible sentence. The game then ends. The cards must then be shuffled and dealt as in Rule No. 1.
6. A player gets five points for each card played in the game (the second card played is worth 10 points, the fifth card played is worth 25 points). The only exceptions are the starter cards and the punctuation cards. The starter cards are always worth 20 points. The punctuation cards are worth the usual number of points, or 50 points, whichever is greater.
7. When the draw pile is depleted, the discard pile is turned over (but not shuffled) and becomes the draw pile.

This is not a difficult game to learn and, in fact, lends itself to sentence structures which are not overly complex. It is not recommended for complicated tenses in some languages because the many different spellings needed for gender and number agreement would require an unsuitably large number of cards in the pack.

The competition in this game is derived from the accumulation of points. Frustration comes into play when students hold cards they expect to be able to use later in the game and find when their turn comes they cannot because someone has played another card in their place.

This game provides some loopholes. Players with foresight or imagination soon learn ways of improving their chances of winning, and any opportunity to use exceptional (and acceptable) combinations of words makes the game interesting. Nothing is more valuable to language students than the ability to manipulate what they know of the target language.

Crazy-Five Model

Although suitable for beginners, this game model is directed toward advanced students. It is especially suitable for drill of variations of three-word grammatical structures (compound tenses, for example). It is very easy to control the players' possibilities because every sentence must fit into a five-word sequence. For this same reason, it is relatively easy to construct.

Let us assume a Spanish teacher wants to design a game to practice the following structures:

    ha buscado
    está buscando
    va a buscar

If these structures appear in a sentence, one can find before the verbs a subject or a negative, or both. After the verbs one can place direct objects or adverbs. With the direct objects and with the noun subjects one can also expect articles. These considerations give ample opportunity to plan five-word sentences. Study the possibilities with the following selection of cards from the game "Loco."

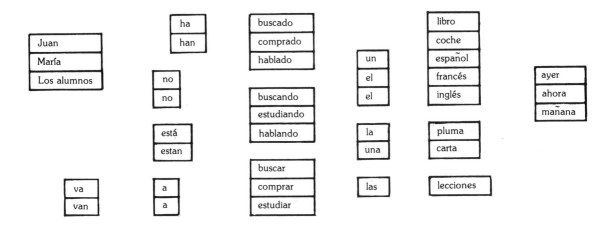

Here are some possible sentences one can make.

1. No ha buscado un coche.
2. Juan no está hablando español.
3. Los alumnos van a estudiar mañana.

Of course, there are also many possibilities for sentences with fewer than five cards. For this reason I recommend that the teacher add five dummy cards that do not stand for a word. In "Loco" there are five *Loco* (dummy) cards. If a player wants to make a sentence with four cards, he must have one *Loco* card to complete his hand. Likewise, a sentence of three words must be accompanied by two *Loco* cards. Here are some examples.

1. Juan no está estudiando *Loco*
2. Ha hablado inglés *Loco Loco*

One more recommendation is that the teacher may include some wild cards. Three may be the optimal number, depending on the restrictiveness of the vocabulary in the game. These wild cards (called *Libre* in the game "Loco") should be used in place of any other card in the pack: word card or dummy card. It is reasonable, of course, to require that the player know what *Libre* stands for in the constructed sentence. Here are some examples of how to use the wild card.

1. Juan no *Libre* estudiando *Loco*
   (Used here for "está")
2. Ha hablado inglés *Loco Libre*
   (Used here for Loco)

The basic rules for the Crazy-Five Model are as follows:

Crazy-Five Model Rules

1. All the cards are shuffled and each player is dealt five cards. The rest of the cards are placed face down on the table and become the draw pile.
2. Each player's turn consists of (a) choosing the card least helpful in making a sentence and placing it face up on the discard pile, then (b) drawing another card from the draw pile to replace it. Players do not reverse the order of steps in this rule.
3. The first player to make a correct sentence with word, wild, and/or dummy cards is the winner of the game.

Some benefits are intrinsic to playing cards. The most noticeable is that shy students enjoy the opportunity to participate actively for lengthy periods of time in small groups, with non-threatening individuals, and without the attention of the rest of the class. It becomes an annoyance to other students when someone has not learned the grammar well enough. Those who need it get scolded by other students, who often give a more thorough scolding than a teacher can. In addition, card games of this type promote discussion of alternatives involving consideration of grammar and vocabulary, as students investigate possibilities for winning. Many students benefit from the need to cooperate with other students. Some need practice in organization. Some benefit from the need to choose which card to discard, and so forth.

A final warning! Teachers using exciting games must do so with their classroom doors closed. Drilling grammar by this method is very noisy at times.

References

Golick, Margie. *Deal Me In!* New York: Jeffrey Norton, 1973.

Taylor, Maurie N. *Classroom Games in French*. Skokie, Ill.: National Text-book, 1982.

Wagner, Guy, Max Hosier, and Mildred Blackman. *Language Games*. New York: Macmillan, 1974.

A Practical Project in Studying Foreign Languages in the Elementary School: Students Teaching Parents

Ivy A. Mitchell

It is generally accepted by foreign language educators that the most favorable time to begin the study of foreign languages is early childhood. Among the reasons given for studying a foreign language in the elementary school is that the earlier students begin studying a foreign language, the better it is for them. Compared with students who begin in high school, for example, the younger students have fewer inhibitions and show greater improvement, especially in oral language acquisition.

When they see a practical reason for studying a language, students perform better. The project I shall describe with fifth graders attempted to provide such a reason for studying Spanish. The assumption was made that practicing until perfection is achieved facilitates the learner's assimilation of the material studied, sensitizes the learner to the potential meanings in the material, and helps prevent him from forgetting. The students in this project taught Spanish to a member of their immediate family—usually a parent—with the anticipated outcome that students would feel a sense of accomplishment and, at the same time, interact positively in a teacher-student setting with their parents.

The Project

The sample consisted of fifty-four fifth graders at the Developmental Research School of Florida State University. At the beginning of the year when parents attended the first meeting of parents and teachers, they were told of the Spanish program, the teacher's role, the students' tasks, and the parental responsibilities. At the meeting they had an opportunity to voice their feelings about the project.

Students studied Spanish for one semester and, at the beginning of the second semester, preparation was made for the teaching assignment. Before beginning the actual teaching, students were asked to prepare lesson plans in which they stated their name, their student, their telephone number, the best time to call, and the material they would be teaching. Two copies of the lesson plan were made:

240

Ivy A. Mitchell is Director of the Developmental Research School at Florida State University.

one for the teacher's file and one for the student's use during his teaching assignment.

When the lesson plan was completed, students were asked to teach Spanish to a family member. The family member was chosen from the following order of desirability: mother, father, or guardian; older sibling; younger sibling; aunt, uncle or grandparent; or a neighbor. The person to be taught was not to have had Spanish previously and the teacher-students were discouraged from moving down the scale of desirable target students.

Students were instructed to teach a five-part Spanish lesson comprising five different things which they had learned in Spanish. Examples of sections were identifying parts of the body, counting, telling time or days and months of the year, learning to respond to questions in Spanish, e.g., ¿Qué Dia es hoy? ¿Cuándo es tu cumpleaños? ¿Dónde vives? ¿Qué tiempo hace hoy? Class time was used to work in pairs or with the teacher to ensure that students were acquainted with the material they were teaching. During the teaching phase of this project, the first ten minutes of class time were used to answer specific questions students had concerning their teaching: pronunciation of words, the number of minutes each day that should be spent teaching, and so forth.

Students were given at least three weeks to teach their parents, at the end of which the teacher tested each student's pupil by telephone at the time specified by the student on the lesson plan. Parents were given immediate feedback on how well they were doing. If for some reason they performed poorly, they could retake the test provided the three-week testing period was not over. The letter grade the parent received was assigned to the student and became an integral part of his grade for that marking period.

241

Results and Conclusion

Thirty-six of the persons taught by the fifth graders and tested by the class teacher received A's, while ten persons received B's. Of the persons taught, twenty-four were mothers, eight were fathers, six were a brother or sister, two were aunts, and one person was a friend. At the end of the exercise, parents were asked to respond to a questionnaire concerning the project. Eighteen of the persons taught by the fifth grader had had no foreign language previously. All but two of the parents reacted very positively, since the project provided time to interact with their child in a meaningful way, in a manner which made the child the person in charge, with the child's grade heavily dependent on the interactive process.

This project served two valuable needs. Unlike the regular teaching-testing situation, it provided the student with a practical reason for studying the language: teaching what he learned to someone else. In addition, there was opportunity for the student to interact with a family member in a positive and unusual manner, an opportunity that many students seldom have.